THE RISE OF THE PLATFORM MUSIC INDUSTRIES

THE RISE OF THE PLATFORM MUSIC INDUSTRIES

ANDREW LEYSHON AND ALLAN WATSON

agenda
publishing

First published in 2025 by Agenda Publishing

Agenda Publishing Limited
PO Box 185
Newcastle upon Tyne
NE20 2DH
www.agendapub.com

ISBN 978-1-78821-819-1

British Library Cataloguing-in-Publication Data
A catalogue record for this book is available from the British Library

Typeset by JS Typesetting Ltd, Porthcawl, Mid-Glamorgan
Printed and bound in the UK by 4edge

EU GPSR authorised representative:
Logos Europe, 9 rue Nicolas Poussin, 17000 La Rochelle, France
contact@logoseurope.eu

CONTENTS

1
INTRODUCTION

In September 2024, the female pop artist Chappell Roan – who rapidly rose first to prominence and then fame following the release of her debut album *The Rise and Fall of a Midwest Princess* in 2023, and especially following her performances as a support act on Olivia Rodrigo's 2024 world tour – cancelled two festival appearances in the United States. Cancelations are not unusual in the live music industry, which can occur for a range of reasons, such as artists being physically unwell, security concerns, or unforeseen scheduling or logistical problems, for example. In this case, the reason given for cancelation was the artist's concerns with her own mental health, and a need to take a break to focus on her own wellbeing. What might have appeared to dispassionate observers as a relatively innocuous act of cancelling a mere two shows for health reasons in fact served to generate a significant and emotive online response from those fans that had already booked tickets and, in many cases, also paid upfront for travel and accommodation, to see the artist perform live. While some responses were supportive, the majority were negative – and some openly hostile – which served to reignite recent debates regarding the relationship between fans and artists and exactly what it is that artists "owe" their fans in return for their support.

The situation in which Chappell Roan found herself, is, we would argue, an insight into some of the changes wrought to the economics of the contemporary music industries by processes of *platformization*; that is, the penetration of economic processes and cultural practices associated with digital platforms which have become increasingly powerful and ubiquitous in the contemporary music industries. For example, live music is now an activity of critical financial value both to the music industries and to musicians themselves. The revalorization of live performances, through the now significant revenues it generates through ticket sales, began with the MP3 file sharing crisis beginning in the late 1990s, which saw a huge reduction in the income received from recorded music. As a result, live music necessarily became an important alternative source of income for musicians, record labels, and music publishers, as well as a range of other intermediaries. Music streaming platforms (MSPs) such as Spotify would eventually stabilize the market for recorded music, returning music corporations to profitability, but the value generating qualities of recorded music would never fully return, especially for artists. This fact, together with the way in which the MSPs made recorded music ubiquitous and accessible as never before, meant that live music gained and retained importance in terms of revenue generation. Even those artists responsible for large volumes of streams on MSPs, and that capture the majority of the revenue pools generated by the MSPs, earn a large proportion of their income from live performance. Whereas prior to the crisis live music was seen largely as a mechanism for exposing audiences to music to drive record sales, in the early twenty-first century there was an inversion of this model which now means that for many artists new recordings are less a way of generating income and more a source of new musical material and media interest which could then be exploited through the sale of concert tickets and related merchandise. As the music industries sought to extract the maximum value of live music, ticket prices increased dramatically: by as much as 82 per cent in the period between 1996 and 2003 alone (Krueger 2005). The result is that, to see artists perform live, fans are often required to make significant financial investments. The two performances that Chappel Roan cancelled were part of The All Things Go music festival, which played concurrently at the end of September 2024 in New York and in Columbia, Maryland (near to Washington, DC), with tickets ranging from $119 to $199 per person. While it was some consolation for those fans that had bought tickets that there were at least other artists playing, it also meant that, unlike cancelled performances within conventional tour schedules, there was no opportunity to seek a refund as most festivals operate an "all sales are final" policy.

This episode also throws light on a further transformation being driven by social media platforms, which have brought about a change in the ways artists and their fans relate to one another. Whether artists are signed to a record label or operate independent of one, there now exists significant pressure for artists to self-promote and develop online fan bases through social media platforms. Indeed, the need to foster and sustain ongoing interactions on social media has increasingly become to be seen as part of the "job" of a musician. Both musicians and record labels have come to value fans and social capital over record sales *per se*, given that it helps artists to better promote themselves, licence their music and sell merchandise and, in relation to the earlier discussion, bring crowds to concerts. Musicians today must have skills beyond mere musical aptitude and creativity; knowing how to use social media platforms – along with a range of other platforms for activities such as crowdfunding and live streaming – to promote their music and communicate with audiences is, for many, now seen as a core competence and so vital to career development. Musicians must employ "relational" forms of labour, which often brings them into direct and very close contact with their fans. Although fans have long sought out feelings of personal connections and exclusivity with artists, due to the affordances of social media platforms, which frame new possibilities for interaction between users, fans often expect forms of openness from, and intimacy with, artists as never before. For the artists, such relational labour has a significant emotional component and often requires them to "give" a lot of themselves. While such connections can be positive and affirmatory, they can also be negative and debilitating. Indeed, Chappell Roan herself, in cancelling the shows, linked her concerns about her mental health to "toxic" social media experiences and "creepy" fans.

Artists would seem to be currently caught in a "perfect storm" between the value that can be extracted from live music in the age of streaming – reflected in the ticket prices paid by fans – and the expectations to develop personal and meaningful connections with fans. But the personal connections which Chappell Roan's fans are encouraged to feel that they are developing with the artist encourage them to make (often considerable) financial and emotional investments in the artist – such as buying expensive tickets for shows – which in turn places particular expectations in return upon the artist, and especially to "be available" for fans. It is this complex relationship of affect and economy that is reflected in the negative reactions of many fans following news of the cancellation, and which also fuelled the significant media coverage that followed (see, e.g., Dailey 2024; Lee 2024; Mier 2024). Yet, it is also in this context that one can understand the exhaustion and mental health issues that can push artists to consider cancelling performances.

While the above case is usefully illustrative of some of the outcomes of the penetration by platforms into the economics and cultural practices of the contemporary music industries – and which we explore in the remainder of this book – it is also more broadly illustrative of the ways in which platforms are transforming economic sectors and spheres of life. The neologism of *platform capitalism* (Srnicek 2016) is one which seeks to capture the rise of a distinctive and powerful mode of capitalist intermediation made possible by a host of socio-technical achievements, or what Langley and Leyshon (2017: 13) describe as "a discrete and dynamic arrangement defined by a particular combination of socio-technical and capitalist business practices". Furthermore, it is a term which also seeks to capture a dynamic set of new work modalities; adjustments in consumption modes, preferences, and behaviours; and changes in how work is conceived (Liang *et al.* 2022). Platforms represent a distinct mode of socio-technical intermediary and business arrangement. At the most general level, platforms can be understood as digital infrastructures that enable two or more groups to interact; that is, platforms position themselves as intermediaries that bring together different users, whether these be producers, suppliers, service providers, customers or advertisers (Srnicek 2016). Or, in other words, "the underlying intermediary logic of the platform is that it solves coordination problems in market exchange by extending the distance-shrinking networking capacities of the internet", and in so doing creates "new opportunities to solve the problem of two-sided or multi-sided markets, where economic agents need to find each other to transact" (Langley & Leyshon 2017: 15). In this respect, platforms represent a new organizational form which is based on a relationship between the platform, the ecosystem of firms dependent upon it, and the users who interact and transact through it (Kenney & Zysman 2020). Platforms provide an open, participative infrastructure for interactions and set governance conditions for them, with the overall aim to create matches between users and facilitate exchange (of goods, services, or even social currency, for example) in such a way as to enable value creation for all participants (Parker *et al.* 2016).

Platform (re)intermediation represents a distinctive form of (re)intermediation due to the ways in which platforms both make the connections to constitute multi-side markets, and to coordinate subsequent network effects (van Dijck 2013). Here, network effects refer to the impact that the number of users of a platform has on the value created for each user. Individuals are not only users of platforms, but also serve as "inputs", with their participation creating value for other users (Andersson Schwarz 2017; McIntyre & Srinivasan 2017). This results in what Cusumano *et al.* (2019: 13) refer to as "nonlinear increases in utility and value", whereby platforms grow with the power and size of the network. Platform businesses are often built on a premise that once they reach a critical mass of users, the existing users on a platform generate self-sustaining growth (Parker *et al.* 2016). This dynamic is underpinned by two major effects, namely network effects and virality, whereby "viral" effects create the possibility to ignite rapid exponential growth (Pussinen *et al.* 2023). All of this is achieved through a platform business model which enrols users through a participatory economic culture, through recruiting "users", and mobilizes code and data analytics to build essential digital infrastructures that is often overlooked and sinks into the business background (Langley & Leyshon 2017). Platforms are simultaneously both mediators and facilitators of economic activity. Furthermore, the intermediary role of platforms in the digital era has positioned platforms as data hubs and data aggregators. They represent an emergent business model which is capable of extracting and controlling immense volumes of data which is then utilized to gain competitive advantage, such as in the optimization of algorithms (Srnicek 2016), to further increase positive network effects.

Taken together, platforms can be understood as governing systems that are capable of control, interaction and accumulation. In this respect, they embody several familiar capitalist developments including consolidation, economies of scale, rent-seeking, uneven distribution of power, and the shift towards more precarious and exploitative immaterial labour (Andersson Schwarz 2017; Nieborg

& Poel 2018). Economies of scale are intimately linked to network effects: the development of *demand economies of scale* (Shapiro & Varian 1999) driven by, for example, efficiencies in social networks, demand aggregation and app development, drive indirect positive network effects that make for bigger networks which are more valuable to their users (Parker *et al.* 2016). This pushes multi-sided markets towards concentration in a "winner-takes-all" effect, as larger platforms are capable of rapidly scaling the value that is derived from network effects. Indeed, as in previous rounds of capital accumulation, we are currently witnessing the development of new forms of oligopoly, this time in the form of a small number of multi-billion-dollar platform corporations, most of which have been incorporated relatively recently (Nieborg *et al.* 2022). Consequently, many studies on platformization processes have emphasized the predilection of digital platforms to accumulate power, to accelerate capital concentration and centralization, while at the same time emphasizing the human, cultural practices related to work, democracy, and creativity which platforms facilitate (Kiberg 2023).

Processes of platformization and platform (re)intermediation have been prevalent across the entirety of the economy and have had a marked impact upon the media and creative industries (Nieborg & Poell 2018; Duffy *et al.* 2019; Poell 2020; Magaudda & Solaroli 2021; Nielsen & Ganter 2022). Nevertheless, we would suggest that the music industries represent *frontier industries* for processes of platformization. Between the late 1990s and early 2000s, they became the first major media industries to be fundamentally disrupted by digital platform innovations. MP3 file sharing, mediated through what were *prototypical* platforms – such as, most notoriously, Napster – fundamentally challenged the recorded music industry's ability to reproduce itself as the volume of revenues earned from the sale of recorded music, hitherto the sector's main source of income, declined precipitously (Leyshon 2014). This "first wave" of platform reintermediation took the form of peer-to-peer (P2P) networks that (illegally) inserted themselves between record companies and audiences in the market for recorded music. Although P2P networks were not digital platforms in the way that they subsequently evolved during the early twenty-first century, they contained many platform-like features, not least the way in which they reintermediated the way music was consumed, as they successfully managed to occupy a position between music and listeners that short-circuited established means of distribution. Such processes of platform reintermediation, which by propagating the open digital format of MP3, initially acted to destroy traditional music industries business models founded on the exploitation of music rights in material music formats such as compact disk, have subsequently been reconstituted to rebuild it. In a "second wave" of platform reintermediation, MSPs helped to undermine the open playback format, with users only able to access music through the platform, which allowed the music industry to reinforce copyright protection once more. In this way, streaming first stemmed, then reversed, the decline in revenues from recorded music. Revenue recovery across the music industries has been largely dependent on the income generated by streaming services, which have become the dominant mode of music distribution. By 2019, total global revenues had returned to levels last seen in the mid-2000s, driven overwhelmingly by the income generated by streaming platforms, which in less than ten years emerged to become the dominant mode of music distribution. By the end of 2023 total music streaming revenues (including both paid subscription and advertising-supported) reached $19.3 billion and accounted for more than two-thirds (67.3 per cent) of the total global market (IFPI 2023). The most recent figures released by the IFPI (2025) demonstrate the global significance of the music industries, and of platforms, to its current success. At the end of 2024, global music industry revenues rose to $29.6 billion, up by 4.8 per cent, with streaming revenues exceeding $20 billion for the first time ($20.4 billion), 69 per cent of total recorded revenues. Paid subscription streaming revenues increased by 9.5 per cent, evidencing the continued stabilization of the industry around the streaming format.

During the early 2000s, the detrimental impacts of early platformization on the music industries resulted in predictions from a range of sources, including major news outlets, industry insiders, academics, and even high-profile musicians that what was being witnessed was "the death rattle of a once-powerful industry" (Fairchild 2015: 469). Yet, observing the music industries in the contemporary period, now stabilized around MSPs as the primary mechanism for music consumption, some of the fundamental underlying dynamics of the music industries remain unchanged. Perhaps most significantly, the music industries remain highly oligopolistic, dominated by a small group of multinational corporations. By 2010, a mere four major multinationals dominated the contemporary global music industry as a result of various mergers and acquisitions: Universal Music Group, Sony BMG Music Entertainment (a product of a joint venture between Sony Music Entertainment and BMG in March 2004, and a subsequent merger in October 2008), EMI Music, and the Warner Music group. A year later, in 2011, when the Universal Group purchased EMI's recorded music division for a figure thought to be in excess of $2 billion, this number was reduced to just three.

For reasons that we outline later, MSPs have quelled anxieties about the long-term survival of the market for recorded music (and also ensured the survival of the major music corporations). But MSPs have also brought to the surface new concerns about the equity implications of this development. A significant body of research has quickly emerged which has focused on MSPs and revealed significant tensions around the uneven distribution of streaming platform revenues, and of the commodification of artists' labour (Hesmondhalgh 2021; Marshall

2015; Meyn *et al.* 2023; Qu *et al.* 2023; Simon 2019; Towse 2020). However, while debates about the moral economy of streaming dominate both media and academic accounts of the music industries, we would argue that a focus on MSPs and the remuneration of artists alone obscures much of the associated complexity produced by concurrent platform innovations. The impacts of platformization go beyond the recorded music industry into other areas of the music industries and include, for example, social media and user-generated content platforms and crowdfunding and investment platforms, which have facilitated the emergence of new groups of music producers, consumers, and influencers.

With this broader framing of platformization in mind, in this book we adopt a perspective for critically understanding the music industries as a *platform political economy* (Guyer 2016; Langley & Leyshon 2021), that is to say that we adopt an approach which views the economy as being increasingly and pervasively constituted through the logics and logistics of platforms. Previous work on the music industries has engaged with platforms to various degrees, and in particular the role of MSPs and social media platforms and their economic logics and affordances (that is to say, the possibilities for action that they provide). However, this book attempts to provide the first holistic evaluation of the contemporary music industries where the notion of the "platform", and of "platform capitalism" more broadly (Srnicek 2016), provides the conceptual entry point. Our aim is to provide a systematic evaluation of how processes of platformization – that is to say, the "penetration of infrastructures, economic processes and governmental frameworks of digital platforms" (Poell *et al.* 2019: 1) – are impacting upon and shaping the contemporary music industries. We shall place the process of platform reintermediation of the musical economy into historical context and examine the economic and cultural implications of the rise of what we term "the platform music industries". We shall illustrate how the interplay of technology, capital and intellectual property seeks to both shape and respond to market changes, and the consequences of this for a variety of actors.

Our use of the term the platform music industries has much in common with the widely employed term "the digital music industries". This is a term which recognizes not only the evolution of the streaming age, but also alongside this the "transformation of the entire media ecosystem, which has seen the rising prominence of social media, and internet technologies facilitating a new digitally connected world" (Murphy & Hume 2022: 217). This idea of a complete digitally centred transformation of the media ecosystem, which has de-emphasized the corporate recorded music industry in favour of attention on a wider range of actors, has underpinned and informed much recent work on the music industries from multiple perspectives and disciplines. Negus, for example, points to "the introduction and rapid adoption of Internet circulation and digital technology as a means of creating and curating, sharing and selling, bundling and licensing access to recorded music" (2019: 368) as being the most significant catalyst of change in the contemporary music industries. A growing body of work in this area has produced vital new insights into the contemporary music industries, and we draw on and critically evaluate much of this literature through the course of this book. However, our central focus on platforms and processes of plat-formization serves to foreground the commercial and institutional configurations of the platform music industries and allows us to identify and elaborate upon the distinct processes of reintermediation and consolidation that are shaping the contemporary music industries. Our account will foreground the role of particular platform technologies, actors and business strategies in shaping particular sets of power dynamics across the music industries, and exactly how these dynamics position different actors and different parts of the music industries in relation to each other. In doing so, we demonstrate how the processes of platformization and political economy at work in the contemporary music industries serve to problematize claims regarding the disruptive, disintermediating and democratizing potential of platforms more generally.

In this book we intentionally use the plural term "music industries" over "the music industry" as a singular term. Here we follow Williamson and Cloonan (2007: 305) who argue that "the notion of a single music industry is an inappropriate model for understanding and analysing the economics and politics surrounding music". They point in particular to two issues with the singular term "the music industry". First, it suggests a homogenous industry, whereas the reality is one of diversity and of "disparate industries with some common interests" (2007: 305). These include, for example, the recorded music industry, the music publishing industry, and the live music industry. Second, and relatedly, this singular term is often used synonymously with the recorded music industry, in such a way as to over-privilege the multinational operations of the major labels and eliminate other smaller firms and individuals from debates. As such, we find this pluralized framing to be crucial to our efforts to examine the social and economic changes that platformization has wrought on the various music industries, allowing us to draw out the complex dynamics, conflicts and inequalities that arise from these changes as they impact upon a range of key actors across the various music industries. This includes not only the major corporations and MSPs, but also independent artists and labels, a wide range of intermediaries, and more recently MusicTech start-ups.

Methodology

Our aim in this book is to develop an account of the platform music industries that is not only theoretically instructive, but also empirically informed.

In this regard, in this text we draw on a number of sets of primary qualitative and quantitative data to inform our account. First, in Chapter 4 we draw on qualitative interviews with MusicTech start-ups and range of related actors and organizations. Between February 2018 and September 2019, 26 qualitative semi-structured interviews were undertaken with individuals working within MusicTech start-ups, major record labels, independent record labels and publishers, incubators and other organizations engaging with start-ups. The start-ups were focused on different aspects of the music industries, including music rights, music creation technologies and live music experiences, as well as artist and repertoire (A&R), music management, music video, music recognition and music investment. The start-ups and other participating organizations were located primarily in London, with a smaller sample taken from Stockholm. London and Stockholm are recognized as primary European agglomerations for music industry activity with a history of collaboration between music and ICT increasingly as hubs of MusicTech innovation. Interviews lasted typically lasted between 30 and 90 minutes.

Second, in Chapter 5, we analyse primary quantitative data on artist royalty earnings and social media platforms in the form of a unique dataset of the royalty earnings and the social media accounts of 255 artists signed to a large UK-based independent music publisher. Growth curve modelling[1] is employed to analyse the relationship *between* royalties earned over three calendar years (2016, 2017 and 2018) and social media statistics, drawn from Facebook, Twitter and Spotify follower counts. The data used in this analysis was collected by the publishing firm for internal research purposes and shared with the research team as part of a Knowledge Transfer Partnership project, with permission given to publish the findings. The value of royalties earned by artists is derived from statements of royalties paid to the publisher by PRS for Music[2] for usages of the musical

---

1   Growth curve models represent a set of statistical methods that allow for the estimation of inter-individual variability in intra-individual patterns of change over time. Put another way, they allow for the estimation of between-person differences in within-person change (Curran *et al.* 2010), in our case individual trajectories of artists based on the above set of observed repeated measures. These individual trajectories then become our unit of analysis, allowing us to identify variance in the trajectories in earning between artists in relation to changes in numbers of social media followers. We employ a random intercept model to allow us to control for the different starting points of the artists and examine only that variance which occurs during our selected period.

2   PRS for Music is a UK music right organization which is home to the Performing Right Society (PRS). PRS for Music collects and distributes royalties to its members and users where their works are broadcast on television and radio, performed or played in public (whether live or through a recording), or streamed and downloaded. They also provide rights management and administrative services to the Mechanical-Copyright Protection

works it controls. Social media indicators were collected via publicly available Application Programming Interface (API) endpoints.[3] The resulting dataset provided a unique opportunity to investigate the relationship between social media and streaming followers and publishing royalty income over time.[4] It allows us to provide the first and only robust quantitative analysis of the correlation between growth in social media followers and income from publishing royalties.

Finally, across Chapters 6 and 7 we draw on two distinct sets of qualitative primary research. The first set of data was produced from 29 qualitative semi-structured interviews with musicians who performed regularly on the Twitch live streaming platform during the Covid-19 pandemic, with interviews undertaken over a 12-month period between May 2021 and May 2022. Data collection took place in two stages. A sample of 55 music musicians were selected (based on evidence that they conducted regular activity on the platform) for an online ethnography, with activity on Twitch channels being sampled for period of nine months. Following this, in-depth qualitative interviews were undertaken with a smaller sample of musicians using the Twitch platform, initially based on the 55 musicians in the ethnographical sample, and recruiting additional participants as required. In total, 29 interviews were undertaken, each lasting between 45 and 60 minutes. Our sample included 16 male and 13 female active streaming musicians. The sample was international in nature; 12 of the 29 streamers were based in the UK, nine were based in North America (USA and Canada), five in mainland Europe (Norway, Germany, Sweden, Austria, Spain), two in South America (Argentina, Bolivia) and one in Australia. Interviews were transcribed, analysed, and coded using qualitative software package NVivo. To protect the anonymity of participants, pseudonyms are used in the attribution of interview material.

The second set of data came from an additional set of 29 qualitative semi-structured interviews with participants working within the musical economy across North West England, undertaken over a five-month period between May and October 2022. Interviewees included record label managers, live music

---

Society (MCPS) who pay royalties to their members when their music is copied as physical products, streamed or downloaded, and used in television, film or radio.

3   API endpoints are URLs that act as access points to an API and its resources. They work as access points to the various resources provided by the API.

4   The data takes the form of a what has variously been referred to in the literature as cohort, longitudinal or perhaps most usefully, repeated measures data (Moskowitz & Hershberger 2002). As the sample is constant over three years, it is possible to utilize statistical models for repeated measures data. In our analysis we employ a two-level longitudinal framework where the repeated measures, (level one) are nested within the artists (level two) in a hierarchical structure.

promoters, music publishers, artist managers, and music advocacy organizations. Interviews were focused on how the Covid-19 pandemic encouraged or forced music businesses to innovate with new digital ways of showcasing, promoting and distributing music, as well as on the support required by such companies to enable them to realize emerging digital opportunities and overcome some of the more significant barriers to doing so. Interviews lasted between 30 and 90 minutes. For all of the interviews on which our discussion draws, transcripts were analysed using systematic coding and recoding based around key themes and common categories emerging from the data, in relation to the overall conceptual framework of the research project being undertaken. Research ethics approval was obtained from the Loughborough University Ethics Review Sub-Committee and best practice was followed at all stages. Quotes are selected for inclusion in our discussion to reveal the key points of concern expressed by the interviewees and are not intended to be representative of all views.

As is reflected above, the empirics on which this text draws come from primary research with, and on, participants in the UK and Europe. As such, while we seek in this text to investigate and critically analyse how the contemporary music industries have been shaped by platformization in as broad a sense as possible, it is important to recognize that our analysis and discussion are underpinned by a particular (Western) geographical specificity and, invariably, its associated theoretical frameworks. Therefore, while much of the analysis outline in this book will have wider relevance beyond the UK, Europe and North America, we would point readers to the work of those music industries scholars from outside of, or otherwise researching outside of, Western contexts, where both the background cultural, economic and political contexts (for example, government policy, censorship, copyright and the prevalence of piracy) – and therefore the impacts of digitalization and platformization – may be notably different. Giving the growing economic and cultural importance of China, we would point readers in particular to the sizeable body of literature that has developed on the digital music industries in that country. This includes studies of government policy, investment and censorship (Morrow & Li 2016); copyright regimes (Herlihy & Zhang 2016; Chen 2021); disruption to value chains (Tang & Lyons 2016); digital platforms and self-releasing musicians (Qu *et al.* 2021); the impacts of Covid-19 (Gu *et al.* 2020); platform-mediated live music performance (Zhang & Xiao 2023); popular music idol industries and fandom (Zhang & Negus 2020); and record label music planning and artist acquisition (Zhang & Negus 2024).

Structure of this book

The remainder of the book is organized as follows. In Chapter 2, we discuss the ways in which platforms have demonstrated a capacity to reconfigure recorded music industry business models, fracturing taken for granted ways of doing business and creating new sets of winners and losers. In particular, we consider the high-profile moral economy debates that continue to take place regarding music streaming and fair remuneration for artists and set these within the context of the ongoing platformization of the recorded music industry. MSPs, we contend, are digital platforms that have their own dynamics of economic transformation, which encourage capital concentration and centralization and at the same time reflect existing structural inequalities and amplify them in new ways, creating a "winner-takes-all" sensibility. We argue that many of the moral economy arguments developed by the recorded music industry in the face of the growing dominance of platforms are flawed, not least because they fail to sufficiently recognize the agency of music corporations in the platform economy and disregard the nature of the platform business model.

In Chapter 3, we build on this discussion by considering the broader framework of music rights in which the platform music industries operate, especially in relation to the relationship that exists between major corporations and the MSPs. We outline a number of consequential changes in the power dynamics of this sector: how controlling the large catalogues of recorded music defines the major corporations as the key rentiers of the music industries; how key actors have become bound together in a system of rent extraction; and how this system results in the protection of the oligopoly of the major music corporations. Furthermore, we argue that the success of MSPs has been crucial in demonstrating the potential of copyright as an asset, resulting in the growing interest of financial markets in investing in music rights. Considering the rise of music investment firms, we point towards a future in which the platform music industries and financial services become more intertwined, whilst changing the established dynamics of music rights ownership. Finally, we consider the emergence of machine learning generative AI music systems, and related concerns with regards to copyright and authorship, distributive justice, and the adequacy of existing copyright regimes.

In Chapter 4, we focus on the business dynamics behind the evolving role of technology in the "third wave" of platformization in the music industries through the examination of an emergent MusicTech sector. We focus on the unique and significant issues faced by start-ups in the MusicTech sector with regards to capitalization, and the ability of start-ups to develop plausible narratives of how investment into a MusicTech business model will leverage returns in an industry characterized by capital centralization, concentration and oligopsony. Drawing on primary data from qualitative interviews, we find there to be significant issues of investor reluctance related to the uncertainty of returns in music-related innovations and the legacy effects of preceding waves of platform reintermediation. Furthermore, we also outline the tensions that exist between the major corporations and MusicTech start-ups with specific regard to intellectual property rights, and in particular the exorbitant rents required to make use of the significant catalogues of music rights owned by the majors. The hardline defence of copyrighted assets by the majors is, we argue, one of the single biggest barriers to launching and subsequently growing a financially viable MusicTech start-up.

Chapter 5 considers social media and broader developments around platforms that seek to mobilize fan enthusiasm for economic ends. We discuss how disintermediation and subsequent reintermediation processes have seen promotion and marketing activities increasingly falling on artists, and how social media platforms present an enabling mechanism for promotional activities and audience building. Yet, we also argue that self-promotion through such platforms places particular requirements and demands on artists and musicians to adopt entrepreneurial approaches to promotion and perform online relational and emotional labour. Through a novel quantitative analysis, we examine whether the labour given to social media promotion provides financial benefits to musicians in terms of fans subsequently streaming music and attending live performances. We also critically consider how fan enthusiasm is increasingly being directly mobilized for financial gain, via crowd funding platforms, with the promise of filling a venture gap in the industry where money to fund the emergence of new music is increasingly the responsibility of musicians. Finally, we consider developments around Web 3.0, the blockchain and the Musical Metaverse that are affording new innovations in the mobilization of fan enthusiasm. We critically consider the role of platforms in the emergence of a decentralized creator economy, and the potential and possibilities of more radical digital autonomous organizations.

Chapter 6 explores the importance of live performance to the music industries, with a focus on the impact of live streaming and its emergence as a mechanism for performance and income generation during the Covid-19 pandemic. We seek to underscore the transformative potential of live streaming in shaping the future of music performance and distribution, highlighting opportunities for innovation, audience engagement and revenue generation. We reflect the complexities of monetizing music through live streaming. Drawing on original research with musicians using the Twitch live streaming platform, we reveal the diverse experiences of musicians, and the challenges music streamers face in balancing relational and transactional labour. Live streaming, we demonstrate, represents a form of live performance in which platform mechanisms privilege presenteeism and the development of intimate connections with audiences. Combined with the precarity that stems from highly variable and uncertain incomes that such performances generate, we argue that online labour is both intensive and demanding, requiring constant presence and engagement.

Building on the discussion in the above two chapters, in Chapter 7 we consider the emergence of data literacy as a key competence within the contemporary music industries, set within a critical framework exploring the relationship between platforms and democratization, access and participation. Specifically, we contend that data literacy, and more broadly the ability of individuals or companies to determine how to capitalize upon processes of digitalization, is dependent upon the wider distribution of various human and financial resources. We consider digital literacy in the context of data and metrics, illustrating the growing importance of data to creative and strategic decision making, and how data creates new divides between the data literate and those who lack the knowledge, skills and financial resources to effectively utilize platforms and leverage the metrics that they provide. We also consider the implications of the algorithmic recommendation and curation systems operated by MSPs, how the curatorial power of MSPs might be exercised with bias, and how attempts can be made to "game" song recommender systems through the creative process. Finally, drawing on primary qualitative data, we examine how platformization is resulting in new ways of working, new opportunities, and new challenges, for small independent record labels and a range of intermediaries.

Finally, in Chapter 8, we conclude the book by emphasizing the new and *distinctive form of platformization* developing in the contemporary music industries. This reaches beyond shifts in the technologies of distribution and consumption to a wider condition in which platformization has permeated the entire musical economy. The most notable characteristic of this, we argue, is the unfolding of new types of relations between the various incumbent corporations. MSPs not only have their own dynamics of economic transformation that encourage capital concentration and centralization, but they have also served to reinforce the power structures of the traditional musical economy, through a copyright-enabled system of rent extraction, encouraging the formation of a very powerful oligopoly in the market for musical intellectual property. Subsequently, we argue that this distinctive form of platformization has important implications in relation to debates around democratization, with contemporary musicians and other music industries professionals working within a business ecology in which large digital platforms own, develop, steer and – critically – *monetize* many of the most influential music industries distribution channels. Finally, we point towards some of the emerging technological developments that have the potential to further shape the economic, social and cultural dynamics of the platform music industries in coming years.

2
PLATFORMIZATION AND THE RECORDED MUSIC INDUSTRY

Introduction

The major corporations within the music industries have, almost since their inception, been focused on technological innovation while also building around themselves sophisticated global networks of marketing, promotion and distribution. As a consequence, the relationship between the music industry and technological developments is long-standing and persistent. From early innovations in sound reproduction, through the reproductive mediums of vinyl, audiotape and compact disc (CD), technological developments in the music industry have in turn provided higher quality audio playback, as well as bringing about economic benefits across the musical economy, especially to record companies and music publishing companies (for example, the reissuing of back-catalogues in new formats) and to electronic companies producing new reproductive equipment. Following the introduction of the CD, for example, the music industry enjoyed about 15 years of steady growth in recorded music sales (Leyshon *et al.* 2005; Forde 2024). Indeed, a mostly symbiotic relationship existed between electronic companies who produced reproductive equipment and created consumer demand for new, higher quality audio playback, and the record companies producing music for new media. In some cases this happened under the same corporate umbrella: Sony, for example, is a major producer of both technology and entertainment.

Given the economic benefits of previous technological developments, the development of the internet as a vehicle for world digital distribution was largely seen as a positive one (Leyshon 2001). It is now widely known that rather than an opportunity for economic gain, this development would present one of the most significant challenges ever faced by the music industry in terms of its profitability. Indeed, it would fundamentally challenge the viability of the music industry in the form in which it had existed for many years (see Graham *et al.* 2004). The causes of the decline and fall of the recorded music industry from the late 1990s onward are now well known (e.g., Arditi 2015; Leyshon 2014; Morris 2015), with the music industry becoming the first major media industry to be fundamentally disrupted by digital platform innovations. The previously productive engagement with technological innovation broke down as MP3 file sharing mediated through what, as argued earlier, can be seen to be prototypical digital platforms, in that they reintermediated the consumption of music, manifested as peer-to-peer (P2P) networks (David 2010). These prototypical platforms fundamentally challenged the music industry's ability to reproduce itself by dramatically reducing revenues from the sale of recorded music, hitherto the sector's main source of income (Garafolo 1999; McCourt & Burkart 2003; Graham *et al.* 2004; Leyshon 2014). The threat posed by an open digital file format was partially abated in the early 2000s by the rise of new pay-to-download services such as iTunes (Arditi 2015), before further disruptive innovations in music streaming technologies presented a novel set of technological opportunities and challenges for the industry (Barr 2013). Streaming would first stem, then eventually reverse, the decline in revenues from recorded music. But it was not until 2016, following nearly 20 years of decline, that revenues across the music industry finally began to increase again after the crisis of piracy.

In this chapter, we discuss the ways in which platforms have demonstrated a capacity to reconfigure recorded music industry business models, set in the context of the high-profile debates that continue to take place regarding the equity implications of music streaming and judgements about "fair" remuneration for artists. Music streaming platforms (MSPs) are, we contend, digital platforms that have their own dynamics of economic transformation. These dynamics encourage capital concentration and centralization while at the same time reflecting existing structural inequalities which are amplified in new ways. Given this, we argue that many of the arguments developed by the recorded music industry in the face of the growing dominance of platforms are flawed because they resort to moral economy interpretations of just returns and fail to recognize the agency of music corporations in the formation of a platform economy, while disregarding the nature of the platform business model which has tipped the balance of power ever more firmly towards them and away from artists.

A recent history of platformization in the recorded music industry

The music industries have pioneered processes of digital transformation and platform reintermediation. These processes first destroyed and then rebuilt a music industry business model based on the exploitation of music rights. In the following sections, we trace the recent history of platformization in the recorded music industry, categorized as three "waves": first, the emergence of peer-to-peer (P2P) platforms in the 1990s; second, the rise of MSPs in the 2000s; and finally, the emergence of a MusicTech innovation ecosystem in the 2010s and onwards.

First wave: MP3 and peer-to-peer platforms

Through the mid- to late-1990s early positivity regarding the possibility of digital music distribution gave way to a growing realization that a world of cabled connectivity was a serious threat to future profitability and the long-term survival of established record companies (Leyshon 2001). The reason for this was a relatively unremarkable technological development: the emergence of the MP3 software format in response to a call in 1988 by the Moving Pictures Expert Group for an international coding standard to facilitate the development of interactive video and audio on compact disks (Musmann 2006). Emanating from research undertaken on audio compression at the Fraunhofer Institute for Digital Media Technology based at Technische Universität Ilmenaum in the 1980s, the software that enabled MP3 was patented by Fraunhofer in 1989 (Forde 2024). But it was not until the mid-1990s, when the compression software had been developed sufficiently, that the psychoacoustic masking techniques deployed were capable of enabling the much smaller MP3 files to pass as more or less accurate copies of their original digital audio recordings (Forde 2024).

For some the creation of MP3 was a seemingly innocuous development: merely the creation of a compressed, standard file format for music, which was playable on most home PCs and a range of mobile music devices, which extended the number of playback devices for music. However, the development of a PC application that was freely given away by Fraunhofer to promote the MP3 format, which could quickly extract data from a CD track and convert them into MP3 files (Witt 2015), made possible the sharing of music online between listeners from computer to computer first through physical storage media and then the internet. The size of these files had important consequences for their mobility, as they were small enough to be transferred from computer to computer via the "narrow-band" dial-up modem connections typical in homes in the late 1990s and early 2000s. The copying of music encoded on CDs into MP3 format, and the subsequent sharing of this music on the internet, would undermine sales of recorded music, impacting directly on the economic viability of the music industries, and tipping the recorded music economy into a full-blown "crisis of reproduction" (Leyshon 2014).

Issues around the breach of intellectual property rights and illegal copying would abruptly come to the fore with the rise of P2P file-sharing networks, which exposed the extent to which the music industry relied on the exploitation of copyright for generating profits, while at the same time throwing into question music's always uneasy status as a commodity (Hesmondhalgh & Meier 2018). Such P2P networks were the earliest examples of platformization in music, distributing (albeit illegally) recorded music online by making digital music files freely available to users that downloaded their user interface. In this way, they acted as a form of two-sided intermediary; on one side of the market were those uploading pirated music files and, on the other, those downloading these files. Most of these platforms failed to make any revenue, nor did the users on either side of the market make money from their activities, but in some cases P2P networks connected users to a third party, namely advertisers, to create a revenue stream. These early platforms destabilized the regime of governance that supported copyright capitalism by creating, and giving mass access to, a series of what were effectively "gift economies" (Leyshon 2003) in which the products of the music industry were given away for free, crowding out sales. The two best known peer-to-peer networks were Napster and Kazaa. Napster operated between June 1999 and July 2001 and which at its peak allowed tens of millions of users to share and download music for free through a user-friendly interface. Meanwhile, Kazaa, which began operating in March 2001, built up a user base of around 140 million users with as many as 4 million users online at any one time. The emergence of these networks meant that "digitized music's immateriality and hyper-mobility as code caused both the economic and legal property regimes associated with the pre-digital era to become outdated and impotent" (Born 2005: 25). In 2001, music sales fell by 5 per cent, and then by over 9 per cent in the first half of 2002, resulting in a reduction in the inflow of capital to the industry and disastrous loses for the leading firms in the sector (Leyshon *et al*. 2005). The outcome was a crisis of funding across the wider musical economy, resulting in significant reductions in rosters of recording artists. As Arditi (2014: 421) observed:

> With the development of P2P software, major record labels were quickly losing their grasp on the control over access to the industry. Without long term structural changes to the music industry, the major record labels realized that they would no longer have a viable business model.

MP3s offered the possibility of a new type of business model, linking artists directly to consumers, which threatened to bypass record companies (Garofalo 1999), and the vice-like grip they exercised over the distribution of recorded music.

The response to the challenge by the industry's major corporations was litigation against both file-sharing services and individual file sharers (see

Bhattacharjee *et al.* 2006; Choi & Perez 2007), along with strong political lob-bying. In 1998, the US Congress passed the Digital Millennium Copyright ACT (DCMA), which made it illegal to circumvent any Digital Rights Management (DRM) embedded into MP3 files (McCourt & Bukart 2003). In the same year the Recording Industry Association of America (RIAA) – the trade organiza-tion that represents the recording industry in the United States – began filing lawsuits against online music distributors, and in 2003 even began suing indi-vidual file sharers (Arditi 2014). Similar bills to the DCMA followed in Europe. In 2006, Loi sur le Droit d'Auteur et les Droits Voisins dans la Société de l'Infor-mation (DADVSI) reformed French copyright law, focused on the exchange of copyrighted works over peer-to-peer networks and criminalizing of circumven-tion of digital rights management protection measures. In 2010 in the UK, the Digital Economy Act was passed by Parliament, which made provision about the online infringement of copyright and about penalties for infringement of copyright and performers' rights. The most significant court ruling came in the case of Grokster and Streamcast (maker of the Morpheus file sharing soft-ware) versus a consortium of twenty-eight large entertainment companies led by Metro-Goldwyn-Mayer studios. The US Supreme Court ruled against both the Grokster and Streamcast P2P networks, ruling that they could be sued for inducing copyright infringement in their marketing of file sharing software. Crucially, the ruling – subsequently known as the "Grokster decision" – meant that any company which actively helped users circumvent copyright restrictions could be held responsible for copyright theft.

The impact of MP3s on the music industry, while extremely negative in the short term given the collapse of revenues from the sale of recorded music, did not result in the major corporations losing control of the music industry as many had predicted (see, e.g., Graham *et al.* 2004). This was for at least two reasons. First, as outlined above, litigation formed an important and highly successful part of the response of record companies to the challenges of software formats and internet distribution systems, particularly with regards to peer-to-peer networks. This litigation, funded by the deep pockets of powerful oligopolistic corporations, proved successful. Second, while paid-for download platforms emerged from the mass of illegal P2P networks and sought to develop business models that complied with copyright law (such as eMusic, for example, which started charging for downloads as early as 1998), it was the launch of Apple's iTunes platform in 2003, powered by Apple's marketing expertise and consumer reach, that created the first mass market for paid-for direct digital content. Apple provided a platform that both gave people a place to easily download music without risking a lawsuit and which could generate revenue for major record labels. It quickly became clear that many consumers were willing to pay for music downloads and that, given that the costs of online distribution are far lower than those required to manufacture and move a physical object, record companies could sell music online more cheaply but retain similar if not higher profit margins (McLeod 2005). In 2008, iTunes became the largest music retailer in the US, and by 2011 controlled over 38 per cent of the retail music market. When set alongside the closure of major high-street music retailers such as HMV and Virgin stores in the UK, and Tower Records in the US, this indicated a huge transition in the way that people were purchasing music. Its success, Arditi argues, was a result not just of the ingenuity of the platform, but also the industry's "desperate need to compete with free music online" (2014: 417).

Second wave: the rise of the music streaming platforms (MSPs)

Even as the music industry began to successfully deal with one technological challenge as revenues began to flow from new pay-to-download services such as iTunes, new disruptive innovations emerged in the form of MSPs, which presented both new opportunities and new challenges for the recorded music industry. Streaming services are platforms: acquiring rights from record labels to distribute recorded music online or via mobile devices, they make music available to consumers either through a paid subscription-based service or free advert-supported service (Towse 2020). Subsequently, MSPs act as two-sided intermediaries (Erickson *et al.* 2019), located between record labels/artists on the one hand, and listeners/consumers on the other. Some MSPs act as three-side intermediaries, with listeners also connected to advertisers. In less than ten years, streaming became the dominant mode of music distribution, and has fundamentally reconfigured the music industry and the way in which consumers purchased music. Streaming brought about a shift from paying for *ownership* of a music library to, instead, paying – either directly, through a subscription, or indirectly, through exposure to advertising – for *access* to a much more extensive archive (Arditi 2019). Bustinza *et al.* (2013: 18–19) describe how the shift to streaming represented "a theoretical shift in understanding what music retail is, presenting music to consumers not as a product but as a service". As music distribution was decoupled from physical formats in the "post-record music industry" (Negus 2019), music-related industries became less focused on selling the ownership of recordings and increasingly focused on offering gated access to digital catalogues of recorded music through rents paid to MSPs.

The potential value of subscription-based services was recognized even in the midst of the P2P induced crisis, with McCourt and Burkart (2003) identifying subscription models as potentially extremely lucrative but certainly capable of generating a steady cash flow sufficient to support the industry. Thomes (2013) suggested that subscription-based streaming services represented the music industry's greatest prospective source of revenue. The emergence of a small number of very successful MSPs helped to undermine the open playback format ushered in by MP3. As the use of music was only possible inside the platforms, this closed the loop that had been opened by the free exchange of individual MP3 files and so allowed the music industry to reinforce copyright protection once more, first halting and then reversing the decline in revenues from recorded music. The successful roll out of MSPs meant that by 2016 music industry revenues had increased for the first time in nearly 20 years. By 2019 total global revenues had returned to levels of the mid-2000s in real terms. By the end of 2022 total steaming revenue reached $17.5 billion, accounting for 67 per cent of total global recorded music revenues for that year (IFPI 2023). For comparison, physical format revenues represented the next highest share at 17.5 per cent, followed by performance rights at 9.4 per cent.

In 2015, the IFPI estimated that there were over 400 digital music services worldwide, many of which were streaming platforms. However, a small number of MSPs have come to dominate the music market. These are Spotify (launched April 2006, 626 million users and 246 million premium subscribers in 2024), Apple Music (launched 2015, 93 million subscribers in 2024) and Amazon's Prime Music (launched June 2015, 79 million customers in 2024). Other streaming platforms include Deezer (launched August 2007, 10.5 million subscribers in 2024) and Pandora (launched September 2005, 45.1 million users and 6 million subscribers in 2024), although these two services have seen flat and decreasing user and subscribers numbers respectively over the past few years, while the major MSPs have continued to grow their numbers. Whilst being more geographically restricted, also notable in terms of user numbers is the Chinese streaming platform Tencent Music (launched July 2016, 571 million users and 117 million paying subscribers in 2024). Although primarily a video streaming service, Google's YouTube also represents a major platform with regard to music consumption, with an estimated 2 billion people consuming music in the platform every month (YouTube music, a dedicated music platform, was launched in May 2018). As Hesmondhalgh and Meier (2018) argue, Spotify has benefited from a first-mover advantage, but Apple, Google and Amazon have considerable strategic advantages given that they are transnational BigTech corporations whose interests span a range of sectors. Rather than music being an end in itself (as it is, for example, for Spotify), music is a means to an end for BigTech corporations, helping to sell devices, apps, or online advertising and serves to support growth in e-commerce more generally. These companies are able to cross-subsidize music streaming with revenues from other products and sources (Towse 2020). Until very recently, and unlike the consumer electronics companies that preceded them, these BigTech companies had not been involved in the production of music: their intervention had been limited to the contemporary equivalent of music retail (Hesmondhalgh & Meier 2018). However, recently there have been emerging concerns around the role of BigTech in supporting innovations in AI-music (and which we discuss further in Chapter 3).

There exists a significant degree of parity between MSPs, that is, these platforms are very similar with regards to price and catalogue content. Many of these platforms run a similar subscription-based business model which allows users access to advert-free streaming as a "premium" offer while also offering a free service supported by advertising, as a strategy to attract new listeners, develop platform loyalty and to target for conversion to subscriber status. As Carter (2024) notes, unlike with streamed video platforms, MSPs are essentially interchangeable market substitutes, where more or less identical catalogue offerings at more or less identical prices ultimately both suppresses competition between platforms and depress prices. Indeed, as Carter notes, the prices for monthly premium subscriptions have barely increased since the launch of Spotify in 2006. At the time of writing, an individual premium plan typically costs £/$/€10.99, with some platforms also offering discounted duo or family plans. Although it wasn't always the case, there is now also parity across the platforms in terms of size of catalogue: Spotify, Apple Music, Amazon Music and YouTube Music all offer users access to over 100 million songs.

Due to this platform parity the basis for competition has shifted from content, price and curation to the engineering of compelling experiences. Hracs and Webster (2021) point to the way in which platforms have "moved beyond a 'one-size fits all' approach to curation to one that seeks to create experiences that appeal to the dynamic needs and sensibilities of different types of consumers simultaneously" and seeks to "convince individuals that their lives are decomposable into a series of moods, moments and need states, for each of which there is an ideal song or playlist to be found" (2021: 246). Here, they point to the ways in which platforms cater not only for "lean forward" experiences for users who are interested in music discovery, but also "lean back" experiences for the casual listener that outsources music discovery to the platform (see also Drott 2018). This "personalization at scale", Hracs and Webster argue, is made possible by the unique affordances of platformization, both in terms of scale, and in terms of how digital personalized data allows platforms to optimize the delivery of personalized recommendations to individuals. In this way, as Kjus (2016) argues, streaming services introduce a "new" relation between exposure and sale, united within one and the same service. All of this has been made possible by the way in which MSPs combine proprietary algorithms and human curators in ways that constitute a new form of *platform gatekeeping*. As Bonini and Gandini (2019) argue, the editorial power of MSPs is augmented and enhanced by algorithms and big data, such that music curation has become a "data-intense" gatekeeping activity, but one which has also allowed platform music curators to become a "new elite" in relation to traditional human intermediaries such as radio programmers and journalists.

Geurts and Cepa (2023) describe the entry of MSPs into the music industry in terms of a business ecosystem envelopment strategy. In contrast to platform envelopment strategies (Eisenmann *et al.* 2011), in ecosystem envelopment digital platforms do not take over or replace the functionality of the enveloped business ecosystem, but rather install themselves on top of a traditional business ecosystem, leaving its existing organization largely intact. This is demonstrated through the way in which the MSPs have not displaced the music industry incumbent corporations but, rather, platforms and music corporations have become bound together through a system of rent extraction (Meier & Manzerolle 2019). In short, MSPs rely on record companies for catalogue access: it is estimated that the major corporations own the rights to some eight million songs. While MSPs are large companies in their own right (as of February 2024, Spotify had a market capitalization of $45 billion) due to the costs of the deals MSPs are required to negotiate with record labels to exploit their catalogues, the MSPs have struggled to reach profitability. Spotify made a net loss in 2023, for example, of $532 million, recording its largest operating loss in the second quarter of 2023 of $247 million. Simon (2019) notes that for 2017, content costs (i.e. licensing and production costs for the music, podcasts and audiobooks on the platform) as a percentage of Spotify's revenue for the premium subscription business was 78 per cent, and up to 90 per cent for the free advertising-supported business. Furthermore, Simon (2019) highlights that Spotify pays two types of music licensing fees: fees related to sound recording licences, which cover the recording rights, and; fees related to musical composition licence agreements, which is paid to song rights holders (i.e. music publishing). These fees are growing with the revenues collected by the platform: $3.3 billion in 2017, $5 billion in 2020, $7 billion in 2021, and $9 billion in 2023 (Dredge 2024c). As such, as Simon (2019) argues, the company is caught in a "scissor effect" whereby the more its revenues grow the more it will have to pay out, leading to questions as to whether Spotify would ever become profitable over time. Nevertheless, in the first three quarters of 2024, Spotify demonstrated significant profitability for the first time in the platform's history: $168 million, $266 million and $454 million respectively, driven by greater than expected growth in both monthly active users and premium subscribers, together with increases in the cost of premium subscriptions which increased average revenue per user (Dredge 2024d).

As we shall argue further in Chapter 3, the music industry represents a distinctive case of platform reintermediation in which a small number of incumbent corporations, through oligopolistic control of intellectual property rights, are positioned as the key rentiers of digital networks, rather than established or nascent platforms.

Third wave: MusicTech

With the music industry now more or less stabilized around the streaming format (notwithstanding significant tensions and disputes about the equity implications of streaming platform revenues) a series of new rounds of innovation are blurring the lines between the music and tech industries. These have been spurred by recent technological transformations including, *inter alia*, social media, streaming, user-generated content, interaction, community content-sharing and collaboration, location-aware technologies, virtual and immersive technologies, and generative artificial intelligence (AI), together with the appetite of angel investors and venture capital firms to fund new technologies and business models that might further disrupt existing industries. Firms innovating in this space have come to be labelled as "MusicTech", mirroring the use of the suffix "Tech" to describe innovation in other areas of the economy, such as FinTech and HealthTech. While the term "MusicTech" first emerged following the emergence of platforms such as Apple's iTunes, Spotify, Shazam and Soundcloud in the early 2000s, the post-streaming stabilization of the music industry has given rise to an explosion of small, highly innovative start-up firms building platforms, services and apps targeted variously at the production, distribution, and consumption of music in the streaming age. Thus, at the time of writing we are currently witnessing a third wave of platform reintermediation in the music industry which is being driven by an emergent MusicTech sector, characterized by entrepreneurial activity and technological innovation taking place largely outside the major music companies. These firms are developing applications that seek new ways to intermediate between artists, music corporations and audiences, and in so doing to generate new revenue streams and a more complex and diverse music industry ecology. The emergence of the contemporary MusicTech sector can be seen as the next stage of the evolution of the music industries in which a small number of existing incumbent corporations, together with the now established MSPs, and a much larger number of independent record labels, intermediaries and MusicTech start-ups, are all engaged in processes of platform reintermediation.

The academic literature on tech start-ups often asserts that start-ups act to challenge the dominance of incumbents through disruptive innovation, as the legacy business models of incumbents plus inertia provide opportunities for new entrants to gain rapid momentum in the marketplace (Crittenden *et al.* 2019; Mallaby 2023). However, with the music industry having recently gone through a series of disruptive innovations, and more recently stabilized around digital formats distributed through a small number of dominant MSPs, MusicTech platform reintermediation has led to firms not challenging but, rather, aligning themselves with, and contributing and innovating in relation to, existing incumbent corporations and platforms. This includes, for example, creating complimentary platforms, such as music licensing platforms that seek to capture rights income currently not being collected from a wide range of users; and record label-facing platforms that look to provide labels with innovative services that improve the ways that data from consumers is gathered and manipulated, and the ways in which data and insights may be used to identify potentially successful artists. Thus, competition in the contemporary platform music industries mainly revolves around start-ups attracting the attention of incumbents. Very few Music-Tech firms appear to be developing the kinds of disruptive technologies which would challenge the dominance of the incumbents *per se*, opting instead to offer themselves up as potential partners with incumbents to jointly source new innovations and technologies (De Groote & Backmann 2020). We review the logics and dynamics of the emergent MusicTech innovation ecosystem in more detail Chapter 4.

The platform recorded music industry as moral economy: user as asset, music as liability

While the rise of MSPs has stabilized the market for recorded music and the revenues returned to the major music corporations, so quelling anxieties about the long-term survival of the market for recorded music, they have also brought to the surface new concerns about the social-cultural economic value of music and of the equity implications of these developments, especially in relation to the fair remuneration of music artists. Public discussion of payments from streaming began almost as soon as the first platforms were launched. We shall consider the specific details of remuneration and streaming business models shortly, but first it is important to note that underpinning these discussions has been "a broader aesthetic and moral argument about what music should be worth" (Marshall 2015: 181). While the "value" of popular music has been subject to controversy across the various sectors of the music industries, Marshall (2015, 2019) notes there is a concern that recorded music has been progressively "devalued", firstly by piracy and then by streaming, undercutting narratives that claim that the disintermediating nature of the internet should be a boon to artists located outside the major label system. Fairness, or rather a sense that structural changes in the musical economy have brought about an inequity that is manifestly unfair to economic agents that have traditionally been most invested in the music industry, namely musicians and songwriters, has emerged as a recurring theme among many commentators and musical economy practitioners (Arditi 2014, 2015).

Practitioners and commentators alike have developed criticisms that implicitly evoked normative arguments about fairness and equity associated with the concept of moral economy. This idea reveals a concern with "the moral norms and sentiments that structure and influence economic practices, both formal and informal, and the way in which these are reinforced, compromised or overridden by economic pressures" (Sayer 2007: 262). In criticizing the rise of digital platforms, and their unerring ability to capture markets and revenue, market participants and commentators have implicitly drawn on moral economy arguments to make the case for some kind of restitution in favour of those who have lost out, either appealing to public policy to seek redress or calling for further rounds of innovation and disruption that might unseat the new incumbents from their dominant positions. One place where one might not have expected to see a revival of interest in moral economy arguments would be in the main professional body for global music, the International Federation of the Photographic Industry (IFPI). Since at least 2016 – coinciding both with platforms assuming a position of dominance within the musical economy and the recovery of global music industry revenues – the IFPI and major record companies have been critical of what they describe as a "value gap" in the industry; that is, a structural underpayment of royalties to artists (Arditi 2020). In 2017, the IFPI's annual Global Music Report even included a dedicated section titled "Rewarding Creativity: Fixing the Value Gap", setting out its understanding of the problem:

> Significant challenges need to be overcome if the industry is going to move to sustainable growth. The whole music sector has united in its effort to fix the fundamental flaw in today's music market, known as "the value gap", where fair revenues are not being returned to those who are now creating and investing in music. The value gap is now the single highest legislative priority as it seeks to create a level playing field for the digital market and secure the future of the industry. (IFPI 2017: 24)

From the perspective of the IFPI and its supporters, the cause of the value gap was initially the decline of revenues arising from the disruption of the record music industry by P2P networks in the early twentieth century, and the failures of direct download and streaming services to adequately restore the rates of return previously delivered by physical formats despite their later contributions to income recovery.

Arguments about the fairness of a new digital settlement within the musical economy have circulated not only within the corporate suites of the large record labels but also among musicians. Numerous leading artists have boycotted, withdrawn catalogue from, or engaged only reluctantly with major music streaming services to signal their opposition to the low rates of return they receive from the playing of their music on such platforms (Hesmondhalgh 2021). However, as Marshall (2015) observes, the majority of concerns about low returns have been raised by independent artists located several rungs down the industry ladder. Such artists have often drawn attention to their position in an ironic fashion through marketing materials and interviews when releasing new music (see Figure 2.1).

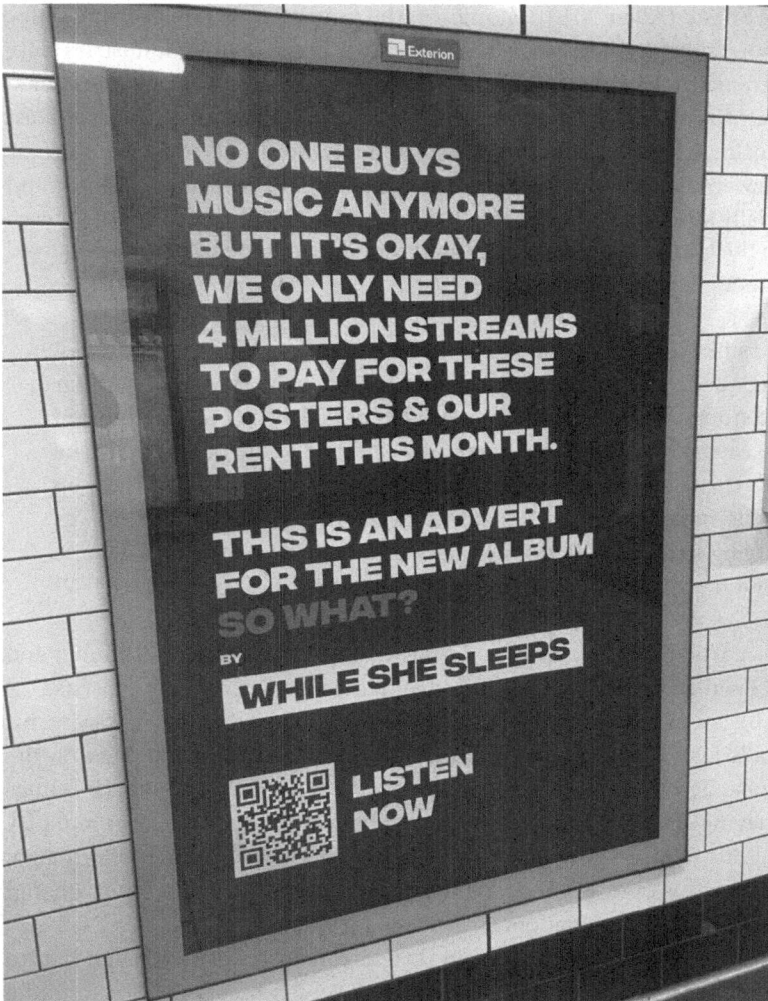

Figure 2.1 Advertisement for album launch referencing the poor financial return from streaming, London Underground, 2019

Source: Allan Watson.

Very few artists have spoken out in support of streaming platforms. Those that did adopted a stance that might be described as "market realist" in tone. For example, Dave Allen, the bassist of Gang of Four between 1976 and 1981, a post-punk band that enjoyed a successful – if not superstar – career, and later an executive with a number of digital creative industry businesses, argued that while the internet certainly brought fundamental change to the musical economy, there is little place for nostalgia given the music industry's history of exploiting artists (Allen 2013). Moreover, the industry has no special case for market protection given the ways in which a wide range of other industries were radically transformed through the advent of first e-commence and later digital platforms. Musicians, like it or not, Allen argued, simply must make the best of the transformations unfolding in front of them. But to do so is by no means straightforward. Jonathan Taplin, previously manager of critically acclaimed and commercially successful act The Band, described how the advent of free downloading in the late 1990s dramatically undermined the standard of living enjoyed by his former employers:

> Groups like The Band had some assurance that, if their music was of lasting quality, they could continue to reap financial rewards long after they'd stopped writing new music. When the CD format was introduced in the early 1980s, their record royalties jumped as old fans bought The Band's classic albums on disc. That royalty stream continued right up until the introduction of Napster in 2000. And then it ended. It was horrifying to see The Band members go from a decent royalty income of around $100,000 per year to almost nothing.   (Taplin 2017: 41–2)

Taplin was particularly aggrieved at the fate that befell The Band's drummer and vocalist, Levon Helm. He was diagnosed with throat cancer in 1998, just as P2P networks began to erode royalty income, and so faced the dilemma of paying his medical bills just as his royalty income withered away: "He couldn't go on the road because he could hardly sing. Eventually he figured out how to do something by having shows at his house, getting a bunch of friends to come and play and calling it the Midnight Rambles. He made a little money, but not enough, just barely paid his bills. It just seemed incredibly *unfair* to me" (Taplin quoted in Schechter 2017; no pagination; emphasis added).

Taplin's (2017) entanglement within this personal tragedy motivated him to develop a critique of Silicon Valley as a whole, which he blamed for enabling free downloading sites that he described as "bloodsuckers who made millions off the hard work of musicians" (Taplin 2012; no pagination). The initial target of Taplin's ire was the first wave of P2P networks such as Napster, the Pirate Bay, and other companies that developed business models based on a flagrant disregard of copyright law that ensured no incomes flowed directly to owners of the intellectual property rights in recorded music. But from the late 2000s onward, Taplin's ire was redirected to the second wave of platforms, the main music streaming platforms (MSPs), as they introduced business models that combined the demand for instant online music created by P2P networks with provision of a regular income stream to copyright holders. Taplin's criticisms gained support within the wider music industry, particularly among musicians and their representatives.

One of the issues for this criticism was the rate at which rights holders were paid per stream, which at only fractions of a cent were also known as "penny streams" (Hesmondhalgh 2021). Such small rates were considered by artists and their representatives as derisory, particularly when compared to the rates per unit for physical products such as CDs. Beginning in 2014, The Trichordist website – "a community blog for those interested in contributing to the advancement of a Sustainable and Ethical Internet for the protection of Artists Rights in the Digital Age"[1] which declares itself to be "working towards defining and setting a fair per stream rate"[2] – began posting details on royalty rates per stream for different music platforms. This data was released to them by one independent record label, with a 150-album catalogue that generated well over 100 million streams from 30 platforms. The latest update is from 2016, and while rates may have changed in the years since, are nevertheless instructive (see Table 2.1). The fact that each play, or stream, of a song generates at best only a tenth of a cent and at worst a thousand of a cent helped fuel arguments about a failure to pay "just" returns. Publishing this information in aggregate form provided some heft to reports emanating from numerous musicians over several years aggrieved about how little income they received from the streaming of their repertoire, especially when compared to CD sales. For example, cellist Zoe Keating publicly revealed that in 2018 that she earned just $21,000 from over 4.6 million streams across 11 platforms (Hesmondhalgh 2021). An artist with a typical contract with one of the major record companies would need approximately 458.3 million streams to earn just £1 in profit, due to the initial advance being recouped by their record label (Carter 2024). On the face of it, it does seem remarkable that millions of streams can produce such relatively modest revenues. However, there are at least three related reasons that help explain this.

First, once a revenue rate is set at a fraction of a monetary unit, then simple arithmetic calculation means that an exceptionally large number of plays are

---

1   See The Trichordist; https://thetrichordist.com/about-2/.
2   See The Trichordist; https://thetrichordist.com/2017/01/16/updated-streaming-price-bible-w-2016-rates-spotify-apple-music-youtube-tidal-amazon-pandora-etc/ (accessed 31 October 2024).

needed to generate significant monetary returns. For example, one figure that has been used by advocates of the value gap is the number of individual streams required to generate the United States monthly minimum wage from streaming alone. With the US rate set at $7.25 per hour, many accounts use a monthly gross minimum wage of around $1,400 as a benchmark, or about 200 hours per month. In 2018, even streaming on Akazoo, the most generous platform in Table 2.1 (paying $0.37847 per stream) would have required 19 steams per hour to generate $7.25, and 3,700 streams to generate a monthly wage of $1,400. But Akazoo was a relatively obscure platform and accounted for a very small percentage of total streams for the label's catalogue, making it an unreliable source of regular income at scale. By 2019, Akazoo was no longer among the top thirty streaming platforms, and the most generous rate was now Peloton, an exercise and equipment platform. At $0.03107 per stream, Peloton offered less than a tenth of what Akazoo had returned in 2016 and required 233 streams per hour to reach $7.25. Given that Spotify accounted for the largest share of the label's total stream revenue in both 2016 and 2019, this platform is a better reference point. At $0.00348 per stream in 2019, it would require over 2,000 streams per hour to generate the minimum wage and over 400,000 streams per month. This is clearly possible, as some superstar artists record tens of millions of streams per month. As of May 2024, the most listened to song on Spotify 2024 had generated over 4 billion streams, with Taylor Swift the highest earner on the platform, having made an estimated $300 million in streaming revenues over the course of her career. But most artists are not superstars and so are unable to generate streams on such a scale. Moreover, streaming rates per song are in decline, falling from an average of $0.00395 in 2016, to $0.00173 in 2019. Spotify, has however, repeatedly argued that it does not sell streams, but rather access to music. As a result, it is argued that it does not make sense to look at revenues per stream, but rather one must consider the overall revenues of the platform, and the total amount of royalties being returned to the industry, and that this requires a change in thinking from unit-based thinking to consumption-based thinking (Marshall 2015). Indeed, this understanding of the allocation or royalties, where the volume of streams determine an artist overall share of a revenue pot, was consolidated in 2024 when Spotify changed its royalties model to ensure more money flowed to the more successful artists, introducing a threshold over which streams must pass to earn any royalties: individual tracks receiving fewer than 1,000 streams in a 12 month period would no longer be eligible for royalties, with withheld revenue being put into the pool that allocated proportionately to tracks that streamed over the threshold (Leight & Stutz 2023).

Second, stream rates are a product of the music platform business model. Streaming platforms were only able to replace P2P platforms as the main intermediary in the consumer market for digital music by ensuring the barriers to entry for consumers were low and would encourage users to move from systems that appeared free at the point of use to another system that would at least commit to providing revenues streams to rights holders. For example, a key part of Spotify's strategy and attempt to enrol the record industry into its project was to present itself as *"the* solution to illicit downloading" (original emphasis, Eriksson *et al.* 2019: 7). To do so, Spotify also had to recruit users who had previously been using P2P networks, which were free at the point of use, exposure to advertising and malware notwithstanding. Weaning users off such networks meant that Spotify and other streaming platforms rolled out dual use membership modes with an advertising-supported "freemium" model on the one hand, and a subscription-based model on the other. A key objective was to move P2P users from the free-advertising model to becoming feepayers in an advertising-free premium tier of membership, but with an understanding that fees needed to be low enough to represent value to users habituated to obtaining such services for free, subject to the inconveniences and disruption of advertising content (Eriksson *et al.* 2019).

However, the recruitment of these assets – advertising consuming users or fee-paying subscribers – needed to be reconciled on the platform balance sheet with liabilities – the payments for each stream made to rights owners. Such payments were never a consideration for illegal P2P networks. Ideally, platforms would have an all-subscription service, facilitating better management of assets and liabilities, with an effective process of capitalization through direct revenue. Some platforms, such as Apple Music for example, have achieved this. Apple was, however, already a large technology company and so had the advantage of having a wider portfolio of revenues that could cross subsidize the new service as it became established. Such breathing room was unavailable to start-up platforms that, while cosseted by large volumes of venture capital funds (Srnicek 2016), were nevertheless on relatively tight deadlines to grow their business and scale to a size that it could be "cashed out" through an IPO providing returns to investors (Langley & Leyshon 2017). For this reason, platforms such as Spotify have exerted considerable effort in attempting to monetize the large number of users that pay no subscription, with non-paying users generating liabilities through streams not covered by subscription assets. Indeed, the process of converting users to subscribers has been a central aim of Spotify's business model since its inception:

> Spotify was founded with the stated aim to mediate between the interests of two conflicting economic actors, the music industry on the one hand, and non-authorized file-sharers on the other ... To do so, they had first to transform the meaning of online music listening, shifting

Table 2.1 Music streaming platforms, revenues, and users for one independent record label (2016 and 2019)

Rank by revenue share (2019)	Music streaming platform	Average $ per stream		Total streams of label roster (%)		Total stream revenue of label roster (%)		Streams per song		Streams per album	
		2016	2019	2016	2019	2016	2019	2016	2019	2016	2019
1	Spotify	0.00437	0.00348	62.97	22.09	69.57	44.33	139	175	1,394	1,752
2	Apple Music	0.00735	0.00675	7.18	6.36	13.35	24.79	83	90	828	902
3	YouTube Content ID	N/A	0.00022	–	51.00	–	6.42	–	2,794	–	27,940
4	Amazon Unlimited	–	0.01123	–	0.83	–	5.35	–	542	–	542
5	Deezer	0.00640	0.00562	2.19	0.80	3.54	2.58	95	108	952	1,048
6	Google Play	0.00676	0.00554	2.36	0.79	4.03	2.54	90	110	901	1,099
7	Pandora	0.00133	0.00203	0.07	1.91	0.02	2.24	456	299	4,565	2,993
8	YouTube	0.00069	0.00154	21.70	1.90	3.81	1.70	876	395	8,764	3,947
9	Amazon Music	0.00402	0.01123	0.63	0.65	0.64	1.60	151	143	1,515	1,431
10	Facebook	–	0.05705	–	0.05	–	1.56	–	11	–	107
11	YouTube Red	–	0.01009	–	0.23	–	1.37	–	60	–	604
12	Peloton	–	0.03107	–	0.07	–	1.28	–	20	–	196
13	TaiHe Music Group	–	0.00044	–	4.92	–	1.25	–	1,386	–	13,862

14	Yandex LLC	0.00016	0.00109	0.77	0.93	0.03	0.58	3,744	559	37,444	5,585
15	Tidal	0.01250	0.00876	0.10	0.11	0.33	0.58	49	70	487	695
16	Rhapsody/Napster	0.01900	0.00916	0.52	0.07	2.52	0.37	32	66	321	665
17	TDC Play	–	0.00994	–	0.06	–	0.37	–	61	–	612
18	LOEN	–	0.00235	–	0.13	–	0.18	–	259	–	2,594
19	UMA	–	0.00022	–	1.17	–	0.15	–	2,779	–	27,794
20	PlayNetwork	0.00065	0.00032	0.07	0.67	0.12	0.12	943	1,916	9,429	19.157
21	Telecom Italia	0.02189	0.01693	0.04	0.01	0.25	0.09	28	36	278	360
22	KKBOX	0.00358	0.00408	0.74	0.04	0.12	0.09	170	149	1,701	1,492
23	VEVO	–	0.00083	–	0.13	–	0.06	–	737	–	7,374
24	Slacker	0.00442	0.00713	0.02	0.01	0.03	0.06	138	85	1,379	854
25	iHeartRadio	–	0.01798	–	0.01	–	0.05	–	34	–	339
26	LINE	–	0.00970	–	0.01	–	0.05	–	63	–	628
27	iMusica	–	0.02247	–	0.00	–	0.05	–	27	–	271
28	Bugs Corporation	–	0.00427	–	0.01	–	0.03	–	143	–	1,426
29	Reliance Jio	–	0.00133	–	0.02	–	0.02	–	346	–	3,463
30	Gaana	–	0.00133	–	0.02	–	0.01	–	457	–	4,575
	Total	**0.00395***	**0.00173**					**154***	**352**	**1,540***	**3,516**

Note: *average includes data from MSPs in leading 30 platforms for 2016 but that did not rank in 2019.

Source: The Trichordist 2017, 2020.

> focus from ownership to access, and then "from access to context" so that a business model based on advertising revenue could take hold.
>
> (Vonderau 2019: 8)

Despite the considerable efforts made in this regard, such as developing strategies for personalization of scale as outlined earlier (Hracs & Webster 2021), or running sophisticated online competitions among advertisers to get appropriate advertisements in front of potentially receptive users, still there is substantial risk in this form of revenue generation as it might not cover the liabilities generated by the streams of unsubscribed users. Seeking to balance assets and liabilities in a new, risky, and volatile market offers some explanation for the low income per stream rates.

Finally, revenues per stream appear low because of historical power imbalances between artists and corporate rights holders in the music industry, which have only been amplified by the platform economy. As Hesmondhalgh (2021: 3599) points out, streaming platforms do not in reality pay according to a pre-determined per stream rate; rather, the rate is better understood as "an analytical construct, an average produced by taking the income generated by an individual recording, by an artist, or by a label, and dividing that income by [the] number of streams achieved by that recording". In fact, the allocation of revenue from the income collected by streaming platforms is allocated on a proportional basis related to an artist's share of total streams, notwithstanding the requirement of tracks to have a certain number of streams to even qualify for a share of the disbursement. This, like much else in the platform economy, is a winner-takes-all model. The higher the share of total streams generated by subscribers, and the higher the volume of advertising revenue generated by non-subscribers, the higher the rate per stream. Although the (variable) per stream rate will determine artist income from streaming, both Hesmondhalgh (2021) and Arditi (2019) emphasize the importance of recognizing these revenues are actually paid to rights holders (record companies and publishers) with only a portion then passed on to the artists: "The value gap is pure ideology. By arguing streaming services underpay recording artists, the IFPI ... and major record labels turn the process of exploiting artists on its head. Streaming services do not pay recording artists, record labels pay recording artists" (Arditi 2019: 20). Therefore, representatives of the music industry are correct in claiming that the rates of return per stream offered by digital platforms are symbolic of a power inequity, with artists on one side and intermediaries on the other. However, record companies and other holders of intellectual property rights holders are themselves powerful intermediaries, with significant financial stakes in many streaming platforms, illustrating how the industry has successfully co-opted digital platforms.

The perceived monopolization of the industry by a small number of large corporations, and the profits being generated by these corporations relative to artist remuneration, represented one of the major points of concern of the UK House of Commons' Digital, Cultural, Media and Sport (DCMS) Committee music streaming enquiry, launched in October 2020. As noted at the opening of this chapter, three major corporations – Sony Music Group, Universal Music Group, and Warner Music Group – form a strong oligopoly within the industry. In terms of recorded music, by 2022 these three controlled an estimated 70 per cent global market share (Universal 31.8 per cent, Sony 22.6 per cent and Warner 15.6 per cent). In terms of publishing, in the same year it is estimated that they cumulatively owned and/or administered over ten million compositions between their respective publishing arms, taking a 60 per cent share of the market (Sony Music Publishing 24.7 per cent, Universal Music Publishing Group 23.4 per cent and Warner Chappell Music 12 per cent) (Dredge 2023). The value which musicians receive from their music is dependent on the deals that record labels strike with the MSPs, and as the industry's major catalogue owners (and, in the case of Spotify, stakeholders through sizeable shareholdings) they are strongly positioned to strike preferential deals with the MSPs (Simon 2019). We discuss this issue further in Chapter 3.

As White (2023) outlines, after the MSP takes its share (30 per cent), the rough split between record label and publisher of the remaining 70 per cent is currently 55/15. Half of the publishing share (that is, half of 15 per cent) goes to the songwriter, but as the publisher share of the overall value is so small, the returns to artists are low. Some record deals specify a 50/50 revenue split between label and artist, but this varies from label to label, with larger labels demanding a larger share, which can be up to as much as 90 per cent of all revenues. Hence, with regards to forming fair deals for artists, campaigners have argued that attention must focus primarily on the revenue allocation to record labels, rather than the share captured by the MSPs. Carter (2024) points to the fact that in Q1 of 2023, the major labels together earned $2.9 million per hour in streaming revenue. Yet, as Hesmondhalgh *et al.* (2021) observe, this is an issue of significant complexity with a number of different views, which are dependent on the relationships between music creators, rights holders and MSPs. On the one hand, they note that there is considerable controversy regarding music creators' earnings, and a sense amongst creators that they should be receiving greater rewards from the system. Yet, at the same time, many rights holders across the music recording and music publishing industries also consider they should be receiving greater amounts from MSPs.

According to White (2023) a number of related issues emerged from the DCMS hearing. First was the matter of whether a stream counts as "communication to the public", as occurs in public spaces such cafes or shops, or whether it is "making available" for consumers to select as they would with their own physical copies of vinyl records or CDs. In the case of the communication to the public, when music is played on broadcast platforms like radio, musicians can claim performing rights, with the allocation of revenues managed by Collective Management Organizations (CMOs). Such payments are allocated on a 50/50 basis between copyright owners and performers (Cooke 2020). Music streams, however, are classified as "making available", which means streams are ineligible for performing rights. Thus, revenue allocation becomes dependent on the deals struck between the recording rights holders (typically record labels) and the platforms. The result is typically a small return for featured musicians. The hearing devoted attention as to whether classifying streams as "communication to the public" might result in more equitable revenue arrangements (White 2023). Second was the matter of other ways in which revenue might be redistributed with the current streaming ecosystem, with specific regard to user-centric payments systems. As mentioned earlier, MSPs currently allocate revenue to artists by the proportion of the entire number of streams on the platform for which their streams are responsible. For subscribers, the result is that the vast bulk of their subscription fee pays for music that they do not listen to, rather than going to artists that they have streamed. As Dredge (2020) explains: "If an artist (Drake, say) got 2% of the streams in that period, then his rightsholders get 2% of the royalties pool. But what that means is essentially 2% of the royalties generated by *every* individual subscriber are going to Drake's music, even if they didn't listen to him at all" (emphasis added).

As such, an artist's direct relationship with their paying fans has been severed. While fans may look to support an artist by streaming more of their music, they can only do so indirectly by increasing the number of streams by that artist in relation to the overall total. The Committee heard accounts from musicians and industry bodies calling for user-centric payment systems (UCPS) in which listeners directly pay artists. Yet as White (2023) points out, it was noted that there is a need for more evidence of the efficacy of such a system in terms of artist remuneration, while such a system also requires a complex data architecture to manage the flow of money between artists and fans. UCPSs have the advantage of re-establishing a direct link between consumers and the artists they listen to on MSPs, and to bring about a significant redistribution of existing revenue flows to artists. Indeed, a study by ProMusik (2023), a German-based advocacy group that works to support freelance musicians, suggests that UCPSs would redistribute over a quarter of total revenues, reducing the incomes of some artists while increasing the income of others. However, while 29 per cent of artists would see an increase in revenues of at least 40 per cent following a switch to UCPS, a larger proportion – 39 per cent – would experience a decline in revenues of 40 per cent or more. The highest gainers were responsible for only

19 per cent of total streams, while the biggest losers accounted for 31 per cent of all streams, indicating that a shift to UCPS would bring about a progressive redistribution of income. But it would also produce more losers than winners, which would disproportionately impact on the more successful artists, indicating the considerable political challenge of bringing about such a change.

While narratives around music streaming have shifted over time from critiques of the MSPs towards critiques of the role of the majors as the largest rights owners, one area in which the grievances of both labels and musicians alike have coalesced has been in relation to YouTube. As Negus (2019) notes, the relationship between YouTube and music companies has been one of mutual antagonism and mutual dependency, with musicians, publishers and labels habitually complaining that they should be receiving greater financial payments for the use of their music on the platform. Indeed, it was in relation to YouTube that the notion of a "value gap" was initially formulated within the music industries, describing the imbalance between the profits being made by the platform and the revenues being passed on to music companies and musicians (see, e.g., RIAA 2017; IFPI 2018). On one hand, complaints that a streamed song is not adequately being rewarded financially are ones that, as we have seen, are levelled at streaming platforms more broadly. However, on the other hand, YouTube represents a somewhat different case where music is often not the primary content itself, but rather used as part of the creation of other video "content" which for the platform attracts audiences which in turn attract advertisers. As such Negus (2019) argues, arguments regarding the value of music in this space are seeing the recording industry and YouTube splitting along a "broader schism": "On one side, the 'business model' of investment in artistic production, remuneration through copyrights and unit sales within the recording and publishing industries. On the other side, a model of generating income from the way 'content' attracts advertising, a model deployed lucratively by the new digital conglomerates" (Negus 2019: 374).

A major point of contention has been YouTube's ability to benefit from "safe harbour" rules, a cornerstone of internet policy over the past several decades, which exempt online intermediaries from liability for materials hosted by their systems. The result of these rules is that YouTube does not take legal or financial culpability for content generated by platform users, even where this includes unauthorized copyrighted material, such as music. Indeed, copyright infringement has been one significant driver for calls in recent years to abolish the concept of safe harbour in relation to internet content.

Yet, in examining the music industries call to revise or remove safe harbour rules, some analysts of cyber law and policy have warned against such a move. For Elkin-Koren *et al.* (2020), even assuming that stakeholders are currently receiving inadequate compensation, this is "not the result of safe harbour but rather a by-product of fundamental social and economic developments that have transformed the way we create and consume creative content" (2020: 5). Claims that YouTube relies on safe harbour immunities and misemploys them as a shield to avoid licensing with right holders is, the authors argue, factually incorrect. Rather, they argue that since 2006, YouTube has been regularly negotiating and executing licensing agreements with publishers, music labels, collecting societies, and artists to shelter themselves against secondary liability claims, while at the same time decreasing the monitoring and enforcement costs of right holders. Further, they point to the voluntary enforcement mechanisms platforms adopt as part of their business models – such as YouTube's Content ID system, which is an automated scanning system that proactively identifies potentially infringing content – which they have no legal obligation to provide. Reportedly, as of 2019, YouTube's Content ID system had already enabled the company to distribute more than $3 billion in revenues to artists and right holders. Finally, they point to the fact that amendments to copyright legislation could end up harming the very group of beneficiaries the music industry is claiming to fight for: musicians. While the rhetoric of the value gap attempts to portray a unified front between right holders, music labels, and artists as allies fighting against YouTube, a hidden part of the narrative remains the distribution of revenues among different stakeholders within the music industry, with the vast majority of income generated through online streaming going to record labels rather than to musicians. This, Elkin-Koren *et al.* (2020) argue, raises some concerns over the alignment of goals represented by the music industry, as well as the ability of changes in the copyright laws to close the so-called value gap.

Conclusions

In response to the MP3 crisis of the early twentieth century, digital platforms have demonstrated a capacity to reconfigure music industry business models, stem overall industry losses, and develop new sources of revenue. But in so doing, they have also fractured taken for granted ways of doing business and created new sets of winners and losers, prompting concerns over fair returns derived from normative expectations forged in an earlier conjuncture. As revenues continue to grow and streaming platforms sink into the background of the music business, new moral economies based on new taken for granted ways of working will be formed. In this chapter, we have argued that the MSPs are digital platforms that have their own dynamics of economic transformation, and which encourage capital concentration and centralization. They also reflect existing structural inequalities and amplify them in new ways. Platforms have served to reinforce the power structures of the traditional musical economy but have added new dynamics based on a winner-takes-all sensibility.

We have argued that many of the moral economy arguments developed around the music industries in the face of the growing dominance of platforms are flawed, because they fail to recognize the agency of music corporations in the platform economy, particularly given their extensive stakes in MSPs such as Spotify (Vonderau 2019). Moreover, such arguments disregard the nature of the platform business model and the need to balance assets with liabilities. Moral economy arguments circulate because there remains sufficient institutional memory within the music industries that remembers all too well the damage done by P2P networks in the early twentieth century. While platforms may be the new corporate titans, they were formed in the libertarian furnace of Silicon Valley, and MSPs share the DNA – and indeed, in some cases, the same code – as the P2P networks that laid waste to the established business models of the music industries (Eriksson *et al.* 2019). It may also be that senior figures in the music industries can see that platforms are coming to colonize all aspects of the diverse "value ecology" of the musical economy. Platforms play an ever more critical role in the mobilization of affect, and the conversion of fan enthusiasm into income. Streaming services are now even making inroads into the final pre-serve of the musical value economy once considered to be immune to the reach of platforms, live performance. These are issues which we shall address in the subsequent chapters of this book. But first, in the next chapter, we expand on some of the issues raised here with regards to the complex relationships that exists between the major corporations, MSPs and other key actors within the music industry, with a particular focus on rights and rent extraction.

3
RIGHTS AND RENTS IN THE PLATFORM MUSIC INDUSTRIES

Introduction

One way of understanding the story of the recorded music industry over a 40-year period is to see it as a process of socio-technological evolution, based around shifting formats. Traditionally, as in the case of the compact disc for example, the recorded music industry organizes to first resist new formats but then negotiates with large technology companies to ensure that a format does not undermine returns on intellectual property rights in sound recordings (Knopper 2009). In this respect, MP3 was an "accidental format", developed as an open compression programme for work on interactive television, which escaped into the emerging online worlds of software programmers and hackers. The format was quickly adopted by an array of rapidly changing peer-to-peer (P2P) networks. As the previous chapter argued, these early platforms constituted the first wave of platformization in the music industries.

In contrast to such a view, Wikström (2020) insists that the recorded music industries are better understood as copyright industries, and that this provides an important starting point for the conceptualization of the music economy in the digital age. Indeed, we contend that the negative impacts of the rise of P2P networks on the music industries can be best understood through this lens. Operating mainly as illegal digital intermediaries and offering the promise of free access to music catalogues that they did not own so as to attract users to their networks, their use of copyrighted material without permission or recompense saw the revenues of the holders of music rights go into a precipitous decline. This was addressed only after the major corporations of the recorded music industry negotiated with large technology companies to reset platform reintermediation on more favourable – and financially sustainable – terms. First, Apple's iTunes store, which began trading in in 2004, built on experiments by firms such as eMusic to allow customers to buy MP3 downloads, which allowed rights holders to be paid. This was shortly followed by the emergence of streaming platforms, as firms such as Spotify, Deezer and Apple Music developed revenue-generating business models, and returned the major corporations to profitability. As argued in Chapter 2, the advance of the music steaming platforms constituted the second wave of platform intermediation in the music industries.

In this chapter, we build on our previous arguments to considering the broader framework of music rights in which the platform music industries operate, and especially in relation to the relationship that exists between major corporations and other key actors in the music industries, most notably the MSPs. As we have noted, the business model of MSPs requires access to the catalogues of recorded music owned by large music corporations, the depth and breadth of which are used to recruit users from whom revenues can be extracted through subscriptions or advertising (Arditi 2019). Yet, MSPs operate within a highly oligopolistic recorded music industry made up of a very small number of incumbent corporations that each prioritize intellectual property protection. And the monetary value of the music catalogues controlled by the large record companies is significant. By 2023, it was estimated that as much as $45.5 billion was generated through an exploitation of the rights vested in recordings, publishing and performance (Page 2024). The rise of digital music distribution platforms has led to claims of structural and organizational inertia amongst the major corporations and an overestimation of the power of the big record labels (Negus 2019). Further, as we shall outline in subsequent chapters, revolutionary narratives have pointed to the possibilities of the democratization of music production and consumption, and to some predictions of even more radical processes of disintermediation (as we shall discuss in Chapter 5, for example, in the context of blockchain-enabled decentralized autonomous organizations).

However, the major label system remains intact. Certainly, the platformization of the music economy has, as Negus (2019) notes, drawn the music corporations into tensions with BigTech digital conglomerates and MSPs. But platforms have certainly not displaced the recorded music industry incumbents; rather, the major music corporations and the MSPs have become bound together through a system of *rent extraction* (Meier & Manzerolle 2019). We consider this system further in the following section, before then reflecting on some of the specific characteristics of music rights, how they function and result in revenues, and how they shape contracts between record labels and artists. Following this, we examine the growing interest of financial markets in investing in music rights, and the drivers that have seen investors, including pension funds, banks and private equity firms, buy stakes in music publishers and catalogues. Finally, we consider the recent emergence of machine learning generative AI music systems and the questions these systems raise about both distributive justice and the adequacy of existing copyright regimes.

Rights, rents and incumbents

Christophers (2020: xxiv) describes rent as "income derived from the owner-ship, possession or control of scarce assets under conditions of limited or no competition". In industries centred on the ownership of intellectual property, he argues, IP rights owners can secure monopoly powers over their assets. Or, to put it in more simply, rent is a payment to an economic actor (the rentier) who receives this income purely by controlling something valuable. It is such a system of rent extraction, we argue, taken together with the volatile nature of the market for music, which has encouraged the formation of a very power-ful oligopoly in the market for musical intellectual property. Indeed, we would argue that the steadfast ownership of music rights exercised by the incumbent music corporations means that it is they, not the streaming platforms, which hold the balance of power in the contemporary music industries, doing so by exploiting an "intellectual monopoly". Yet, as Christophers (2020: xxv) argues, in rentierism "income derives simultaneously both from the control of an asset and from the work involved in delivery of the product or service underwritten by it". That is, assets only generate income when they are "put to work". In this respect, while the major record labels play a crucial role in marketing, it is the rise of MSPs that has allowed large music corporations to better marshal rents from their assets. In many markets, platforms seek entry to take advantage of their ability to become key intermediaries in multi-sided markets, to become rentiers of the network (Langley & Leyshon 2017). In the platform music industries, rent takes the form of the licence fees paid by MSPs to the corporations. MSPs face a powerful oligopoly with whom they must directly negotiate rights agreements to access the most commercially successful music on their platforms, for which they function as an intermediary, allowing audiences, in return for a subscrip-tion fee (or otherwise be exposed to advertising, which also generates income for the platform), access to a vast and ever-expanding musical archive. It is from these fees and advertising revenues that MSPs pay for the licences granted by the music corporations.

For Christophers (2020: xviii), business models based on rentierism represent a kind of "balance sheet capitalism". In the contemporary music industries, the role of recorded music on the balance sheet differs between its major corporate actors. For the large music corporations, their back catalogues of copyrighted music are incontrovertibly seen as assets, which generate income through use, either through sales of licensing agreements with other media organizations or streaming platforms. However, for the streaming platforms, while access to these back catalogues certainly serves as business-critical asset (by generating income for each stream initiated by users) as we argued in the previous chapter it is also a liability, as platforms are obliged to make rental payments to rights owners for each stream. In this regard, the accumulation and maintenance of a population of users that will pay a regular subscription represents an important asset to streaming platforms. This is reflected in the innovations in user interfaces and services that are designed to keep audiences engaged. Furthermore, the major record labels have used their incumbent positions to negotiate preferential licensing agreements with, and acquire equity stakes in, a range of streaming platforms and companies (Negus 2019). In the case of Spotify, for example, the three major corporations together control about two-thirds of its streaming catalogue; if combined with Merlin – a digital rights agency for independent record labels with a membership of some 20,000 independent record labels and distributors – just four organizations hold the rights for the music that makes up 87 per cent of Spotify's streams (Simon 2019). This has further strengthened the position of the major music corporations as incumbents. While MSPs continue to post significant net losses despite significant increases in paying users, the record label oligopoly has reaped significant profits from the digital music boom. This, as Meier and Manzerolle (2019: 555) argue, is demonstrative of how platform accumulation "is structurally biased to support existing capital".

Music rights represent intangible assets that allow the leading firms to enhance their market power, restricting the use of music both within production and consumption (Durand & Milberg 2020). Intellectual property aims to create an artificial monopoly over assets to enable the capture of monopoly rents (Montgomery & Potts 2009). As Meier and Manzerolle (2019: 548) argue, although users of streaming services have access to a seemingly non-depletable resource (music), "copyright regimes are used to (attempt to) maintain artificial scarcity", and in this way, legal monopoly rents artificially ration the use of the protected intangible asset (Durand & Milberg 2020) as a "pure source of rent and distortion" (see Montgomery & Potts 2009: 247). This is an example of what Pagano (2014) has termed "intellectual monopoly capitalism" where monopoly is not only based on market power due to skills and management, but on a legal monopoly exercised over some items. In this case, intellectual monopoly infers the right to control subsequent use of music as exercised through "downstream licensing", as opposed to the right to own and sell music (Boldrin & Levine 2002).

Furthermore, as the focus of value generation in the music industries has shifted towards driving users towards MSPs, the entrenched commercial and promotional logics of the industries' "superstar economy" (Rosen 1981; Krueger 2005) have persisted, with superstar performers receiving the lion's share of promotion and attention (Meier & Manzerolle 2019). The rights of superstar artists tend to be controlled by the major corporations, and a very small proportion of all the music available on MSPs accounts for most of the streams generated. This asymmetry is likely to increase over time, given that in 2023 there were an estimated 120,000 new music audio files added to streaming services every day

(Stassen 2023), which was more than twice the number than as recently as 2020 (Page 2020). This means that nearly all of these tracks are more likely than not to lose the battle for attention (cf. Wu 2016). The power that the major corporations exercise over their catalogue gives them significant control over MSPs as "chokepoints" of digital music distribution.

Yet the complex relations between major music corporations goes beyond MSPs alone. The role of the major corporations as major catalogue owners, and strict enforcers of the related copyright, has brought them into conflict with a range of other platforms that use music to support content. In January 2024, for example, Universal Music Group (UMG) issued an open letter to TikTok – the Chinese owned social media platform that allows users to make short-form videos, many of which are soundtracked with licensed music – which accused the platform of attempting to "bully" and "intimidate" the music group into accepting a new rights deal that offered less than fair market value and not reflective of the platform's growth. UMG warned that if a fair deal were not reached, then their significant catalogue of music would be removed from TikTok. Furthermore, UMG were highly critical of TikTok's arguments regarding the value of the "free promotion" of the music group's artists, arguing that it represented an outdated view that did not recognize the need to fairly compensate artists. Subsequently, in March 2024 with no deal reached, TikTok began removing music that had been written or co-written by songwriters signed to Universal Music Publishing Group (UMPG). This was significant in terms of the availability of the most popular music on the platform: an analysis by Billboard suggested that in the final quarter of 2023, 41 of the top 100 tracks on TikTok were released by UMG labels, and that UMPG has an ownership interest in the compositions for 61 of the top 100 (Dredge 2024a). Yet, by May 2024, the dispute was settled and TikTok in a position to restore millions of songs to the platform. UMG claimed that TikTok had agreed to several changes to the use of copyrighted material that delivered better financial compensation for artists and songwriters than did the deal in operation prior to the dispute (although the financial details of the new deal were not released). This resolution also included commitments from TikTok to work with UMG to remove unauthorized AI-generated music from the platform, and to provide new tools to improve artist and songwriter attribution, which had been the source of related concerns for UMG (Gerken 2024).

Examples such as this would seem to support Wikstrom's (2009) assertation that decision makers in the music industries continue to defend their old core businesses despite an ongoing radical transformation of the media environment. Business models and fundamental industry structures remain more or less as they were when music was consumed through physical formats, and therefore, as discussed earlier, copyright remains the key mechanism through which this defence of assets takes place. As Scharf (2022) argues, technologies and intermediaries in the music industries have now evolved around copyright law, as opposed to the other way around. In the era of streaming, copyright is centrally important in establishing the initial proprietary rights that enable subsequent digital rights management and licence-based online exploitation. As the key mechanism for protecting and managing the content offered on such platforms, the strict defence of copyright has enabled the major rights-holding corporations to successfully exploit both the volume and the popularity of the content they represent during the emergence of the streaming era (Kjus 2022a). In this regard, it can be seen as indicative of a re-establishment of power in the music industries that is now allied with streaming platforms (Scharf 2022). Yet, as discussed in Chapter 2 in relation to artist remuneration and legal under-standings of what type of consumption music steaming represents, this has not been uncontentious.

Concerns have also been expressed that the operation of digital rights man-agement in conjunction with licence agreements with a keen eye to rates of return and cash flows may have future implications for music chart diversity (Scharf 2022). Wikstrom (2009), for example, argues that within the wider economy it is not by developing intellectual properties more efficiently than its competitors that will make a copyright firm prosper in the long term, but rather by continuously developing new intellectual properties. In the music industries too, he argues, successful new products are typically produced by firms that embrace the intrinsic high-risk nature of the music business. However, in the post-crisis recorded music industries of the early 2000s, firms typically adopted defensive and risk reduction strategies that have more immediate results with regards to short term financial goals, rather than revenue-enhancing strategies, which are associated with considerable time lags before returns are accrued. Such risk aversion, he argues, has had an impact new talent development and reducing long-term competitiveness. Such an observation is echoed by Benner and Waldfogel (2016) who argue that major labels have responded to recent technological changes in the recorded music industry by shifting their efforts away from the discovery of "new-to-the-world" talent in favour of a focus on leveraging previously successful artists. In a book that focused on the growing ranks of what might be described as a popular music gerontocracy, made up of artists with careers spanning 50–60 years, many of whom were still perform-ing in their eighth and nineth decades, the journalist David Hepworth asked the question, "How did pop music, which was once supposed to be exclusively about the shock of the new, come to have such a comfortable relationship with its past?" (2024: xii). The tendency, identified by Benner and Waldfogel, of re-cord labels to increasingly promote artists that have already been successful on the Billboard top 200 and top 50 lists, is clearly one of the reasons. They suggest that:

This persistence in deploying high cost complementary resources and capabilities by the major labels likely arises due to the continued value of incumbents' complementary assets specifically for the most promising, broadest in market appeal, and therefore highest-revenue segment of the market. The most promising artists that are leveraged by the major labels as they become increasingly selective are likely to benefit from – and demand – the higher cost distribution and promotion capabilities of the major labels. In turn, in the face of declining revenue, the usefulness and value of these interlinked traditional capabilities likely pushes the major labels to continue to select the types of predictably promising talent that will benefit from these relatively expensive and interrelated capabilities.   (Benner & Waldfogel 2016: 124)

At the same time, Benner and Waldfogel argue that this greater selectivity coincides with an overall decline in the number of major label music releases. This contrasts with their analysis of independent labels which, they suggest, are producing more music and adopting lower cost approaches to activities enabled by technological change. Digital technologies, they note, have also reduced costs associated with production, distribution, and promotion, lowering barriers to entry for new independent entrants. The major corporations, in contrast, are "continuing to deploy expensive interrelated resources and capabilities, now in the narrower segment of the market where they are likely to retain their value" (Benner & Waldfogel 2016: 145). We see this as being reflective of one of the broader characteristics of rentier capitalism whereby rent-based asset incomes are associated with the *extraction* rather than the *creation* of value, or what Christophers (2020: 171) describes as particular mode of rentierism that invests "time and money more in sweating existing rent-generating assets than in carrying out the research and development necessary to create new ones".

The economics of music rights

Tschmuck (2017) argues that the recorded music industry is not a pure monopoly. Rather, music markets are shaped by monopolistic competition. Record companies act as monopolists in the sense that copyright grants an exclusive right to market recordings. However, a given recording by a given artist released on a given record label competes with other artists and record labels. As such, Tschmuck argues, while each company has a monopoly over its products, other record labels make similar products that compete for the same consumers. From this perspective music markets can be understood as a monopolistically competitive market characterized by many sellers, with product differentiation, which allows for free entry and exit. Yet, the conditions within the recorded music industry are not the same for all, being shaped (as are other sectors of the music industries including publishing and the live music business) by a few large dominant major corporations. Unlike the significant number of other smaller independent companies in the market, who operate within a monopolistically competitive market, these major corporations exist within an oligopoly, making strategic business decisions set in the context of the decisions of the other large and dominant companies. As Tschmuck (2017) points out, this oligopoly has characteristics that lie somewhere between monopoly and perfect competition: output is greater than the level produced under conditions of monopoly but lower than the level of perfect competition. Meanwhile, the oligopoly price is lower than the monopoly price but higher than it would be if the market were fully competitive. As a result, oligopolistic firms do not seek to maximize profits at all costs but look to maximize their market share, to increase the size of the company relative to the other firms with the oligopoly. Thus, it is common for a major record label to grow by buying independent labels to enlarge their catalogue of copyrighted master recordings, or to undertake other forms of catalogue acquisition, such as buying directly from artists or other rights holders.

Copyright can be understood as a kind of "bundle" of "rights" that can be sold or licensed (Marshall & Frith 2004). This "bundle" typically centres around the right to reproduce a work, to recreate a work, to create derivative works, to perform the work and to distribute the work (Galuszka & Legiedz 2024). Two main types of intellectual property exist in the music industries. First, there are what are referred to as "composition", "publishing" or "song" rights, through which music publishers control the distribution of written compositions (the music and accompanying lyrics), either on behalf of songwriters, or for music which they themselves own. This form of musical intellectual property is the oldest, predating as it does the birth of the recording industry (Attali 1985). Second, there are "recording" or "master" rights, through which record labels or recording artists control a particular recording of a song, track or sound performance (see Cooke 2020). These rights generate a number of different revenue streams, including for example *mechanical royalties* (when a song is reproduced and sold or streamed); *public performance royalties* (when a song is performed publicly); and *synchronization royalties* (generated when music is synchronized with visual images such as in movies, video games, television and advertisements). We shall revisit these revenue streams in Chapter 5 in the context of music publishing, social media and the incomes of independent artists. For now, it is important to note that music publishing has been central to the major corporations' oligopoly: having both record labels and publishing arms within the same corporate organization has allowed music companies to consolidate control over both master and song rights, managing these rights to maximize revenue.

Control of copyright holds a vital importance within the recorded music industries because of the way music is configured as a cultural product. For record labels, music recordings represent highly specific investments with particular characteristics. Recordings represent sunk costs for labels, in the sense that if the recording is not commercially successful, the financial capital invested within the recording is lost. This issue is exacerbated by the high levels of uncertainty surrounding commercial success in the recorded music industry, with only relatively few recordings breaking even. Therefore, as Tschmuck (2017) contends, copyright represents a form of "insurance" against poor business decisions as it allows labels to exploit a recording over a longer timeframe, helping to decrease the uncertainty around the original investment. The uncertainty around commercial success in music results in record companies seeking to gain control over almost all intellectual property rights linked with music creation (*ibid.*), through contracts that are "tipped" in the label's favour (Cooke 2020) so that they capture the majority of revenues from sales and streaming. While in many cases record deals specify a 50/50 split between label and artist, larger labels command a share greater than that of the artist and it is not unusual for contracts to specify a revenue split of 90/10 in favour of the label.[1] Contracts often centre on the exclusive transfer of the copyright for a recording (excluding the composition rights) from an artist to a record label *in perpetuity*, completely monopolizing a musician's creative work. In return, the record company typically provides the artist with an advance against future royalties (typically around 13–14 per cent of streaming and other sales revenues), whilst also allocating money and resources to marketing the artist's work (Krueger 2019). However, nine out of ten artists who sign to a major label will not cover their advance and expenses and therefore will not collect any royalties (*ibid.*), but nor will they be responsible for any financial losses.

Spurred by a decline in recorded music industry revenue caused by illegal file sharing, record companies began to explore so-called "360 deals" which expanded their access to more profitable fields of industry activity (Marshall 2013). The "360" deal is so named because it "encircles the contracted artist so that non-record-related activities and revenues formerly beyond the reach of the recording contract become subject to "participation" by the contracting company" (Stahl & Meier 2012: 442). Such activities are inclusive of a range of revenue streams, such as, for example, music publishing, touring, merchandising and endorsement, but can even go as far to include the corporate licensing of names, images and logos, and other new-media-enabled opportunities for monetization

---

1   This is comparable with other rights-based industries; for example, in the traditional book business, publishers absorb the majority of book revenues, typically paying authors royalties that range between 10–15 per cent (Parker *et al.* 2016).

of the artist persona. As Stahl and Meier (2012) describe, within 360 deals the record company may adapt an "active" or "passive" role in controlling these activities vis-à-vis the artist. Yet in either dynamic they note how these deals positioned record companies to take an increasing share of incomes which were previously collected entirely by artists and off-limits to record companies.

Since the emergence of these deals in the early 2010s, the shift towards streaming as primary method for music consumption, together with new marketing and branding opportunities made possible by a variety of other platforms, encouraged changes in the structure and focus of 360 deals. Kjus (2022b), for example, notes how there has been a rise in the issuing of record contracts for single tracks at the expense of the traditional album project, due to the way in which streaming encourages the consumption of individual tracks through flexible playlists. Kjus also finds that where longer-term contracts are signed, the traditional two to three albums deal has frequently been replaced with one that stipulates to up to nineteen singles, committing artists to shorter but more frequent projects. This, he argues, represents a refining of the economic logic of option contracts such that record labels can review the success of each single before deciding whether to invest in the next. Such contracts are designed to reduce the economic risk faced by labels, while at the same time expressing "more exhaustive claims to the exploitation of copyright-protected work in the digital context" (Kjus 2022b: 475). The risk offloaded by labels falls elsewhere, mainly on artists. Such contracts reduce the scope and predictability of their work, and the amount of funded time and other resources available to develop music projects. As such, 360 contracts in the digital era represent a continuation and extension of the "deep-seated imbalances in artist-label relations (Kjus 2022b: 475) that are longstanding within the music industries.

Music rights and financialization

As well as a kind of insurance, copyright also functions as a market entry barrier in the music industries (Towse 2011; Tschmuck 2017). The only way a competing firm can legally obtain and exploit an existing copyrighted recording is by buying the rights from the owner – or indeed acquiring or merging with the firms that owns the copyrights – or by acquiring a licence to use them (which, as we shall discuss in Chapter 4 in relation to MusicTech, has issues of both permissions and cost). As argued above, the monopolization of control over music works by the major corporations has led to a decline in the level of competition in the music industries and a tendency towards the oligopolization of music industries structures (Tschmuck 2017). This includes not only the control of catalogues of songs released through their labels but is also underpinned by their financial ability to purchase other catalogues. As recently as June 2024, for example, Sony Music paid over £1 billion to purchase the rights to the catalogue of the band Queen outside of North America,[2] along with a variety of other rights, representing the largest purchase for a single artist's catalogue in history (McIntyre 2024). In October 2024, Sony Music purchased the recorded music catalogue, name, and likeness rights of the band Pink Floyd for $400 million.

Nevertheless, recently we have seen a series of new players emerge in music markets, centred around the growing interest of financial markets in investing in music rights. While investment in music rights is not new, it traditionally came from within the music industries. However, since the late 1990s investors, including pension funds, banks and private equity firms, began purchasing music publishers and catalogues (Galuszka & Legiedz 2024). A series of new companies emerged which made substantial investment in the catalogues of high-profile artists and offered investors the opportunity to invest in the funds that owned songs and their associated musical intellectual property rights. The capitalization of copyright assets in fact foreshadowed the later roll out of the 360-degree deal because both are driven by the same logic, which is to buy the rights to an income stream, at a discount. A discount rate is a standard financial calculation which is used to convert future cash flows in an equivalent one-off up-front sum or present value. It reflects the time value of money, accounting for the idea that a sum of money today is worth more than the same sum in the future due to its potential earning capacity. The discount rate is used to equate future cash flows to their present value, making it easier to compare and evaluate the value of money received at different times. Factors influencing the discount rate include the risk-free rate (such as the rate paid by US and UK government bonds, for example), inflation expectations, and the risk premium associated with the uncertainty surrounding the cash flow.

For music companies, 360-degree deals were attractive because they could take the risk that they would be better able to exploit the opportunities around an artist's varied income streams over time, purchased at a discount now to what the income streams might generate over time. For the artists, such deals were attractive because although they gave up the right to a future sum of money that might be in excess of the sum they were paid by music companies in exchange for these rights, the discounted sum of money was brought forward in time. Purchasing the rights to the back catalogues of music by artists is based on a similar logic with a similar discount rate; artists are able to bring forward in time

---

2   Which, according to Simpson (2024), are owned by Disney "in perpetuity", although some of the band's remaining royalties from them will go to Sony once the deal closes. Similarly, the group's distribution deal, which is currently with Universal, will transfer to Sony in all territories outside North America when that expires in a couple of years

the income they might earn in the future which, particularly for older and more established artists, is at least delivered in their lifetime.

The first example of the capitalization of music rights is broadly accredited to David Pullman, a financial trader who began his career buying and selling mortgage-backed securities. In 1997, as managing director of Fahenstock & Company's Structured Assets sale group, he pioneered the securitization of music rights when he converted the future income of David Bowie's royalty and publishing income into a $55 million ten-year bond issue (Chen 2000). The financial engineering involved has been succinctly described by McCrum:

> Bowie struck a licensing deal with EMI for his back catalogue giving the group the rights to release 25 Bowie albums from between 1969 and 1990. These included his most popular work – *Ziggy Stardust, Aladdin Sane, Hunky Dory* and *Let's Dance* – as well as unreleased studio and live recordings. He was guaranteed more than 25 per cent of the royalties from wholesale sales in the US. Those rights were then securitized, turned into $55m of Bowie Bonds, offering a 7.9 per cent annual coupon. The bonds were "self-liquidating", meaning the principal declined each year, and the rating agency Moody's blessed the deal with an investment grade credit rating.   (McCrum 2016; no pagination)

The self-liquidating quality of the bonds meant that the money invested would be paid back to investors at the end of the ten-year term, which required borrowers to ensure that they either put the money received to work, by purchasing even higher yielding assets or having access to other income streams or sources of debt to ensure that funds are available to repay the principal when the bonds expire. The interest rate, at 7.9 per cent, which was paid on top of the principal, was higher than background rates of interest, but was necessary to attract money to an investment inherently riskier than risk-free government debt. But the interest rate was also based in part on an estimation of the income that could be gleaned through the royalty and publishing payments accruing to an artist with the status and fan base of David Bowie. By the mid-1990s, a typical CD retailed at $18 in the US, and at around $25–30 in Europe and Japan (Strauss 1995), while Bowie sold around 1 million albums per year, which promised lucrative returns. Encouraged by the uptake of the offer, similar securitizations were quickly arranged by Pullman for the rights of other storied artists such as James Brown, Holland-Dozier-Holland, the Isley Brothers and Ashford & Simpson (Chen 2000).

These financial instruments strongly resembled existing forms of securitization, not only in their design, but also in the way they shifted risk from sellers to investors, who were nevertheless attracted to the bonds because of their promised returns over prevailing interest rates and inflation. As Chen (2000) notes, even as these financial instruments were developed, there were concerns about the wider applicability of such deals due to the high levels of information asymmetry in the music industries, and the fickle nature of taste and fashion that means that the demand for music is very volatile. But it was not individual artists waning in popularity that ultimately threatened such deals, but rather the broader structural changes underway in the music industries as MP3s and P2P networks laid waste to much of the royalty and publishing income that underpinned the bonds. According to McCrum (2016), Bowie Bonds evolved out of an initial interest expressed by the artist in selling the ownership of his Master recordings in exchange for an upfront free, which given his later prescient pronouncements on the implications of the internet on music revenues, may have been prompted by an intimation that, as far as music rights were concerned, he was currently at the top of what would be a rapidly deflating market. Persuaded otherwise by Pullman in favour of securitization, Bowie not only kept the ownership of his Masters but benefitted from the multi-million investment in exchange for revenue income which, as the recorded music industry fell into crisis, declined precipitously, bringing the sales of his records down with it. By 2004 Bowie Bonds, originally deemed to be a high-quality investment, were downgraded to junk bond status, a form of investment that has a high rate of default due to the weakness of the underlying payments upon which they are based.

However, although the bonds came under stress, they did not default, and at the end of their ten-year term in 2007 they were liquidated, investors were repaid, and the income from royalties and publishing reverted back to David Bowie and his management company. But investment in such celebrity bonds proved to be a chastening experience against the background of the ongoing crisis of the recorded music industry. These were amplified by the breaking of the global financial crisis in 2008, particularly as they revolved around forms of securitization that provided the templates for Bowie Bonds and the like, namely mortgage-backed securities. As a result, there was understandably very little immediate appetite for similar attempts to capitalize music royalty and publishing income. Yet, during this wider crisis, the seeds of renewal in music capitalization were taking form, through the rise first of digital platforms that enabled legal downloads, and then music streaming platforms (MSPs) that not only ensured a steadier flow of funds. This once more made music amenable to capitalization through the ownership of music rights.

New forms of investment have emerged which reflect the changing financialized realities in which artists and music industries operate since platform-based music streaming became the dominant form of music consumption in the major music markers of the Global North (Galuszka & Legiedz 2024). The success of streaming services has been crucial in demonstrating the potential of copyright as an asset: not only did streaming demonstrate that music could once again generate revenue following the MP3 crisis, but it generates steady and predictable revenue over an extended period of time. As Leyshon and Thrift (2007: 98) argue, the early twenty-first century heralded a period of contemporary financial capitalism in which processes of securitization sought to "identify almost anything that might provide a stable source of income, on which speculation might be built", and in this respect music rights, in theory at least, provide such a stable and continuing income stream. Thus, MSPs have played a pivotal role in music rights becoming an attractive asset in financial markets. Unlike physical formats, streaming monetizes consumption rather than transactions, and furthermore streaming services are able to provide detailed data on the profitability of particular songs and particular catalogues of music. This data, Galuszka and Legiedz (2024) argue, allows investors to see the performance of these "assets" and thus is central to earning the trust of financial markets, along with a belief that platform-based music streaming will remain the dominant form of music consumption into the future.

One of the most high-profile of the companies purchasing the rights to music in the post-Bowie Bond period has been Kobalt Music Group, which was founded in 2000, and describes itself as an independent music rights management and music publishing company. The corporate history recounted on its web site tells a heroic story of its founders' ability to successfully lean into the digital transition that was disrupting the traditional music industry to bring about a more efficient – but also lucrative – reintermediation of rights and revenues:

> The start-up built a platform to maximize efficiency, accuracy, and transparency across the billions of micro-payments collected in today's highly complex digital world. As traditional music companies fought technology and contracted, Kobalt embraced it and grew, building a global digital music infrastructure and world-class creative team purposely designed to usher in the streaming era and a more fair, rewarding music business for creators.[3]

Initially focusing on music publishing, Kobalt sought to exploit the complexities and lags in the system for collecting royalties on behalf of publishing rights holders, caused by the legacy system of rights collection, which passed through largely national based organizations. For example, the Paris-based International

---

3   See Kobalt Music; https://www.kobaltmusic.com/who-we-are/.

Confederation of Societies of Authors and Composers (CISAC) contains as many as 133 national based performance rights collection societies within its music division.[4]

> The ... efficiency and accuracy of its electronic royalty collections and reporting system ... is at the core of its administrative services. This system – designed, owned and operated solely by Kobalt – automatically communicates with and collects directly from the majority of its international content users; the data from these transactions being managed by a singular database. Given the lag time inherent in foreign sub publisher reporting and remittance of licensing and royalty monies owed, Kobalt's ability to bypass these entities allows it to pay its clients more quickly (an estimated 50 per cent faster) and more accurately than publishers doing so by more traditional means.
>
> (Alberti 2011; no pagination)

It was the success of this model that encouraged the firm to move into other areas of rights management, and in 2011 create a record labels services division (Peters 2023), and establish Kobalt Capital Ltd (KCL) as an investment management focused on music rights. This was the world's first regulated music royalties investment fund, raising $350 million to spend on music rights. In 2017, KCL closed its second managed fund (Fund II) to invest in music copyright, with a capacity of $600 million through $345 million of equity commitments plus debt, led by the UK railways pension scheme Railpen, along with other institutional investors (Ingham 2017). Subsequently, in December 2017 KCL acquired Songs Music Publishing's catalogue for a reported $150 million, competitively bidding against other major players in the music publishing business (Paine 2017). In 2021, leading global investment firm KKR, together with Dundee Partners, purchased Fund II – which owned more than 62,000 copyrights by artists across pop, rock, hip hop, country and other genres – from KCL for approximately $1.1 billion, with sister company Kobalt Music Publishing administering and servicing the works under a multi-year agreement (Kobalt 2021). In November 2023, KCL announced a new partnership with investment funds managed by Morgan Stanley Tactical Value to invest more than $700 million to acquire music copyrights, with Kobalt managing the creative, synch, licensing, administration, and investment services for the copyrights (Morgan Stanley 2023). Soon afterwards, in March 2024, Kobalt increased its total funding capacity to over $1 billion,

---

4   See International Confederation of Societies of Authors and Composers (CISAC) membership list; https://members.cisac.org/CisacPortal/annuaire.do?method=members DirectoryList&by=directory&alpha=&rme=&domain=domain.music.

having obtained $266.5 million from an asset-backed securitization (Smith 2024b). The success of Kobalt in raising such sums is demonstrative of the rapidly growing interest from financial markets in music assets during this period.

More recently, 2018 saw the launch of Hipgnosis, a British music intellectual property investment and song management company, which has rapidly gained prominence through an aggressive campaign to purchase music catalogues over a relatively brief period of time (Galuszka & Legiedz 2024). This buying spree, which exceeded $2 billion (Sisario 2024a), was enabled by the successful and repeated raising of money from new investors, which included for example the Church of England's investment arm. Hipgnosis Songs Fund (HSF) was established as an investment trust and listed on the main market of the London Stock Exchange in July 2018, before transferring to the premium segment in November 2019, and since March 2020 it has been a constituent of the FTSE 250 Index. HSF, the listed entity, operates as an investment trust that owns the song rights, while a separate company, Hipgnosis Song Management (HSM), acts as is its "investment adviser" and does much of the work of acquiring assets. HSM is part owned by investment firm Blackstone (perhaps most well-known for real estate investment, see Christophers 2022) which in 2021 invested $1 billion in the company to take majority control (Sisario 2024b). In November 2020, Hipgnosis acquired 42 catalogues from Kobalt Capital's first fund (Fund I) for $322.9 million, which was made up of 33,000 songs by 1,500 songwriters. Kobalt acted as Hipgnosis' main publishing administrator, demonstrating the complex interdependencies within this developing financial sector. By the end of 2022 HSF held rights to over 65,000 songs, valued at some $2.6 billion.

These are just two of the most high-profile investment companies amongst a plethora of new firms emerging in the last few years which have raised significant sums of money for catalogue purchases and begun selling music royalty shares. In May 2023, for example, South Korean investment firm Beyond Music announced that it had raised a further $170 million for catalogue acquisitions, taking it to a total of $400 million, with the company owning some 27,000 songs (Peoples 2023). Companies and funds of this type have made considerable efforts to establish music as a recognized asset class. For example, HSF's strategy of only investing in commercially successful catalogues sought to ensure that investment in music would offer predictable, reliable and "uncorrelated" revenues – that is, that would generate income regardless of macroeconomic conditions – over a long period of time. However, as Galuszka and Legiedz (2024) point out, HSF were required to become deeply entangled with the financial sector to fund catalogue purchases, using debt and leverage to fund its acquisitions. Moreover, Galuszka and Legiedz were also critical of HSF offering its investors uncorrelated revenues, noting that increases in interest rates would both increase the interest it must pay on capital, as well as making its assets comparatively less attractive to investors. An additional risk in HSFs approach was that if investors believed that HSF paid more for the catalogues than they were actually worth, the company's valuation would fall, making it harder for it to obtain new capital need to purchase further catalogues.

As the period of low interest rates came to an end in 2022, the relative attractiveness of the investments in music assets in the firm's funds declined. In the two years up to March 2024, the price of Hipgnosis shares was halved as investors started to reconsider the value of its underlying music assets, centred on concerns that the group had overpaid for catalogue acquisitions. Further, concerns were raised over the governance and debt levels of the group. In March 2024, a reassessment of the firm's assets in the context of higher interest rates resulted in a 26 per cent devaluation from its position only six months earlier (Sisario 2024a), which estimated a midpoint value of the music rights portfolio at $1.9 billion. As the company's share price fell, it became more difficult to raise money to fund further additions to its portfolio of rights. The company's board was subsequently charged with overseeing a strategic review that could lead to the sale of the group (Thomas 2024). In July 2024, following a bidding war, Hipgnosis announced its sale to Blackstone – which, as previously noted, already part owned Hipgnosis Song Management – for $1.6 billion (Bloom 2024; Sisario 2024b; Ingham 2024).

Artificial intelligence, music and copyright

As we have seen in the discussion presented so far, the music industries can be characterized in relation to their tendency to lurch from crisis to crisis. These arise in part because the music industries are often at the sharp end of the creative and media industries' encounters with technological innovation. This has often seen the music industries considered as the "canary in the coal mine" for a range of socio-technical innovations. In Chapter 2, we discussed the period of *relative* stability that has now developed around music streaming as the primary mode of music consumption, in particular with regards to the return to profitability of the industries' major corporations. Building on this, in Chapter 4 we discussed how this stability has enabled the emergence of a platform centred MusicTech innovation ecosystem. Yet, as we write this, a new set of concerns has begun to develop regarding new developments in a potentially fundamentally disruptive technology – namely artificial intelligence (AI) – and its potential impacts upon the music industries. Although such technologies have existed for many years (Wooldridge 2021), it is only since the 2010s that new developments in AI technologies around automation, deep learning and generative AI, together with increased computing power and the commercialization of distributed computer networks, have seen these technologies become more widespread and accessible (Bonini & Magaudda 2024). Furthermore, there has been a notable improvement in the quality of the music generated by AI due to advances in machine learning together with the accumulation of now massive datasets of digital music upon which machine learning systems can be trained (Drott 2021).

Two related sets of concerns are developing. First, there are fears that generative AI technologies may soon replace artists and musicians within the creative process, effectively "turning music creativity into something cold and functional" whilst at the same time favouring "a new way to make profit for online platforms and financial investors in the digital sector" (Bonini & Magaudda 2024: 122). There have been concerns, for example, that recent experiments by MSPs and BigTech companies in generative AI – seen in the recent formation of research groups such as Magenta at Google and the Creator Technology Research Lab (CTRL) at Spotify (Briot & Pachet 2020) – are leading towards a situation where significant amount of AI-generated music may flood on to platforms. For the MSPs, such a development would have significant financial benefits, given that it would avoid having to pay licensing costs to record labels. As discussed previously, these licensing costs represent a significant barrier to the MSPs achieving profitability. However, at the same time AI-generated music would likely displace the work of artists and musicians, competing against them for the limited pool of attention and streams available on the MSPs, whilst also diminishing the income of record labels, music publishers and other intermediaries. Furthermore, as part of the emerging MusicTech ecosystem we discuss in Chapter 4, there has been notable growth in the number of start-ups seeking to commercialize music produced using AI in respect of a variety of different applications and uses. As Drott (2021) notes, computer generated works can be sold or licensed at very low prices, undercutting the market for human-composed production music.

Second, and of particular relevance to this chapter, there are growing concerns around issues of copyright and authorship, which raise questions both with regards to distributive justice and the adequacy of existing copyright regimes. As Drott (2021) outlines, there are two particular considerations here. First, there are issues relating to whether AI-generated music should be copyrighted, and if so, to whom (or what) rights over the music produced should be awarded. Most copyright regimes are based upon human-centred understandings of intellectual property (Clancy 2022; Li 2022) wherein machines cannot be designated as the legal authors of the works they generate. Therefore, debates about AI authorship tend to revolve around who is the most suitable among the human actors involved in AI music composition to be assigned copyright: this might include, for example, a machine's programmers, its proprietors, or perhaps the client for whom the work is produced. For most AI start-ups and research labs, this leaves them in a position where they are required to cede any claims to the music being produced, whilst carefully controlling the system that produced them (Drott 2021). Second, there are issues related to the music that constitutes the training set necessary for machine learners to learn. As Drott argues, much of the efficacy, and hence much of the value, of machine learners depends on the datasets on which they are trained (2021). The key question here then is centred on whether the material being used for training is under copyright. As Drott argues, it is highly likely that at least some of the training data used by generative AI music programmes falls under copyright. Therefore, copyright claims to the work produced by music AI are not limited to the people (or machines) producing the music, but also include the producers of the music used to train AI machine learning or those otherwise holding the right to this music.

Growing awareness of these issues has prompted major rights holders to develop a series of defensive responses to threats to future income streams. In the same way that the immediate response of the music industries major corporations to illegal file sharing was to turn to litigation, major corporations are now bringing legal action against AI companies producing music trained on copyrighted material. In May 2022, for example, the Recording Industry Association of America announced that lawsuits were being brought by the three major labels against AI music generators Udio and Suno, accusing them of copyright infringement. The lawsuits claimed that Suno and Udio's software were trained on copyrighted music without permission and asked for compensation of $150,000 per work produced, arguing that outputs from AI music generators are derivative works of copyrighted recordings. The lawsuit claimed a pattern where users of Udio's service could generate outputs with vocal replicas of specific artists by entering prompts based on genres and descriptors of copyrighted recordings, replicating specific artists' vocals (Berger 2024). In 2024, Universal Music Publishing Group sued Anthropic, an artificial intelligence company backed by the likes of Amazon, Google and Zoom, because of its use of copyrighted song lyrics (Paterno & Deneen 2024). Anthropic's primary product was a chatbot which, when asked to generate song lyrics, provided responses containing lyrics extracted from copyright material. Such cases are indicative of ongoing battles between the music industries and generative AI companies over the unauthorized use of copyrighted material, and the outcomes will shape the future relationship between the music industries, BigTech and AI start-ups.

Yet, as Drott (2021) argues, legal action against AI music generation is not straightforward. Demonstrating that a piece of work is derivative, for example, requires demonstrating substantial similarity as a key test for copyright infringement; yet, the musical output of machine learning AI systems is more akin to a recomposition than a copy, meaning that in most instances output is not substantially similar to any of the materials used to train the system (Deltorn & Macrez 2021). In addition, there is a significant practical challenge in "identifying all the relevant copyright holders whose creations have been used to train an AI, determining the contribution their works made to its training, and apportioning royalties accordingly" (Drott 2021: 200). Nevertheless, despite the challenge, there is evidence of a significant anxiety and concern among creative artists of all kinds about the implication of AI. For example, in October 2024, over 11,500 creative professionals added their name to the following statement on AOI training: "The unlicensed use of creative works for training generative AI is a major, unjust threat to the livelihoods of people behind these works and must not be permitted".[5]

Such issues and concerns question the adequacy of existing human-centred copyright regimes in their treatment of both authorship and originality in the face of the advance of AI and suggest a re-evaluation of copyright rules and established norms is urgently required (Li 2022). This may result in either amendments to existing copyright laws or the passing of new *sui generis* rights that directly target AI-generated products (Sturm *et al.* 2019). In March 2024, for example, the European Parliament passed a landmark AI Act which had received widespread and longstanding support from the music industries. The act includes measures relating to training-data disclosures and the rights of creators to opt out of training. For example, the act stated that use of copyright protected content to train AI systems requires the authorization of the rightsholder concerned (unless relevant copyright exceptions and limitations apply), as well as requiring that the providers of such models draw up and make publicly available a sufficiently detailed summary of the content used for training (Smith 2024a).

Conclusions

Paying specific attention to music rights is necessary in order to fully understand many of the key dynamics and tensions that have developed as the music industries have transitioned into a digital and platformized era. In the case of the music industries, a copyright-enabled system of rent extraction has encouraged the formation of an enormously powerful oligopoly in the market for musical intellectual property: for large music corporations, immense back catalogues of copyrighted music are significant income generating assets. The control of these assets, through strict enforcement of copyright, positions the major corporations as the key rentiers in the networks of the music industries. It is in this

---

5   See "Statement on AI training"; https://www.aitrainingstatement.org/ (accessed 22 October 2024).

context that one can make sense of the nature of relations between the major corporations, MSPs, and artists. These include both the ways in which the key actors have become bound together in a very particular system of rent extraction, and how they work together to ensure the protection of the oligopoly of the major music corporations. In the next chapter, we shall consider how this protectionist system of rent extraction plays out in relation to a wider range of other technology firms within an emerging MusicTech ecosystem, in ways which are often considered to be detrimental to innovation.

Meanwhile, the growing interest of financial markets in investing in music rights has seen a series of new players emerge in music markets which have made substantial financial investments in their aggressive purchases of music catalogues over a relatively brief period of time. It is the success of streaming services, we argue, that has been crucial in demonstrating the potential of copyright as an asset and that music can generate steady and predictable revenue over an extended period of time. The two examples of such new entrants provided in this chapter demonstrate how a deep engagement with the financial sector has been necessary to fund catalogue purchases. As such, this new development points to a future in which the platform music industries and financial services have become more intertwined, whilst changing the established dynamics of music rights ownership. Moreover, the emergence of machine learning generative AI music systems has raised significant concerns about copyright and authorship and prompted complex questions about distributive justice and the adequacy of existing copyright regimes. Who or what should be credited as the authors of AI-generated music? Who should receive credit and associated rights-related compensation with regards to the music used to train AI machine learning? As the dynamics of the relationships between the recorded music industries and generative AI companies over the unauthorized use of copyrighted material take shape, we are seeing new legal actions being brought by the major rights holders. At the same time, we are also beginning to see the re-evaluation of copyright rules and established norms in relation to AI-generated products in such a way as to provide protection for right holders (Sturm *et al.* 2019; Li 2022).

4
MUSICTECH AND "THIRD WAVE" PLATFORM REINTERMEDIATION

Introduction

As outlined in Chapter 2, the music industries – and the recorded music industry in particular – have a long and complex relationship with technology.
Since the late 1990s the music industries have pioneered processes of digital
transformation and a process that, borrowing from Langley and Leyshon (2021),
we describe as "platform reintermediation". This process destroyed established
business models based on the exploitation of music rights before they were rebuilt in new ways as emergent music streaming platforms (MSPs) and developed
productive working relations with music corporations to enable streaming to
become the main digital distribution format. The revenues generated by MSPs
helped to plug the hole created by the rise of P2P networks. As streaming pulled
the music industries out of crisis, notwithstanding ongoing tensions and disputes
about the equity implications of streaming platform revenues, it created the
conditions for new rounds of technological innovation which began to blur the
boundaries between the music and tech industries. If, as we argued in Chapter 2,
the first wave of platform reintermediation in the music industries was focused
on P2P networks, and the second on the rise of streaming platforms, a third
wave was initiated by an emergent MusicTech sector, characterized by entrepreneurial activity and technological innovation taking place outside the major
music companies, in areas such as music production, publishing, consumption,
and distribution (Dumbreck & McPherson 2016). These firms developed applications that sought new ways to reintermediate extant connections between
artists, music corporations and audiences, to find ways to locate themselves in
the music value chain that links music industries firms to consumers. In doing
so they generated new revenue streams cultivated a more complex and diverse
music industries ecology.

MusicTech also figures within wider policy narratives developed around
the importance of technological innovation across a range of sectors (such as

BigTech, FinTech, InsurTech, RegTech, MedTech and HealthTech, etc.). As such, government organizations have been quick to promote particular cities or even their national music industries as "leading" centres of MusicTech innovation. In the UK, for example, a Department for International Trade report, *British Music Innovation: Hitting the Right Notes for the Future* (Department for International Trade 2018), offered a compelling account of revitalized music industries embracing technological innovation and showcased several start-ups to demonstrate the "global impact" of UK MusicTech. Similarly, Invest Stockholm, the city's official investment promotion agency, published *Stockholm: The Powerhouse of Sound* (Stockholm Business Region 2016), a report which advertised the city as "the world's MusicTech capital", similarly drawing attention to locally-based MusicTech start-ups.

In this chapter, an analysis of qualitative data collected through interviews with MusicTech firms, and a range of linked actors, allows us to provide a critical appraisal of the key dynamics of this emerging sector within the music industries, revealing important features shaping the opportunities and challenges faced by platform tech entrepreneurs and start-ups. More specifically, we outline a series of unique interrelated challenges faced by MusicTech entrepreneurs and start-ups, centred on issues of capitalization and copyright. The challenges to which we refer are, *inter alia*: scaling technologies; defining user bases and markets; recruiting and renumerating skilled tech developers; mentoring and accessing networks within the music industries; issues with securing licensing deals for copyrighted music; and identifying innovation gaps related to potential investment by large music industry corporations.

Third-wave platform reintermediation in the music industry

The academic literature on tech start-ups often asserts that start-ups act to challenge the dominance of incumbents through disruptive innovation, as the legacy business models of incumbents plus inertia provide opportunities for new entrants to gain rapid momentum in the marketplace (Crittenden *et al.* 2019). However, with the music industries having recently gone through a series of disruptive innovations and now recently stabilized around digital formats (Drott 2024; Leyshon 2014; Lotz 2021; Hesmondhalgh 2021; Peitz & Waelbrock 2006) distributed through a small number of dominant MSPs, MusicTech platform reintermediation has led to firms not seeking to challenge but to align with, and contribute and innovate in relation to, existing incumbent corporations and platforms. This activity includes, for example, creating complimentary platforms, developing data applications or producing content. Unlike the period from the late 1990s onwards, when the competitive bases of the industries were transformed following the growth of unlicensed file sharing through P2P networks, an accommodation between tech firms and traditional music industries companies has seen the construction of mutually beneficial business models. In other words, a third wave of platform reintermediation has been characterized by the emergence of a series of firms developing ancillary digital services that offer new opportunities for revenue capture in a music ecology shaped by the incumbent power of the large music corporations and dominant MSPs. Examples range from firms that offer new ways of tracking music rights to discover otherwise forgone royalty income,[1] through firms that offer AI-assisted search process to assist with artists talent identification,[2] to firms enabling video content creators to license music and to track unlicensed use of music.[3] Developments such as these resonate with wider narratives developing in the music industries around the growth in digital music revenues, the transformative power of tech and its potential to create buoyant and sustainable digital music industries in the twenty-first century (see, e.g., Department for International Trade 2018). The broadly positive coverage given by the music industries media to firms innovating in MusicTech, and the prominence of MusicTech start-ups at music industries trade events such as Midem and the Music Week Tech Summit, can be understood in this context.

The emergence of a MusicTech sector made up of small, entrepreneurial start-up firms can be seen as the next stage of the evolution for music industries not only experiencing platform reintermediation but also operating on reduced budgets and coping with the loss of technical expertise due to corporate retrenchment in the era of declining overall revenues within the incumbent major corporations. Innovation that might previously have been undertaken internally has effectively been delegated to start-ups and scale-ups (Simon 2019). Yet, a new dynamic has emerged whereby competition in the contemporary platform musical economy centres on start-ups gaining attention from the incumbents of the music industries, as both controllers of music rights and as potential investors or buyers of innovations. Very few MusicTech firms appear to be developing disruptive technologies which would challenge the dominance of the incumbents per se. As such, dynamics in MusicTech are akin to a process of open innovation, where start-ups offer themselves up as potential partners with dominant incumbents as a means of sourcing new innovations and technologies (De Groote & Backmann 2020). The actions of incumbents in cultivating a wider ecosystem to draw in the necessary disruptive innovations and innovators to expand their platforms – for example, through the release of public Application

---

1   Such as Blokur; https://blokur.com/.

2   Such as FrtyFve; https://weareinstrumental.com/.

3   Such as Lickd; https://lickd.co/.

Programming Interfaces (APIs) – and to preferentially lock-in developers, is a strategy seen in other areas of the economy where hitherto dominant firms have been threatened by disruptive tech starts-ups (see, e.g., Hendrikse *et al.* 2018, 2020, on FinTech). Examples of this are evident in the music industries: Spotify offers a "Spotify for Developers" service, whereby developers can use the Spotify Web API to create applications that can interact with Spotify's streaming service, such as retrieving content metadata, getting recommendations, creating and managing playlists, or controlling playback. Indeed, most major MSPs now make APIs available to developers, including Apple Music, Amazon Music, YouTube, TIDAL, Deezer and SoundCloud, as do other music platforms such as Songkick and Bandsintown (live music) and Shazam (music discovery). All these platforms open their APIs for the purposes of capitalizing upon the innovations of external software developers.

Table 4.1 illustrates a typology that attempts to position both established and nascent MusicTech platforms and start-ups in relation to both domains of circulation and their relationships to the music industries' incumbent corporations. To be clear, we are *not* arguing that all MusicTech firms are platforms. Far from it. As MSPs were stabilizing the music industries, but before an overall return to profitability, there was a search for all manner of technological applications that might produce new markets and revenue streams. But the attempt to embrace new music technologies cast a wide net and adopted an inclusive definition of the technology part of MusicTech, to include ventures as varied as new musical instruments, holographical representations for virtual live performances and new forms of immersive listening.[4] However, as MSPs have become the dominant mode of music distribution, so they have set the structure and context within which a new generation of platform based MusicTech innovations have emerged. This "overarching framework" of platform reintermediation in the music industries has two key elements. First, there are online exchange markets, which are centred upon MSPs, several of which have preferential licensing arrangements with incumbent corporations, while others are part-owned by the majors. MSPs represent a fundamental shift from ownership to access models

---

4   As an illustration of this, in 2014 one of us attended an event hosted by the University of Westminster's Music Tank, a knowledge transfer unit established to forge better links between academic research and the music industry. The title of the event, "Is tech the new Beatles?", a phrase attributed to professional musician Kevin Godley, illustrated the ways that in the midst of the breakdown of established business models, and prior to the industry fully restabilizing around streaming, there was an eagerness to explore alternative revenue streams that might be delivered through a host of tech-led business models. Of all the putative business models presented at the event, the only one that has any notable visibility ten years after the event is Sofar Sounds, which sought to capitalize on the revaluation of live performances (see Chapter 6).

as the dominant channel of delivering recorded music to consumers (Barr 2013). Second, there are social media platforms, which function as one of the most prominent domains of the new form of digital economic circulation (Bleier *et al.* 2024; Fuchs 2015; Fumagalli *et al.* 2018; Langley & Leyshon 2017; Rigi & Prey 2015). Both domains facilitate the distribution and creative use of music and generate significant audiences for music. There also exist a range of music industries-specific domains of circulation that include music rights, record label-facing companies, artist-facing companies, and live music.

In common with platform capitalism more broadly, firms in MusicTech can broadly be divided into those firms focused on providing business-to-business (B-2-B) technological solutions, and those producing new technological innovations aimed at consumers (B-2-C). However, while some B-2-B innovation focuses on providing services for record labels, most innovation is primarily focused on B-2-C which, in the case of the music industries, includes independent creators of music (such as music artists, producers and engineers, for example) and consumers of music (listeners, as well as other creatives wishing to licence music such as video producers and games developers). Alongside record-label facing and artist-facing domains, two more music industries-specific domains include platforms innovating in the areas of live music and music rights, which blur the B-2-B/B-2-C distinction.

"No one wants to invest in music": start-up capitalization and investment in MusicTech

One of the most important challenges facing entrepreneurs in technology start-ups is access to capital (Conti *et al.* 2013). As Langley and Leyshon (2021) have argued, a significant and integral feature of platform capitalism is that many digital platforms are highly capitalized by investors. In outlining the central importance of platform capitalization to the emergence of FinTech, for example, they describe how an era of low interest-rates, together with the promising revenue prospects of platforms within the financial services industries, encouraged risk-embracing investors to invest in platform businesses. Our findings, however, suggest that start-ups in MusicTech, with far less certain revenue prospects (for reasons that we shall subsequently discuss) have experienced a set of dynamics and barriers around investment which are very specific to the music industries. In the critical early stages of investment, MusicTech start-ups are largely supported by funding provided through founder, friends and family (FFF) investors, small business loans and other innovation-related loans (for example, accelerator programmes), which then, in turn, may act as important signals to attract individual angel investors (Conti *et al.* 2013).

Table 4.1 Platform reintermediation in the music industry

Domain of circulation	Platform type	Indicative platforms	Relationship to incumbent major music corporations
Online exchange markets	Platforms which provide a marketplace for music. The music industry has stabilized around a small number of music streaming platforms, which have brought about a major shift from ownership to access models as the dominant channel of delivering recorded music to consumers and have played a fundamental role in returning the music industry to profit.	– Spotify – Apple music – Amazon music – Deezer – Bandcamp – SoundCloud	While these platforms have become incumbents in their own right, they are significantly dependent on the major music corporations for the licences to stream music on their platforms. Many of the largest platforms have preferential licensing arrangements with major record labels, and some are part-owned by the majors.
Social media and user-generated content	Platforms which provide a host site for communities to post user-generated content in the form of text, images, videos and live streaming. Dominated by BigTech companies but new platforms are frequently entering this domain. Social media influencers are playing an increasingly important role in this space.	– Facebook, Twitter – YouTube – Instagram – TikTok – Twitch	Social media platforms are now hugely important both with regards to the promotion and marketing of artists and users, and for the licensed used of music. There are however many complexities around rights, with various platforms having various licensing agreements, and emerging platforms often do not have licences in place (see also below).
Music rights	Platforms innovating in the area of music licensing for those wishing to use music in situations where licensing music is problematic or not currently possible, for example content creators on social media platforms (e.g. YouTube) and live events. Also covers platforms innovating in the area of rights management and licensing for business, in specific relation to the use of blockchain technologies.	– Lickd – Click 'n' clear – Jaak – Blockur	Through creating solutions for the legal use of music, these platforms have the potential to capture rights income currently not being collected, and therefore provide significant potential gain for the major rights holders. More efficient management of music rights and the simplification of licensing will benefit both rights holders and start-ups.

Domain of circulation	Platform type	Indicative platforms	Relationship to incumbent major music corporations
Record label-facing	Platforms innovating in the area of marketing and promotion, including closed social media platforms, social media audience development (e.g. platforms targeting social media influencers), location and context-aware marketing, and bot-building platforms.	– Landmrk – Fanbytes – The Bot Platform – Number Eight	These platforms look to provide the major labels with innovative services that have the potential to improve: business models; the way data from consumers is gathered and manipulated; the way in which data and insights are used to identify potentially successful artists; and the way in which artists are marketed and promoted. These platforms provide complimentary rather that disruptive technologies and play a potential role in the corporations retaining their position as the incumbents of the music industry.
	Platforms providing a variety of management services and data services for record labels, including for example music management platforms for record label sync teams and music supervisors; and companies using platforms to provide data science services and insights from music, for example for A&R departments.	– Disco – Instrumental	
Artist-facing	Crowdfunding platforms for donating or pledging money to artists, often in return for exclusive merchandise, experiences, and even cryptocurrencies. New innovations are seeing the appearance of investment platforms offering the opportunity to financially invest in music with a potential financial return on this investment.	– Kickstarter – Patreon – Corite – Riteband – Blockpool	Play a significant contribution in the sustainability of contemporary artist's careers and their ability to produce and distribute music, and as such help to sustain a significant independent music sector from which major corporations are able to scout and sign artists.
	Music publishing and distribution services which assist independent artists in collecting publishing royalties and distributing their music on streaming platforms, social media platforms and across physical outlets.	– CDBaby – Distrokid – Tunecore – Amuse	Independent music publishing and distribution platforms are largely not viewed as competing with the major corporation publishing divisions and distribution networks, and successful independent artists may be signed by the majors.

Table 4.1 *(continued)*

Domain of circulation	Platform type	Indicative platforms	Relationship to incumbent major music corporations
	Companies producing platforms and software to assist with music creation, including audio recording apps, music video creation platforms, and artificial intelligence music creation and adaptive audio solutions.	– Topline – Rotor – AI Music – Bandlab	Help to sustain a significant independent music sector, through supporting and enabling music production, from which major corporations are able to scout and sign artists. Yet, at the same time, AI music creation offers a potentially cheap way for streaming platforms and other music licences to create music, bypassing artists, labels and publishers.
Data analytics		– Audigent – Next Big Sound, – Kworb – ForTunes, – Viberate, – Soundcharts, – Songstats,	The development of biga data and other analytical tools to help record companies, management companies and artists provide insights into audiences to market more effectively and develop more targeted and efficient engagement in the search for increased revenues and profits.
Live music	A significant area of innovation, this domain includes platforms facilitating live music performance streaming, including virtual reality experiences; platforms facilitating the sale and re-sale of gig tickets; and festival apps including those allowing for virtual community building and interaction.	– Sofar Sounds – Mbryonic – Melody VR – Chew.tv (Bandlab) – Dice – SecondScreen	Prior to Covid-19 much innovation in this area was focused on ticketing for physical live music events. The Covid-19 pandemic has subsequently accelerated innovations already underway in live music performance streaming, along with increasing the use of social media platforms such as Twitch for live performances.

Source: After Langley and Leyshon (2017: 16).

Yet, interviewees also noted significant issues related to investor reluctance, which is related to the perceived ability of start-ups to progress from seed and early-stage investment to venture capital investment at Series A[5] and beyond. For example, one of our interviewees noted how:

... investors love intellectual property, [but] no one wants to invest in music ... because "it's just not enforceable". Because people have struggled with the enforcement side of the rights. And I think when you [achieve] that ... investors are going to be a bit more supportive and understand more of the value, because they know that they're not going to be cheated away by the general public stealing music.

(CEO, music rights start-up, London)

Here we see direct reference to the legacy effects of preceding waves of platform reintermediation and on-going issues around copyright enforcement which, despite the stabilization around MSPs, practitioners consider to be a lingering concern for investors. Similarly, the founder and director of product at an independent record label in Stockholm noted the difficulty of approaching investors as a music start-up, going as far as to say that reference to music was a "bad word" in pitches to potential investors. Many interviewees observed that most investors did not understand the music industries, and so certainly not the nature of the innovation they were pitching nor the investment opportunity. As one interviewee noted: "In terms of finding investment, it was quite a difficult road. And it's hard for people to take you seriously because, one, I'm in a market that they just don't understand, and two, no one's ever done this before, so you don't necessarily see the potential" (CEO, music rights start-up, London).

For several of the start-ups interviewed, recognition of investor reluctance and the difficulties of building a sustainable model around music resulted in companies either avoiding promoting themselves explicitly as music start-ups and platforms or sought to broaden the applications of their platforms and services to increase their appeal to potential investors. Others noted that the small economic footprint of the music industries in comparison to other industries encouraged tech firms to work on developing platforms and services that had utility across other sectors. The chief marketing officer of a social media and music start-up in London noted the glaring absence of successful exemplars of novel music industries business models in the streaming era that could be used to attract investors. In this regard, the matter of investor reluctance is not only

5   Series A funding is the common term for referring to a company's first significant round of venture capital financing. This is funding usually sought after an initial investment round where common stock and common stock options have been issued to company founders, employees, friends and family and angel investors.

about legacy issues around copyright, but a lack of success stories alongside some high-profile failures of MusicTech start-ups.

One high profile example was Crowdmix, a social music discovery company,[6] which in 2016 entered administration despite obtaining investment of £14 million while employing 160 staff across offices in London and Los Angeles. While some of the reasons for the failure were specific to the firm, such as bad financial management and a poor HR policy, other reasons were more generic and are instructive for an understanding of the challenges facing MusicTech firms more generally. Neither of the two founders of Crowdmix had a background in any of the music industries, while its main investors came from an entirely unrelated industry: property development (Forde 2016). As such, the company may not have possessed a sufficient understanding of the music business to be successful. But, more than this, given the importance of informal social networks to successful business operation in the music industries (see, e.g., Watson 2008), the company almost certainly did not have the required networks of social connections into the music industries to enable them to negotiate appropriate deals around music rights. Due to this, their initial business model was flawed,[7] and by the time the company hired people with better connections, it was too late to reorientate their business model and give the start-up sufficient legitimacy within the sector.

It is clear from the sheer number of MusicTech start-ups within contemporary music industries clusters across major western cities that a preponderance of small business loans and other innovation related loans, friends and family investors, and individual angel investments have funded the development of a diverse start-up ecosystem. Relatively modest levels of investment are often sufficient to place many MusicTech start-ups in a position where they can make initial hires and work on proof of concepts and prototypes of platforms. Yet, as the chapter will later address, the inability of many start-ups to raise venture capital investment even at Series A level results in significant issues when it comes to scaling up platforms, users and markets, and recruiting and renumerating development teams. As Langley and Leyshon (2021) note, due to the way that platforms aspire to remake markets, multi-sided platforms must have strong "demand economies of scale" or "network effects". As discussed in Chapter 1,

---

6   Social music discovery platforms are a form of social media platform premised specifically on the discovery and sharing of music amongst users with shared musical tastes.

7   The company planned to operate on the basis of a 50/50 split of revenues with artists around their music and content. Revenue was to be generated by selling advertising space and making income around secondary streams. However, the company had not negotiated with other services, such as Spotify for example, regarding the secondary streams happening from these services, and therefore had no agreements in place to be able to use the content which they then planned to remonetize.

for users, the benefits of a platform increase as a function of the total number of users (Cusumano *et al.* 2019). As such, one of the early key strategic objectives for MusicTech firms is to rapidly recruit and retain user populations – and to harvest their data – to leverage network effects to "scale up". This strategy is exemplified by MSPs.

Yet, in the case of MSPs, aggressive scaling is about more than simply remaking markets. In his critical examination of Spotify, Vonderau (2019) points to the co-dependence between constant growth imperatives and debt finance, arguing that the platform's growth strategy "does not primarily aim to turn songs (or audiences) into commodities but to treat them as a form of collateral that can be mobilized to secure loans" (2019: 15). For platform start-ups, scaling offers the promise of future income streams that provide venture legitimacy in the present. In his analysis of digital start-ups in music, Hodgson (2020: 429) points to the importance of "imagined metrics", including assumptions about the behaviour of future customers, which "parade as stable and fixed indicators yet are in fact provisional and highly contingent", but are of fundamental importance in attracting investors. Many of those interviewed were acutely aware of the need to scale to demonstrate the financial viability of their platforms, and to provide a return to their investors. Start-ups are also required to vigorously communicate the intermediary advantages of their platforms and technologies to both potential users and content providers.

Yet, the need to scale presents significant challenges in terms of financial and human resources, both with regards to technological development (an issue we shall return to shortly) and marketing and reaching new users and new territories. Thus, while scaling is an important indicator to potential investors of a platform's future viability, often it is difficult to scale without sufficient investment in the first place. A range of responses were given relating to this challenge when start-ups were asked why their next round of investment – typically, Series A venture capital investment – was important to them. Many referenced the need to grow their marketing teams. The co-founder and CEO of a music rights start-up from London noted how "the marketing budget will be a much higher percentage ... how do you reach two million kids in their bedrooms all around the world?". Similarly, the marketing manager of a music streaming start-up from London noted that "we know we've got a product that works, we just need to raise the funds to be able to go into those markets to sell it". For some companies, future investments were considered crucial to having a physical presence in particular markets, with one interviewee noting the importance of having a "local presence" in markets and "experienced people on the ground ... to understand local factors" (founder and CEO, music investment start-up, Stockholm). Several start-ups in both London and Stockholm referred to the large and potentially lucrative US market, but also noted the costs associated with developing a physical presence there.

Recruitment of skilled labour and the need for "smart" investment

As illustrated above, start-ups in MusicTech face a dilemma: while scaling offers the promise of future income streams that provide venture capital legitimacy in the present (Vonderau 2019), the opportunities for scaling may not be realized without significant initial investment. But there are other ways in which issues of capitalization impact upon MusicTech start-ups' ability to realize innovations and demonstrate the efficacy of their technologies. Most notable from our interviews were problems relating to the recruitment and remuneration of key personnel, and especially chief technical officers (CTOs) and developer teams. Talent shortages are a widely recognized feature of labour markets in technology-based clusters (Davis *et al.* 2009). There is a scarcity of skilled labour globally across the technology and software sectors in general (see, e.g., Bachtiar *et al.* 2022; Hyrynsalmi *et al.* 2021), and this can be particularly acute in technology-facing creative industries due to relatively low rates of pay. In the UK for example, there are noted skills shortages across the film, television, animation, visual effects (VFX) and videogame industries, which were exacerbated by the UK leaving the European Union (Ozimek 2021). In the case of MusicTech start-ups in London and Stockholm, the issue of a limited availability of people with requisite levels of technical knowledge is further exacerbated by the need to match levels of staff remuneration and rewards offered in other sectors with greater start-up capitalization. In the creative industries, the prospect of high profits for workers in the future – mainly by the possibility of converting stock options into cash – can allow companies to attract highly skilled employees prepared to take risks despite relatively low basic wages and employment insecurity (Teipen 2008).

As Hodgson (2020) notes, it is a common approach among pre-revenue music start-ups to attempt to attract engineers through a "double-pronged approach" of selling them a vision of company development and offering them remuneration in the form of equity. However, the wages and potential value of equity that MusicTech start-ups are able to offer are often not particularly attractive vis-à-vis those being offered by start-ups in other areas of the economy. One interviewee noted that:

> That's the hard part for the whole tech scene, there is not enough talent that can work with it. And of course, a MusicTech company is for sure not making as much money as a FinTech company. So as a developer, you might not take the chance to join a start-up in MusicTech because obviously you want your shares, and you might be rich … They can select whatever they want to do. Like someone can pay them a huge salary and options, you know.
>
> (Founder and director of product, independent record label, Stockholm)

Some interviewees suggested that the distinctive challenges being addressed by start-ups in the music industries, along with the disruptive ethic of some start-ups, can be attractive to developers. Many of the start-up founder-entrepreneurs interviewed described their own lack of technical know-how in relation to realizing their innovations. Accordingly, some interviewees highlighted the importance of recruiting a sufficiently qualified and experienced CTO who could be relied on to direct technical development. The founder and CEO of a music rights start-up from London reflected that "I made one good hire: the CTO. That's the first. And then after that you take his lead". Another interviewee, currently interviewing for a CTO, reflected on their need for technical direction, stating that "it's been difficult to really understand what it is that we need, because I don't know. And that's where I fall down (founder and CEO, music rights start-up, London).

Yet, many participants reflected on the difficulties inherent in recruiting developers more generally. Another interviewee, for example, explained that: "[Programmers] are bloody hard to find … For every month worth of someone solidly looking we might get one person … our last CTO spent about the last 90 days of being in this company trying to find people. And we eventually employed three people, two of which just couldn't cut it" (founder and CEO, music creation start-up, London). One of the strategies adopted by several start-ups to address problems of developer recruitment and remuneration was to recruit from outside their base city, and in many cases outside of their home country, often on a flexible, hybrid-working basis. The above interviewee also noted how, for example: "I've got a chap who's a professor of deep learning in Athens, who's doing two days a week for us … our head of MIR [music information retrieval] is based in Seville, simply because she prefers it to London, and I'm not going to argue with her because she works brilliantly no matter where she is, she just gets on with it" (founder and CEO, music creation start-up, London).

Two interviewees based in Stockholm explained the financial challenges of locating a developer team in the city, which is also the origin city of Spotify. One noted that: "We have a tech team outsourced in Bosnia, a pretty significant tech team. Cost, and setting up the team is so difficult. Spotify takes all the developers – and they take a lot! – so it's extremely hard to recruit developers. It's probably any start-up in Stockholm's biggest problem. Yeah, extremely competitive to hire talent in tech" (founder and director of product, independent record label, Stockholm). The other, whose start-up had a development team based in Ukraine prior to the invasion by Russia, noted that Ukrainians:

> … they are as good as Swedes, they speak great English, and the cost for having a team there is much less. They're very competitive! It would be lovely to have all these guys in the same room because that's always

better, but the competitive situation in Stockholm to get developers means the price level of those developers increases. So, I think for us this is a perfect fit, and I think as we also grow global, there is no reason for us having development in Stockholm.

(Founder and CEO, music investment start-up, Stockholm)

Meanwhile, a scarcity of investors is amplified by the need to find investors that also have suitable experience to mentor entrepreneurs and, ideally, the capacity to unlock networks and connections within the music industries. In the case of second-wave streaming platforms, their disruptive impact effectively forced the incumbent music industries corporations to build relationships with these platforms to first protect, and then maximize the value of, their intellectual property. However, in the case of third-wave MusicTech platforms and start-ups, the need to collaborate and cooperate with the major corporations, in particular to licence music, along with the sheer number of innovations in the market, places the emphasis on start-ups to build networks with major corporations. The case of Crowdmix, the failed MusicTech start-up mentioned earlier, is held up as an example of the importance of gaining investors experienced in the music industries. Such a perspective was expressed by a number of our interviewees. For example, an interviewee noted how music is different to other disruptive technology spaces within which investors typically invest:

Our investor networks don't sit in music typically, most of their businesses are in FinTech or disruptive technology spaces but not music … I think in terms of music technology consultation, especially when it comes down to the challenge of what is the correct user experience for a music B2B company, it's an area which gets misunderstood quite a lot because it's something where you really need to be in the music industry to understand … It's a very different type of industry.

(Senior account manager, online artist and repertoire start-up, London)

In his study of early-stage investors and entrepreneurs in the United States, Lee (2022) notes how social ties are critical in enabling entrepreneurs to connect to venture capitalists. The lack of such ties, he argues, can exclude viable business ideas from funding whilst distorting capital allocations in favour of those entrepreneurs with greater social capital. However, one interviewee noted how unlocking access to the right networks often requires connecting with the right investors who are able to provide mentorship and guidance on how to navigate the music industries:

> I don't have a specific music mentor, and that is something that I feel like I'm missing and could really benefit from. He [current investor] is more business side ... he's very business strategy ... he kind of acts as like my COO. I've learnt a lot from him ... But yeah, in terms of actually music and then getting connected with some of the higher people that you can't necessarily get to, that's where I'm struggling. I need someone who's well connected, who's kind of like quite high up in that industry, who's got a lot of experience really. To kind of teach me you know, well don't go talking to these guys without talking to these people, or don't go saying this thing to them, and you know, how to play the game.
>
> (Founder and CEO, music rights start-up, London)

A noted characteristic of the emergence of Tech innovation ecosystems is the founding of new firms by former employees of industry related firms or technologically related industries, who subsequently transfer knowledge and capabilities from pre-existing companies and industries into the emerging entity (Chen & Hassink 2022). Yet, few of the people interviewed had come directly from the music industries themselves. Rather, a number had managed to find investors experienced within the music industries and were quick to explain the benefits of this. Another interviewee explained how: "Fundamentally, the only reason why [investor name] invested is he's got a place to take it [the business]. He's very well connected in the music space ... he knows everyone right to the top of the music industry. So, the reason why we've been able to walk into many of the largest companies we need to, is simply because of that connection" (founder and CEO, music creation start-up, London). Several interviewees noted a tension between, on the one hand, a need to obtain any investment available and, on the other, being more selective with accepting investment to consider the longer-term implications of not attracting an appropriate investor, with the *right kind of money*:

> So, I think that's something really important to sort out when you start raising money, they call it *smart money* or *strategic money*, but making sure that you know that you've got a route ... Everybody just wants to get the money, but make sure it's the right money or else you might as well not even bother taking it because all you're doing is kicking the can down the road. And then you are stuffed because the smart money that you wished you'd have taken you then can't.
>
> (CEO, music creation start-up, London, emphasis added)

Similarly, another interviewee described the need to look for "further value" from investors:

> If they only provide the money, that will be good in the short term, but then after the first money starts to end, you have no value from that investor ... it gets no further value. But if you have right people, the money is good in the start but then eventually they could be the one that actually open up the big commercial deal for you, so I think it's super important to try to find the right ones.
>
> (Founder and CEO, music investment start-up, Stockholm)

However, the above interviewee also recognized the tension that exists, noting that "it's very easy to say [that investors need to provide additional value] because in the beginning you need the money, so if somebody comes up with a cheque, it's tough to say no".

One potential source of investment for MusicTech start-ups are the major corporations of the music industries. Returning to profitability through the incomes being received from MSPs, all three major corporations have been making strategic investments in MusicTech (MusicAlly 2019). One of our interviewees noted the potentially key role of the corporations in relation to investor reluctance at Series A stage, the reasons for which were outlined earlier:

> ... [the major music corporations] have got to actually be the people who provide funding because otherwise those [MusicTech] companies might struggle to get funding. The one thing we're hearing is that it's still a bit awkward, I think, if you're going to a venture capital company and asking for a Series A round ... but in terms of seed funding and angel investors, I get reports back that there's lots more of them. It seems to be quite a good time for that ... [but] then they have to figure out how to make the jump to Series A. And I think that's where major labels are figuring out how they fit into that. That the major labels are the next round of funding perhaps, or are they the people who are participating in Series A to convince investors?
>
> (Editor, music industries news and analysis publication, London)

There are many examples of recent investment by the major record labels in MusicTech while all of the three major corporations operate start-up incubator programmes in one form or another. Universal Music Group (UMG), for example, operates a number of incubator schemes, including the Abbey Road Studios Red incubator in London, where UMG takes a small share of equity in the start-up in return for the start-ups' participation in the incubator; there is also the Capitol Innovation Centre in Los Angeles, which is a collaborative workspace for artists and tech innovators/entrepreneurs; and, in addition, there is the Universal Accelerator Network, which is a series of partnerships with tech accelerators across the globe (Forde 2016). One interviewee, whose start-up was part of one such programme, described how this provided benefits not only in terms of mentorships and access to networks, but also in terms of investor confidence:

> It's a massive complement. They've only taken two companies so far this year, and for us going into a series A, it's the sort of good PR and sort of vindication you need to keep investors confident and happy. We are also in contract with Universal and, if we can keep that, we are hoping it will put wind in the sails ... it gives us access to lots of their senior management who aren't directly involved in our contract process. So, like marketing, like their PR teams, like their tech teams, you know.
> (Co-founder and CEO, music rights start-up, London)

Music, copyright and innovation

MusicTech start-ups are also inhibited from scaling up their userbases by their inability to secure the necessary music rights that would enable them to provide music to the users of their platforms and services. Start-ups entering the music industries found themselves faced not only with a complex licensing landscape, but also one in which incumbent corporations were highly defensive of their main asset – control over intellectual property. Within the innovative ecosystem of MusicTech start-ups, it was the B2C start-ups that were most exposed to the limitations and challenges imposed by the oligopolistic intellectual property arrangements of the music industries. B2Cs included both start-ups that wished to licence music directly as content on platforms, such as streaming services, and firms that sought to provide innovative solutions for licensing purchasing, especially for use on social media where platform users wish to licence music for user-generated content (such as, for example, creating YouTube or TikTok videos). In the case of the latter, start-up interviewees argued that their platforms would be able to provide additional income to record labels from rights which labels are currently unable to exploit themselves, due to a lack of appropriate technologies to both issue and monitor appropriate licences for the use of music on these platforms. Nevertheless, agreeing licensing deals with the major corporations was challenging.

In theory, many start-up platforms could seek to avoid licensing music from the major corporations, and instead seek to agree licensing arrangements with independent publishers or even directly with artists. However, the users of these platforms – which include those who wish to licence music for use as part of user-generated content on social media, or as part of other creative projects and events such as sports and performance events – expect to be able to use and licence music from the most popular artists, which tends to be controlled by the major corporations. Several interviewees highlighted the reluctance amongst corporations to provide licences to start-ups unless they could give definitive proof of their ability to produce additional revenues. One interviewee revealed a classic causality dilemma: there is need to demonstrate revenues to secure the licences, but a need to obtain the licences to generate revenue:

> Because we don't have top 40 hits or the popular content, we're play-ing this chicken and egg game. So, the music industry is just like, "Oh well, we need to know revenue figures", and I'm just like, "You need to give me your music and then I can make money from your music. But until you give me that, I'm telling people [users of the start-up's music licensing platform] that they need to license music that they've never heard of".
>
> (Founder and CEO, music rights start-up, London)

There is a similar causality dilemma over music rights in relation to capitaliza-tion and investors. Our interviews revealed that even in cases where majors of-fered licensing arrangements, the up-front cost of these deals was prohibitive for many start-ups,[8] with several interviewees discussing the prohibitive pricing of music licences for start-up firms. One interviewee noted that, "you're not going to build a B2C proposition without very, very deep pockets" (former founder and CEO, live experiences start-up, London). Start-ups with limited funding were unable to obtain the necessary licences required to access music assets that would allow them to scale. The larger volumes of venture capital investment available at Series A stage has the potential to allow firms to obtain the required music rights, but without demonstrating scale, it is unlikely that firms can at-tract such investment. Indeed, such funding is often conditional on licensing agreements already being in place.

These examples are indicative of a broader problem. When interviewees were asked about the key barriers to start-up formation and growth, a recurring issue was the way in which incumbent music corporations policed and enforced intel-lectual property, including their recourse to legal action. The above interviewee revealed how the major corporations exercise their power:

---

8   The cost of licensing music varies based upon several factors, including the number of songs being licensed, the songs being licensed, the type of licence being sought, the intended use of these songs and the medium in which they are used. In some cases, the licence may include in the contract a percentage of the revenue earned through that licence.

No one's done rights for the internet age properly yet … The legal structure around copyright is just an utter shit show and is … wielded to great effect by the majors who have lots of money and … so if the majors don't like what you're doing, they'll shut you down … But that's unfortunately how they play. They're on such tight margins these days, it's "litigate first and play nice later".

(Former founder and CEO, live experiences start-up, London)

Indeed, difficult relations with publishing departments of major corporations and the involvement of lawyers were raised by several interviewees. In many cases, start-ups had successfully developed relationships with record labels and marketing teams within the corporation, only to find that once the potential innovation/collaboration was passed onto the publishing or legal department it was blocked. Many start-ups and major labels found themselves in a position where they wanted to do business, but the publishing department refused to create a licence, either because it was judged to be too risky, too difficult, or "impossible". Such a situation was described by one of our interviewees as follows:

The problem with the majors is that if you talk to anyone outside of [the] legal [department], they love you; they love what you're doing … we had really good relationships with the marketing teams at [major corporation] … But as soon as it gets big enough [to get to the stage] where the lawyers get involved, it's either a lawsuit or it's just, "No way, we can't do it, it's too complicated".

(Co-founder and CEO, music rights start-up, London)

There was an issue not only with the willingness to issue licences, but also with the availability of appropriate frameworks for licensing in a digital age. The CEO of an AI music start-up, for example, described how they were not able to secure the necessary rights that would allow users to edit and adapt music on their platform because the rights frameworks that might allow this practice simply did not exist: "I'd have loved to [have] done the licences but you couldn't buy them, they weren't set up to do this in such legacy companies". In one case, senior executive in a major corporation advised a start-up to purposively breach copyright to trigger a legal test case that might resolve once and for all the copyright issues preventing a deal:

… we were speaking to the senior vice presidents of Sony, Universal and Warner. And they were all saying, "Well, we don't even have a department to send you to for this stuff". The guy at [major corporation] said, "Look the best thing you can do is just release this, then we'll sue you but then at least you're connected to the legal team that would deal with this. And then out the back of that we'll do a deal, we can sort it out."

(Founder and CEO, music creation start-up, London)

Unsurprisingly, this was not seen as a practical solution by the start-up. Even in cases in which majors offered licensing arrangements, the up-front cost of these deals was prohibitive for many small start-ups. One interviewee forcefully expressed frustration at the barriers to entry imposed by large rights owning organizations:

… the licensing mindset has been, "Fuck you, pay me!". It's been, "Sure … here's the minimum guarantee, $200 million"! And we say, "What?! But can't we just try to see if we can scale, and you will have your revenue share?" and they are like, "No, if you want our catalogue, it's this much in minimum guarantees. If you can't fix that, we won't give our catalogue to you".

(Founder and director of product, independent record label, Stockholm)

Several other interviewees also discussed the prohibitive pricing of music licences for start-up firms. One interviewee described, for example, how the company received a bill for €250,000 from a major corporation alongside an accusation of copyright infringement, which in turn generated additional costs by consequently paying for a legal team to contest the accusation and then negotiate licensing: "It's very grey, copyright … we had the best music rights lawyers that money could have, and it got us as far as we needed to do, but for someone that couldn't afford a £600-an-hour lawyer, it's just not going to happen" (former founder and CEO, live experience start-up, London). Another interviewee, noted how:

if you're an innovator to consumers, you're always going to be beholden to the major record labels who have the music that the consumers want. So, they're always going to make it really difficult for you, only because they've been burnt so many times … It takes a lot of money to invest in a start-up, to pull all of your music over … do all the payments, to do the negotiation, do the contracts. If a company hasn't got 25 million quid, they haven't got the ability to be able to do those deals, they'll go bust.

(CEO, independent music publisher, Liverpool)

Here we see reference to the collective institutional memory within the music industries that remembers all too well being "burnt" by the damage done by P2P platforms in the first wave of platform intermediation, and which explains the defensive stance taken over intellectual property rights. Start-ups with limited funding are unable to obtain the necessary licences required to access music assets. As noted, for some Music Tech start-ups their first wave of external funding might be conditional on licensing agreements already being in place, so the unwillingness of established music corporations to provide licensing solutions can prevent access to the funding needed to get the business off the ground.

As Andersen *et al.* (2007) note, while large scale changes to copyright law would require complex collective action through government intervention, less complex individual action could be undertaken between music industries firms which could potentially harmonize the needs of technological innovators with existing copyright frameworks. A potential solution here would be the use of a "sandbox", mirroring those created in the FinTech sector, a protocol which enables start-ups to test innovations in the market with actual customers under strict conditions and monitoring. The first FinTech sandbox was created in the UK in 2016 (Brown & Piskora 2022) and has since proven successful to the degree that it has been adopted across multiple regulatory environments (Truby 2020; Wójcik 2021). As one of our interviewees argued, "some sort of [MusicTech] sandbox agreement would be really helpful to everyone that's got an idea and wants to innovate" (CEO, music rights start-up, London argue). While music industries sandboxes have been trialled, major corporations appear to be reluctant to enter into a wide-ranging sandbox agreement for MusicTech firms. The reasons for this include: the desire to maintain artificial scarcity, potential reputational damage from the use of a label's music in a low-quality application, and the difficulty inherent in transferring a start-up to a full licence if its business model might not be viable under currently licensing regimes (Music Ally 2019). Furthermore, unlike in FinTech where central banks encourage and facilitate sandboxes, there is no such overarching regulatory authority in the music industries.

The major corporations as "innovation resistant"?

Given the difficulties faced by start-ups when working with major corporations, several interviewees were critical of the corporations with regards to a perceived lack of understanding of the situation facing MusicTech start-ups: "The labels don't really have any empathy for what it takes to run a start-up, and the risk you're taking and the investment you're putting [in] and the livelihoods you have on the line. They could send you broke. Just through bureaucracy" (CEO, music rights start-up, London).

There was a sense amongst participants that while the departments of the music corporations that are initially tasked to liaise with start-ups are open and responsive to innovation, they are ultimately restricted by the bureaucracy of the legal frameworks that surround rights. Moreover, from the perspective of the majors, engaging with emerging MusicTech businesses can be problematic. One reason was capacity. For one interviewee there was no shortage of willingness amongst the majors to be innovative. Rather, the problem lay elsewhere: "first of all, internal resources. There aren't that many people who have the skillset to go out and make the deals and also evaluating them properly" (commercial director, major corporation, Stockholm). While major labels often employed staff with appropriate skills sets around innovative technologies – often those within specialized tech teams within labels – the vast amounts of data being provided from streaming and social media platforms requires significant resource to analyse. As another interviewee put it: "Most of the tech team's time at the label level is taken up with Spotify, as well as Instagram, Facebook, etc" (director of policy, major corporation, London). Recent research into the use of metrics and decision making by Maasø and Hagen (2020) suggests that this has been a significant challenge for major labels, which has led them to gradually build up dedicated global analytics teams, of often hundreds of people, so that "major labels are dominating the metric race" vis-à-vis independent labels and artist services, with major labels having "the resources and skillsets to interpret this data in ways that others do not" (2020: 29). Yet, while this may be the case, the significant amounts of new data being provided means that major labels must allocate significant capacity and resources, allowing little time for appraisals of other kinds of external innovations.

A second and related issue is one of being able to communicate in the right manner with the major labels. There was a broad sense amongst both major label interviewees and those start-ups who had been successful in developing relationships with the majors that many start-ups lack sufficient connections in, or cultural understanding of, the music industries. Amongst the start-ups interviewed, we found a mix of businesses that had been started by an entrepreneur with a background in the music industries and those which had been started by those with a background in tech or another area beyond music. Very rarely did individual entrepreneurs have experience across both domains:

> Well, the difficulty I think in ... tech and music is ... you either get the music people who ... have a background in tech, or you get the tech people who don't really have anything in music, and you need to kind of have someone who has the understanding of both ... I've advised for some companies who are trying to start up, tech people trying to start these music companies, and they don't understand the intellectual

property ... like it's great to innovate but ... essentially your business is almost always going to be tied to whether or not the majors are going to sign up with you.

(CEO, music rights start-up, London)

Interviewees recognized that MusicTech start-ups needed at least one key person able to act as a "bridge" between the start-up and the large music companies. Accessing the relevant people within the music industries, and knowing how to communicate in appropriate terms, was often acknowledged as a problem within many MusicTech start-ups. As the same interviewee put it:

... if you don't have those relationships or you don't understand how to talk the talk, you're going to really struggle. Because [record labels are] ... very protective and very sensitive with their rights and, yeah, if you've got someone who just walks in, "Hey, I have this whole business idea and this is how it's going to work", they're just like, "Well no, we can't do that, we don't have the rights for that or you're going to run into this, this and this complication". I think that's probably one of the biggest issues for more tech-focused rather than music-focused start-ups.

(CEO, music rights start-up, London)

Perhaps the most significant determinant in the development of a working relationship between a start-up and music corporation is whether the latter judges that the innovation being proposed is worth the time, effort and often money that will be required to make it work. For many interviewees, a sense of major record companies as being "resistant to innovation" and giving "lip-service" to innovation while not demonstrating a commitment to this through their behaviour, came from the lukewarm responses their own approaches to majors had elicited. However, as another of our interviewees noted:

I think you shouldn't have unlimited sympathy for those tech founders, right, because ... I think that there's a lot of naivety ... to think, you know, that "The people who actually work in this industry are just all idiots and therefore I can do something, and I can come in from the outside" ... but if they don't really understand the problem or don't really understand how they're going to communicate the solution or whatever, that can be a barrier in and of itself.

(CEO, blockchain start-up, London)

The issue of being able to identify which innovations are needed by the music industries, rather than simply those which are technically possible – or what

De Groote and Backmann (2020: 2) describe as the "asymmetric goals" of incumbents and start-ups – was linked by one interviewee to the issue of understanding the music industries: "I think there are a lot of people that don't know how the music industry works, but have an assumption about it, that make bad decisions on what they should build for the music industry and it's not needed" (CEO, independent music publisher, Liverpool). The same issue was also raised by another interviewee who had previously worked at a major label, along with the issue of major being inundated with pitches from start-ups:

> I think that's the main problem, with music tech in general. When I was at [major corporation] for like ten years ago, and we built a bunch of services in-house ... these were actually things that we wanted to do because it was good for us. But at the same time, I think I got like hundreds of pitches from different music tech companies ... But they very seldom saw the real problem whatsoever because they really wanted to build something cool within music.
>
> (CEO, crowdfunding start-up, Stockholm)

The premise that the majors are innovation-resistant was strongly rebutted by another interviewee:

> I also think it's a pretty naïve approach that just because we're big doesn't mean we're not innovative. But we can't innovate with the same rapid pace because our internal revenue, our internal rate of return, is just higher ... we have budget meetings every, you know every year, and it needs to be funded. It's like you have a boss who says, 'When is your return on investment?' And look, we make a lot of bets ... [but] if you make your budget why would you take part of your cashflow and invest it? Because you'll need to justify it.
>
> (Commercial director, major corporation, Stockholm)

Smaller, nimbler MusicTech start-ups do provide an important source of innovation for the major corporations, but majors are focusing their limited internal resources on those innovations which meet immediate strategic needs. A recent report on major corporations and innovation produced by the music industries think-tank Music Ally (2019: 2) suggested that "rather than scrabbling around for the Next Big Thing, the labels are quietly seeking unsexy, powerful, niche pieces of technology to augment their existing businesses". Many acquisitions are aimed at further leveraging the oligopoly powers conferred on the majors by their control of large catalogues of music, or what the above interviewee described as "future-proofing our revenues". In 2020 Sony Music Group, for example, invested in Tracklib, a service that provides legal clearance for the use, in new releases, of samples of already licensed recordings, while Universal Music Group acquired Soundsgood, a platform which allows music influencers to create and distribute their playlists across MSPs, including streaming early access new music releases (Music Ally 2019).

Conclusions

In this chapter, we have focused on the business dynamics behind the evolving role of technology in the "third wave" of platformization in the music industries. One of the most important challenges facing entrepreneurs in technology start-ups across a wide range of industries in general, and the creative industries in particular, is access to capital (Conti *et al.* 2013). This chapter has pointed to the unique and significant issues faced by start-ups in the MusicTech sector in particular with regards to capitalization, and the ability of developing a plausible narrative of how investment into a MusicTech business model will leverage returns in industries increasingly characterized by capital centralization, concentration and oligopsony. Our findings suggest that early-stage capital in the forms of small business loans and other innovation-related loans, friends and family investors, and individual angel investments, has resulted in a diverse and well-populated MusicTech ecosystem. Yet, we also found there to be significant issues of investor reluctance related to their ability to progress from seed and early-stage investment to Series A funding and beyond. We have also focused on the related tensions that exist between the incumbent corporations and MusicTech start-ups with specific regard to intellectual property rights, set within the context of capitalization issues. The progress of the third wave of platform reintermediation is being determined in part by the legacy of earlier waves, which served both to make large record companies cautious of the implications of platformization and of the demands that innovation around platforms make on their resources. The strong institutional memory of the devastating impacts of internet file sharing in the early 2000s is reflected in the majors' stout defence of key historical assets, namely extensive catalogues of music. Our findings suggest that the major corporations are unwilling to bend or adapt legal frameworks to the needs of many start-ups, including the widescale adoption of a sandbox methodology for exploring the new use of music rights, or are otherwise constrained by the nature of the existing legal frameworks for which they previously lobbied.

The hardline defence of copyrighted assets by the major corporations would appear to be one of the single biggest challenges in launching and subsequently growing a viable MusicTech start-up, especially where initial funding is limited.

Yet, it would be wrong to suggest that majors are innovation resistant. Where the major labels identify a technology that offers potential benefits within the context of their own strategic priorities, they are highly likely to collaborate with – and subsequently acquire – relevant firms. There is also evidence that, where new technology significantly threatens the business models of the majors, they can take a more proactive and collaborative approach. A recent case in point concerns Universal Music Group's experiment in generative artificial intelligence (AI) with Google. In YouTube's DreamTrack programme, a select group of 100 YouTube creators will get to use the AI-generated voices and song writing styles of nine well-known singer-songwriters – three of which were signed to Universal – to create YouTube Shorts of up to 30 seconds. At the same time as taking a strong moral and legal position on the use of copyrighted music in AI-generated music, Universal has also recognized that properly licensed AI music services have the potential to generate revenues that could be distributed back to songwriters and labels according to consumption (Seabrook 2024).

5
MOBILIZING FAN ENTHUSIASM: SOCIAL MEDIA, CROWDFUNDING AND THE BLOCKCHAIN

Introduction

Chapter 2 outlined the "crisis of reproduction" (Leyshon 2014) which faced the recorded music industry in the early 2000s, and its subsequent stabilization around music streaming. The recorded music industry that emerged from this period of transition was one of reduced capital flow, smaller artist rosters, and substantially reduced record label budgets. These changes resulted in the independent artist sector – that is, the sector of the music industries made up of artists operating without formal record label contracts and that typically own the rights to their own music – gaining much greater economic significance. A 2019 report by music industries data and insights firm MIDiA Research, undertaken in collaboration with independent music label and distributor Amuse, suggested that revenue generated by independent artists was the fastest-growing segment of the music business, generating $643.1 million in revenues in 2018, a 35 per cent increase from 2017 (Mulligan & Jopling 2019). While this still only represented 3.3 per cent of global revenues from recorded music, the independent sector continues to grow. One outcome of this is that many of the tasks previously performed by music label representatives, including promotion, marketing, and distribution, have fallen to artists (Kribs 2017). This, in turn, has left many artists in a more precarious position *vis-à-vis* income generation. The MIDiA report suggests that nearly three quarters of independent artists earn less than $10,000 a year from music, compared to 61 per cent of label artists (Mulligan & Jopling 2019). Using the standard referred to first in Chapter 2 in relation to streaming income, given that the US federal minimum wages rate is $7.25 per hour, and assuming a monthly gross minimum wage of around $1,400 as a benchmark, and by extrapolation an annual gross minimum salary of $16,800, then these artists fall well below this threshold. The shift to streaming as the primary mode of distribution may have exacerbated this issue. According to recent figures from Spotify, around 200,000 artists on its platform are "professional or professionally aspiring". Yet, while there are as many as 8 million artists on Spotify, 98 per cent of them have fewer than 10,000 monthly listeners. Some 16,500 artists generated over $50,000 in royalties from Spotify in 2021, but this was just 0.2 per cent of artists on the platform (Music Business Worldwide 2022).

At the same time, the growing importance of the digital distribution and promotion of music has seen an optimistic discourse develop that emphasizes developments in social media as a means through which artists can potentially reach new global audiences and, in turn, monetize their fan base to generate income to facilitate more stable, financially self-sustaining independent careers (Haynes & Marshall 2018).[1] Indeed, as Bonini and Magaudda (2024) point out, music acted as an accelerant for early innovations in social media. For example, MySpace (established in 2003) provided opportunities for musicians to post their profiles online, interact directly with their fans and have significant control over the content they were posting. However, this was subsequently supplanted by the platforms that have come to define the social media age, Facebook and Twitter (now X). Although these platforms allow for similar functionality – such as profile posting, network building and interaction – their popularity, large number of users and the range of interests covered saw music and musicians become far less prominent on social media as a whole, at least until short-form video platforms such as TikTok and Instagram helped reprioritize music in alternative ways. With the widespread uptake of social media, discourses and practices of self-branding have become a pervasive feature of social and economic life (Scolere *et al.* 2018), and subsequently these platforms have redefined the rules of music promotion in the age of social media.

The dominance of particular social media "super-platforms" means that musicians increasingly must rely on the affordances of such platforms – that is, the kinds of social and communicative practices and habits that they enable or constrain (Bucher & Helmond 2017) – to reach potential fans and to build audiences for, and communities around, their music. Given the growing importance attached to an online fanbase, especially for independent artists, the need to foster and sustain ongoing interaction on social media as a form of modern-day promotion has increasingly become to be seen as part of the "job" of a musician (Baym 2015; Gee & Yeow 2021). For example, despite achieving a top chart position for their debut album in 2021, and a top three position for its follow up in 2023, the Scottish band The Snuts were pressured by their record label to do more self-promotion on social media:

---

1 Some artists have even taken to the platform OnlyFans to exploit images of their body in return for regular income. For example, in late 2024 it was revealed that both Lily Allen and Kate Nash provide subscribers access to pictures as a way of generating regular flows of income, despite significant back catalogues of music and large volumes of streams of MSPs (Cockerill 2024).

"By the time of the second album, we were expected to do marketing jobs rather than be musicians", says the band's singer Jack Cochrane. "We went into a boardroom where someone held up their phone and flicked through examples of how many videos pop stars posted each week, what time they posted them, which demographic was connecting with which content. And I thought, whatever happened to making the music you wanted to make?"   (Hodgkinson 2024)

This chapter considers social media and broader developments around platforms that seek to mobilize fan enthusiasm for economic ends. In the first section, we discuss how disintermediation processes have seen the emergence of the "artists as intermediary" (Kribs 2017) and how promotion and marketing activities are increasingly falling on artists. We consider how social media platforms present an enabling mechanism for promotional activities and audience building, but at the same time place particular requirements and demands on musicians to adopt entrepreneurial approaches to promotion and performing online labour. We also point towards the problematic rhetoric around social media platforms, user empowerment and unfettered production. The second section of the chapter presents a quantitative analysis that examines whether the labour given to social media promotion financially benefits musicians by increasing the number of fans that subsequently stream music and attend live performances. In the third section, we critically consider how fan enthusiasm is increasingly being directly mobilized for financial gain, via crowd funding platforms. While these platforms promised to fill a venture gap in the industries where money to fund the emergence of new music is increasingly the responsibility of musicians in a way that it was not in the past, we argue that many artists with limited fan bases continue to be constrained by a funding gap that crowdfunding cannot viably fill. We then consider developments around blockchain, Web 3.0 and the Musical Metaverse which are generating further innovations in crowdfunding and the mobilization of fan enthusiasm. Finally, we discuss the potential for the emergence of a decentralized creator economy underpinned by these technologies and intermediated by platforms, and more radical visions of blockchain-enabled decentralization in the form of distributed autonomous organizations (DAOs).

The "artist-as-intermediary" and the demands of online labour

As noted above, the contemporary recorded music industry operates a business model centred on reduced capital flow and smaller artist rosters, which is focused particularly on those few artists with strong cross-marketing potential

(Leyshon *et al.* 2005). Pre-MP3 crisis, music production tended to be collaborative between a range of actors and featured cultural intermediaries and a specialized division of labour. Major record labels provided their musicians with an integrated suite of services as part of record deals, enabling them to record, distribute and market music in exchange for the rights to the recording (Arditi 2020). However, reductions in record label budgets together with ongoing processes of disintermediation and subsequent reintermediation by platforms in activities such as artist and repertoire (A&R), production, marketing and promotion have acted has given rise to what Kribs (2017) has termed the "artist-as-intermediary". This term describes how new responsibilities have fallen on many musicians who not only have to create new music but who also are increasingly undertaking promotion and distribution duties to attract the attention of more powerful actors in the music industries:

> ... [the] elimination of middle men does not liberate artists from industry shackles but forces artists to occupy the role of intermediary should they aspire to be commercially successful. The artist-as-intermediary does all her/his own creative and promotional work, establishing a monetizable fanbase in the hopes that label executives (or, rather their interns) scanning the web for the hottest trend will sign him/her to a recording contract. (Kribs 2017: 8)

Because the internet is considered to have lowered barriers to entry into the music industries both by allowing easier access to marketplace and distribution platforms and providing the means by which artists can reach audiences independent of traditional marketing campaigns, disintermediation and the platform reintermediation which followed it are often celebrated as potentially empowering for musicians. This argument has been frequently circulated throughout the mainstream media and given credence within the wider music industries (Strachan 2007). However, for the artist-as-intermediary, one consequence of this development is that new forms of unpaid and often invisible labour have emerged. Musicians now increasingly carry both artistic *and* entrepreneurial responsibility for their careers, with autonomous and entrepreneurial modes coming to define popular musicians' careers (Stahl 2013; Gee & Yeow 2021). As Frenneaux argues, for artists "the development of skills beyond musical aptitude and creativity is essential, such as knowing how to use social media platforms, streaming services and other digital tools to promote music and communicate with audiences" (2023: 136). Yet, as Tessler and Flynn (2016) note, there is a subtle distinction between "being free to" and "having to": the latter demands that artists adopt a fundamentally entrepreneurial mindset. Frenneaux (2023) points to a skillset that includes qualities of self-sufficiency, resourcefulness,

entrepreneurialism and adaptability that artists working in the new music industries are expected to possess.

An emancipatory and optimistic discourse has emerged that emphasizes developments in social media as a means through which artists of all kinds can
potentially reach new global audiences. Such a discourse has its origins in the
early web optimism literature of the 2000s, such as Chris Anderson's (2006) trea-
tise on the "long tail" economics of the internet. What is certain is that online
platforms are fundamentally reconfiguring relations between performers and
their audiences (Beer 2008), such that not only are some performers moving
closer to their audiences, but they also allow for closer connections and interactions between fans. Some scholars have gone as far as to argue that fan sharing
of recommendations and user-generated content through social media acts as
a new form of marketing that has the potential to supplant music industries
companies as intermediaries entirely (Benkler 2006; Simon 2019), with online
audiences having significant potential to be monetized to the benefit of the artist
(Haynes & Marshall 2018). As such, social media is considered to have changed
the rules of music promotion and self-branding, and artists must maintain con-
sistent engagement with their audiences through high-quality media and content (Morrow 2018).

Certainly, the role of social media users as collective tastemakers has become
stronger at the expense of top-down promotion from record labels, with social
medial influencers and user-generated content taking on a new importance in
this respect (Dhar & Chang 2009; Morris 2014). Not only are musicians com-
pelled to sell themselves through their artist "brand" (Meier 2015), but they must
also seek to create "buzz" and an online community of fans through social networking sites (Scott 2012). Daellenbach *et al.* (2015) argue that social media offers fans an opportunity to engage with and connect to musicians that may lead
to greater purchase intent, while for Baym (2018) both musicians and record
labels have come to value fans and social capital over record sales *per se*, since
this helps artists to grow their brand, sell merchandise and bring crowds to concerts, which can be a source of higher revenues. Put another way, the symbolic
capital created by online buzz is valued over the immediate economic capital of
the sale of songs in commodity form (Scott 2012).

More recent developments with social media platforms have seen artists
being able to financially benefit from the buzz developing amongst online communities of fans in more direct ways. The video-focused social networking platform TikTok, for example, pays royalties to songwriters based on the number
of videos in which a song is used (notwithstanding some of the controversies
around royalties and TikTok outlined in Chapter 3), while Instagram does the
same for uses of songs in the stories and reels of users. But more than this, such
short-form video social media platforms have recently fundamentally changed

the way artists brand themselves and interact with their audiences. Rauchberg (2022) examines the case of Olivia Rodrigo, a Filipina-American pop star who used TikTok to launch her music career in early 2021. On this platform, popular viral trends often emerge from dances or performances that reuse sound or visual content. Artists such as Rodrigo, Rauchberg argues, use their social media influencing and self-branding skills to remix and remediate already-existing ideas, text and sounds, in a form of "open borrowing" that creates a new form of "platform authenticity" that appeals to followers.[2] This, she argues, represents a strategy for standing out in an era of hyper-individualism, with users such as Rodrigo relying on "the platform's playful affordances to challenge the universality of dominant cultural conversations and situate dialogue in different, distinct ways" (Rauchberg 2022: 1292). TikTok's algorithmic infrastructure and user interface work to promote forms of remixing, restyling and repetition, which in turn are crucial to going "viral".[3]

Given the earlier discussion regarding the potential of social media for artists branding and promotion, some commentators have argued that "the entrepreneurial opportunity independent artists have to add value to their projects and careers" through such platforms "comes with the responsibility of using digital platforms effectively and advantageously" (Tessler & Flynn 2016: 60). For Rauchberg, Olivia Rodrigo's success on TikTok "reveals how personal branding and other forms of content creation are *mandatory public relations practices*" (2022: 1293, emphasis added). Indeed, the need for artists to "foster and sustain ongoing interaction" with fans via social media has increasingly been seen as "part of the job" (Baym 2015: 14) and something that independent artists "must navigate to achieve economic viability of their music" (Nickell 2020: 49). However, the successful use of social media comes with an imperative to possess or at least develop entrepreneurial skills (Morris 2014) and to be an "entrepreneurial attention seeker" (Tessler & Flynn 2016). As such, a lacklustre online presence might be understood in terms of an "entrepreneurial failing" that inhibits a band's ability to "scale up their listener base" (Nickell 2020: 52).

Yet, work in the online realm represents an additional and mostly unpaid (at, least in a direct sense) form of labour for the artist as intermediary. The labour required to maintain online interaction in the music industries has been variously described as "relational" (Baym 2015), "emotional" (Watson & Beaverstock 2014) and "aesthetic" (Hracs & Leslie 2014). These concepts recognize the

---

2   This is an approach which has also however caused significant controversy; see, for example, Savage (2021) on the arguments surrounding Rodrigo's use of the music of Elvis Costello, and Costello's subsequent defence of Rodrigo.

3   We return to the matter of the affordances of new video and live-streaming platforms in Chapter 6.

emotional and physical demands online labour places on artists and other music professionals. In her work on musicians and audiences, for example, Baym (2015, 2018) extends Hochschild's concept of emotional labour (see Hochschild 2012) to develop the term *relational labour*, seeking to illustrate how performers build ongoing connections with disparate audiences. The concept encourages us to consider how the issues raised by emotional labour play out when focused not on particular interactions, but rather on the unending connectivity which social media demands. In the music industries, Baym argues, there is significant pressure to build relationships across social media for career reasons, which actually increases as some measure of success is achieved; as Baym observes, "when more and more people feel their livelihood depends on how well they self-brand, self-promote and connect, relational labour becomes less and less optional" (Baym 2018: 193).

In recent years, critical internet scholars have sought to problematize the debates that have emerged around social medial platforms in relation to user empowerment and unfettered production (Jones 2020). For example, Haynes and Marshall (2018) argue that despite the circulation of discourses that celebrate the internet as a facilitator of democratization and empowerment, there is reason to question some of their core assumptions. Independent musicians are, they argue, "at the sharp end of the 'crisis of the music industry'" and further "online success does not easily translate into material sustainability" (2018: 1989). In a study of 43 independent musicians, they discovered that musicians rely heavily on income derived from selling music and tickets to in-person audiences, and as such, traditional means of accessing and developing audiences are more effective in generating the income needed to survive. Social media, they suggest, is more effective for maintaining established audiences than building new ones. For established artists, social media provides opportunities to leverage their following, but for unknown artists an oversaturated online marketplace makes building an audience from scratch extremely difficult. As Sargent (2009) argues, without connections to formal music industries institutions, artists encounter significant limits in trying to reach broader audiences, while Verboord and van Noord (2016) suggest that "offline inequalities" in the field of music – that is differences in social, cultural and economic capital amongst artists – are not that easily undone via online resources.

For these reasons, traditional music intermediaries such as managers, live music agents and promoters, PR, pluggers and sync[4] teams continue to remain important in connecting artists either directly or indirectly with audiences

---

4   Music "sync" is the use of a piece of music in conjunction with moving images. It represents a form of music licensing whereby a music publisher or copyright owner and a client agree to attach a song onto visual media, such as film, television, advertisements or video games.

through labels, platforms and venues (see, for example, Hracs 2015, on the importance of freelance music managers for independent artists). Further, not only is running a successful media campaign exceptionally labour intensive (Banks 2007) but if one also considers the "viral" nature of music promotion in the social media age, those campaigns that are successful have tended to be highly coordinated with large budgets and that span multiple platforms across old and new media (Wikström 2020). As such, while the internet would seem to offer the opportunity for artists to reach an international audience, which subsequently could be monetized , there would seem to be little evidence to suggest that independent artists have benefited from the shorter value chains afforded by disintermediation (Wallis 2006; Leenders *et al.* 2015).

Does social media pay for artists?

Centred around the above debates, a growing body of research has examined how and why artists and labels are motivated to engage with fans, fans with artists, and fans with other fans online for mutual benefit (see, e.g., Théberge 2006; Choi & Burnes 2013, 2017; Baym 2018; Edlom & Karlsson 2021a, 2021b). However, no empirical evidence exists to confirm that the work expended to build followers on social media platforms results in an increase in income for artists. Indeed, in the most comprehensive qualitative analysis to date of artists' interactions with fans through social media to date, Baym (2018) notes that despite the pressure on artists to build relationships across social media to enhance their careers, it remains unclear as to whether the online labour invested in social media work rewards artists financially. This can be considered more broadly as being as part of what Hesmondhalgh (2021) describes as the "problem of evidence" in critical accounts developed around artists and the complex ways in which they assemble income from a variety of sources to make a living. In seeking to address this issue, this part of the chapter reports on a quantitative analysis of the correlation between social media audiences and artists' incomes. More specifically, in the analysis which follows, we focus specifically on royalties associated with music publishing. While publishing royalties are relatively small compared to recording royalties,[5] they nevertheless represent a crucial source of income for independent artists in their own right, as well as reflecting the variety of activities from which artists derive income.

---

5   In their report produced for the UK Intellectual Property Office, Hesmondhalgh *et al.* (2021) calculate distributions based on average per-stream rates and find that approximately 55 per cent of stream revenues go to recording rights holders, with just 18 per cent going to music-publishing rights holders.

The business model operated by the publisher providing data for this study gives important context for the subsequent data analysis. The company operates an "everyman" publishing model which any and all songwriters and performers to sign up for their publishing service. Historically, the royalty split between a songwriter and publisher was 50/50, with the publisher retaining rights to that musical work until copyright expired (in the UK, this is currently 70 years after the death of the last remaining author). Currently, although terms vary between publishers, deals are often more in favour of the artist, with longer terms and control of copyrights varying between contracts, such that more successful artists are often able to negotiate better deals. In the case of this particular publisher, the split is allocated 80/20 in favour of the songwriter for all artists, and the arrangement between the company and the artist is based on a rolling 28-day contract. In this sense, the company operates more as a publishing intermediary – or "administrative publishing company" (Alberti 2011) – charging a fee for the collection of licensing revenue on behalf of the copyright owner. Whereas a traditional publisher which would require songwriters to assign their rights to the publisher (Cooke 2020), rights are retained by the songwriters. While this business model generates a lower financial return per song than the traditional model, this is offset by the high volume of songs administered. By the end of 2020, over 100,000 songwriters and catalogue owners used the service. In our sample of 255 artists, all were the rights holders for their music, so the artists in this sample can be considered as representative of independent artists more broadly (that is, having not signed away their song rights to a "major" publisher). The subsequent analysis of data reflects this context.

The growth-curve modelling employed used two key sets of variables. The first variable was the cumulative royalty earnings in British pounds sterling (GBP) of musical works attributed to the 255 artists as of the end of three given calendar years: 2016, 2017 and 2018. We use cumulative royalty earnings rather than snapshots of earnings at given points to take account of the different starting positions of artists in terms of earnings and to negate the volatility that can be experienced from royalty income. These figures were aggregated from royalty statements received by the publisher from PRS for Music and detail the amount of money earned by these musical works over the course of the agreement with the music publisher up until that point in time. The second variable was the number of followers on two major social media platforms (Facebook and Twitter) and one major music streaming platform (Spotify), based on the numeric count of followers that the artist had as of the end of the 2016, 2017 and 2018 calendar years. In the sample, for any given year the *mean* royalty income for an artist is much larger than the *median* royalty income, showing this variable to be positively skewed; that is, there are frequent small values and just a few large values. In this case a positive skew indicates that more artists earn towards the lower end of the range of royalty values with relatively fewer artists earning royalties approaching the maximum value in the sample. This skewness is a common feature of income data and so we use a standard statistical transformation to derive the natural logarithm of the royalty income in order to reduce the positive skewness. Accordingly, we analyse percentage rather than absolute increases.

Three different models were run to achieve a nuanced understanding of different income streams, the results of which are displayed in Table 5.1. The first model included all sources of royalty income reported on the PRS statements for artists in the sample. Two other versions of the model focused on specific, individual sources of royalty income, to control for the risk that an examination of total earnings alone obscured a link between social followers and particular kinds of royalty income. First, we focused on income from streaming royalties (that is, those monies collected by the company from streaming services and via collecting societies, and subsequently paid to artists based on the 80/20 split). Secondly, we focused on incomes from live music royalties (that is, those monies collected by the company from live music venues and other sources,

Table 5.1 Model results

		Model 1 All sources	Model 2 Streaming	Model 3 Live
Fixed Part	Constant	4.795 (0.502)	−4.778 (0.770)	4.803 (0.507)
	Facebook followers	−0.032 (0.073)	0.367 (0.127)	−0.024 (0.073)
	Twitter followers	**0.049 (0.007)**	**0.203 (0.079)**	0.044 (0.038)
	Spotify followers	**0.323 (0.030)**	**0.391 (0.063)**	0.278 (0.028)
Random Part	Variance in royalties earned between time periods:	1.597 (0.144)	**2.203 (0.226)**	**1.918 (0.172)**
	Variance in royalties earned between artists:	0.072 (0.005)	0.509 (0.036)	0.065 (0.004)

Notes: Model parameters estimated using MLwiN 3.05 (Charlton *et al.* 2020). The table displays parameter estimates, with associated standard errors shown in brackets. Where parameter values are more than twice the value of the standard error, there is considered to be a strong correlation between the total number of social media followers and an artists' total cumulative royalties over the three-year period of our measures (indicated in bold). Where a strong correlation is identified, the parameters are then used to directly calculate the relative potential financial implication of an increase in follower numbers on royalty income, in percentage terms. A parameter value of 0.1 represents a 1 per cent increase in total royalty income corresponding with a 10 per cent increase in followers on a particular platform over the three-year period, with all other variables constant.

via collecting societies, on the basis of "public performance" and paid to artists based on the 80/20 split). These represent two of the primary income streams for independent musicians with regards to publishing royalties.

Data from the sample of 255 artists suggests that streaming is forming an increasingly significant share of the publishing royalties received by independent artists. Over the three-year period covered by the data, the contribution made by streaming royalties to the total royalties of an average artist in the sample increased from 12 per cent in 2016 to 30 per cent by 2018. This figure corresponds closely with that reported in a 2019 survey of 254 independent artists undertaken by MIDiA Research/Amuse which found that streaming, at 30 per cent of the total, represented the primary source of income for independent artists (Mulligan & Jopling 2019), giving some confidence to the proportions represented in the royalties in our sample. The total monetary value of streams increased by 37 per cent between 2016 and 2017, and by 52 per cent between 2017 and 2018, indicating an accumulating increase in streaming royalties paid by the music publisher to independent artists. Conversely, the royalty revenue from live music as a share of the total royalty revenue decreased over the period from 50 per cent in 2016 to 37 per cent in 2018. However, it is important to note that most income for live music performance will be derived from the up-front fees paid to artists to play in front of live audiences, rather than from royalties.

The first stage of the analysis employed a growth curve model to analyse the correlation between royalties earned over three calendar years (based on cumulative royalties for each year) and the following social media statistics: total number of Facebook followers; total number of Twitter followers; total number of followers on Spotify; and the Spotify Popularity Index[6] (see Table 5.1, model 1). The modelling finds no correlation for our dataset between the total number of Facebook followers and an artists' total royalties from their publishing agreement over the three-year period. Furthermore, while our modelling did find a correlation between the total number of Twitter followers and an artists' total royalties, it is not significant in terms of the size of the impact on earnings; a 10 per cent increase in followers over the three-year period, with all other variables constant, corresponds with just a 0.5 per cent increase in royalties. These are important findings, as they challenge the more optimistic discourses around social media that suggest artists can monetize this fan base to generate income to facilitate more stable, financially self-sustaining independent careers (Haynes & Marshall 2018). If the premise holds that artists can, or indeed must, work

---

6   The Spotify Popularity Index is a 0-to-100 score that ranks how popular an artist is relative to other artists on Spotify. A higher score results in artists getting placed in more editorial playlists and increases their reach on algorithmic playlists and recommendations.

to develop an online audience on social media platforms to generate enough income to sustain their careers, then one would expect to see a clear link between growth in follower numbers on these two major social media platforms and growth in income from royalties. However, our modelling did find a strong correlation between the total number of followers of an artist on Spotify and total cumulative royalties. Moreover, this relationship is much more significant in terms of impact on artists' royalties; a 10 per cent increase in followers on Spotify over the three-year period, with all other variables constant, corresponds with a 3.2 per cent increase in royalties. Having a follower on Spotify is much like having a subscriber to a channel on YouTube in the sense that an artist's content will then show up more in a user's Home/Browse windows, while also triggering user notification/alerts, and influencing other algorithms (such as Spotify's radio stations and Release Radar) that promote an artist's music (Joven 2018). As such, the number of followers on Spotify has the potential to directly influence the number of streams an artist receives, and thus also the amount of royalties received from streaming. However, as there is no capacity for social interaction between artists and fans on the Spotify platform, artists cannot work directly through the platform to attract and retain followers as is possible on actual social media platforms.

The second stage of the analysis sought to obtain a more nuanced understanding of different income streams through growth curve models which separated out streaming royalties and live music royalties. Each income stream was modelled to examine their respective potential relationship with the social media statistics. With streaming royalties separated out in the modelling (see Table 5.1, model 2), there is a strong correlation between the number of followers on all three platforms and streaming income. The most significant impact in terms of an artist's royalty income comes from increasing followers on Spotify; a 10 per cent increase in number of followers over the three-year period, with all other variables constant, corresponds with a 3.9 per cent increase in streaming royalties. We also find that increasing followers on both Facebook (a 10 per cent increase in followers, with all other variables constant, corresponds with a 3.7 per cent increase in streaming royalties) and Twitter (a 10 per cent increase in followers, with all other variables constant, corresponds with a 2.0 per cent increase in streaming royalties) has a significant impact on artist royalty income. With streaming income forming an increasing proportion of artists income, these findings indicate that an important and positive co-evolution is occurring between social media following and the incomes artists are receiving from streaming.

Interestingly, there was a much greater variation between artists in our sample in terms of income levels derived from streaming royalties than from total royalties; in model 2 (streaming only) 18 per cent of the variance is accounted for by variances between artists in terms of their total royalty incomes over the period, compared to just 4 per cent in model 1 (all sources). This suggests a higher level of variance in royalties earned from streaming amongst our artists than for other sources of royalty income such as, for example, from live music, for which income might be considered more stable and more predictable for many musicians, especially those performing regularly. Furthermore, in our sample, artists beginning with a below average number of Spotify followers in 2016 demonstrate a steeper increase in number of followers over the three-year period than those beginning with an above average number, and alongside this they demonstrated a higher growth rate in royalty earnings in percentage terms. This further supports our assertion of a co-evolution of social media and streaming, while also suggesting the potential for faster growth in both followers and royalty earnings in the early stages of an artist's career, both of which will then subsequently slow over time.

In addition, our findings also suggest that a connection exists between the number of followers on music streaming platforms (MSPs) and the royalty incomes received from live music (see Table 5.1, model 3). With royalties from live music separated out in the modelling, we find a strong correlation between the total number of followers of an artist on Spotify and total live music royalties. Here, a 10 per cent increase in the total of number of followers on Spotify over the three-year period, with all other variables constant, corresponds with a 2.8 per cent increase in total royalties from live music. These results suggest that listening to artists on a streaming platform may subsequently result in fans watching an artist live or, conversely, that watching an artist live will encourage fans to listen to that artist on a streaming platform supporting the notion of a "co-evolution" between streaming and live music (Naveed *et al.* 2017).

For artists, there are many positives to online interaction with fans that go beyond simply building follower numbers in search of financial reward. Baym (2018) argues that the value in the relational labour of social media lies primarily in the "enriching, and profoundly validating" social ties that can be formed. Yet, whilst recognizing these emotional and symbolic rewards, the relational labour necessary is additional labour to be undertaken by the "artist as intermediary" (Kribs 2017), and there are going to be limits to the benefits gleaned from such non-monetary rewards, especially in conditions of financial precarity (Frenette 2016). As such, this additional labour will not be equally valued nor welcomed by all. However, our findings suggest that building a social media following is becoming more important for independent artists in relation to the royalty incomes received from streaming. Set in the context of the high level of income precarity experienced amongst independent artists (Mulligan & Jopling 2019), and the increasing influence of MSPs on artist's careers in music, our findings suggest that a positive co-evolution is occurring between a social media following and the incomes artists receive from streaming. Similarly, it would seem that a connection exists between the number of followers on MSPs and the size of live audiences for artists, supporting the notion of a positive co-evolution between streaming and live music incomes (Naveed *et al.* 2017).

Mobilizing fan enthusiasm from crowdfunding to the blockchain

Running alongside – and indeed propelling the development of social media platforms – there has been a broader change in the contours of capitalism which has made the harnessing of fans to the interests of capitalism not just a business proposition but an integral part of generating business propositions. Driven by the networking capacity of the internet and mobile technologies, since at least the early 2000 pervasive communications have been transforming consumer practices (Rheingold 2002) such that what were once seen as makeshift alliances and inspired improvizations are gradually settling into a new pattern of producer-consumer relations that have the power to redefine what is understood as innovation and markets. This has given rise to what might termed an *internet-enabled enthusiastic consumption*, which has blurred the boundaries between firms, consumers and the creative process. Consumers are increasingly taking cues from one another rather than from conventional channels such as large corporations or media outlets, catalysed in part through means of communication and consumption such as social media platforms, web sites and blogs, wherein "influencers" wield considerable agency in determining taste and "followership" (Harrigan *et al.* 2021). These technologies have transformed atomized, individual "sovereign" consumers into connected consumer collectives which, we argue, is important in theorizing the fusion of production and consumption of value (Kiss & Bichler 2008). Fan communities can be seen as tribal collectives, affective assemblages of neo-tribes searching for shared sentiments, or at least approval of their assumed narrations of self (Duffett 2013; Hetherington 1998; Maffesoli 1996). The solidarity made possible by the internet provides shared experience; validation is both sought and found. Labels, or groupings, become organizing factors in the lives of members, who seek support and affirmation by bonding with others of a similar kind (Sundararajun 2016).

Academic research on fandom has sought to understand why fans make considerable emotional investments in the objects, subjects and texts that they follow. The recognition of the importance of emotion and affect within the performance of fandom led Sandvoss to define a fan as an individual who undertakes "the regular, emotionally involved consumption of a given popular narrative or text" (Sandvoss 2005: 8). Abercrombie and Longhurst (1998: 121) meanwhile define fans as a "skilled audience", arguing that the competencies and skills of fans differ, as do the actions that stem from their fandom. They argue that differences in the skills and competencies of fans constitute an "audience continuum"; thus, fans may be distinguished from general consumers but also, in turn, from what they describe as "cultists" and enthusiasts, representing a deepening of the "division of labor" of fandom. Sandvoss argues "that [while] fandom at its core remains a form of spectatorship" (2005: 53), based on the fact that studies have revealed that "fans," as defined above, overwhelmingly out-number the more active and engaged cultists or enthusiasts, the activities of the latter groups indicate that in some cases the emotional investment within the subjects of their fandom drives them to acts of textual production or other forms of active engagement. It is this tendency that is being harnessed by eco-nomic agents to augment and refine their production of cultural goods and ser-vices. In the following section, we consider this in relation to the emergence of crowdfunding platforms as a way in which musicians, through developing their own set of fans, cultists and enthusiasts, can generate new sources of income or funding. We subsequently expand on this discussion further in Chapter 6 in relation to new developments in online audience engagement.

Towards the co-creation of value: the rise of crowdfunding

In opening this chapter, we noted that the recorded music industry which emerged from its crisis of reproduction is one of reduced capital flow, smaller artist rosters, and substantially reduced record label budgets per project. This has created something of a wider venture gap in the music industries, where money to fund the emergence of new music is increasingly the responsibility of musicians in a way that it was not in the past. Partly in response to the more par-simonious position taken by record companies following the MP3 crisis, there has emerged a greater awareness of alternative funding options open to artists, from traditional means such as seeking grants from charities and associations, or borrowing from friends and family, to newer developments such as commer-cial funding in the form of debt and investment (Harris 2013) and crowdfund-ing. Crowdfunding seeks to leverage the power of affect and emotion which, by targeting fans, has the potential to provide the investment needed to develop new music and establish musical careers but without the need to generate mar-ket standard returns on investment as demanded by more traditional funding routes. Crowdfunding seeks to align the interest of producers and consumers through a campaign to raise money to fund new ventures of various kinds: it is an online collective action through which initiators seek to gather funds from a large number of contributors, often using crowdfunding platforms to facilitate contact and flow of resources between parties.

Crowdfunding covers a spectrum of activity. At one end, crowdfunding represents an analogue of the financial sector, making it possible to arrange personal and business loans, and even equity finance. At the other end, crowdfunding is driven by gifts and donations or where money is offered in exchange for a non-pecuniary reward. It is this later kind of crowdfunding that has the most relevance for music, representing a means of funding creative and innovation-related projects by tapping into the enthusiasms and passions of motivated fans and enthusiasts (Bennett *et al.* 2015). In this respect, crowdfunding seeks to take advantage of the internet's long tail (Anderson 2006), by aggregating geographically distributed sources of supply and demand to form markets with viable critical mass. Crowdfunding has the potential to inculcate long-term relationships between musicians (as borrowers) and fans (as lenders/donators) through the intermediation of the P2P platforms on which they are based. Through such platforms, musicians have the opportunity to develop narrow but potentially temporally deep and repetitive sources of funding, particularly given that fans provide money for motivations related to fandom and affect. In this way, crowdfunding mobilizes what Lewis (2002) has described as "interest group" economics and what Sundararajan (2016) describes as crowd-based capitalism.

Within the music and entertainment field, a number of crowdfunding sites have come to prominence. Indeed, it was in this field that the principle of crowdfunding emerged, as in the late 1990s the out-of-favour neo-progressive rock band Marillion used an incipient online network of dedicated fans to raise $60,000 they needed to fund a US tour. The band turned to their fans when, being without a contract with a record label that would pay for investments in their career, they lacked the funds necessary to underwrite the costs (Lewis 2002). Emboldened by this fundraising success, the band turned again to its fans to provide investment for a new record. Estimating that they needed an advance of £100,000 to pay for recording costs, the band raised £200,000 in weeks from 16,000 fans (Lewis 2002: 132). It took almost a decade for the ideas forged by the likes of Marillion to be formalized into crowdfunding platforms that would attract funds to support the musical economy. SellaBand was established in 2006, followed by Slicethepie (2007), Indiegogo (2008), and Pledge Music (2009). However, the best-known crowdfunding platform in this field is Kickstarter, established in New York in 2009, and which now has additional offices in Los Angeles, London, Berlin and Vancouver. Kickstarter allows artists of all kinds to make appeals for money to fund their "projects", with the donor's reward being the successful completion of a project to which supporters were committed or at least interested in seeing bear fruit and even – although this is not obligatory – obtaining a copy of the output of the project or, in the case of performance art, for example, participation in it.

An examination of the music section of Kickstarter quickly establishes that the activities for which artists seek funding are those formerly undertaken by record companies. These include the recording, mixing, and mastering of new songs, album artwork design, the manufacturing and printing of CDs, promotion and publicity, and website design. The amount of money requested varies, from modest amounts to levels of investment that even record companies at the height of their financial powers may have hesitated to approve. For example, a former member of the band Dresden Dolls, Amanda Palmer, used Kickstarter to raise $100,000 to record her first solo album. The appeal period for all artists is strictly limited – if artists do not raise the target fund in a maximum of 90 days all investments are returned to supporters – yet Palmer managed to earn more than ten times her target figure, generating a total fund of $1.2 million. The ability of Palmer to leverage the affect and loyalty of fans into investment capital was particularly impressive given that she was seen as a having only a narrow market appeal. The money raised was used to record an album, which sold enough copies in its first week to make the Billboard top 10. In addition, Palmer hoped to bank $100,000 of the $1.2 million as pure profit (Lindvall 2012).

However, while this form of fund raising may enable some artists to circumvent the gatekeeping role of record companies, obtaining money this way is not without its own cost. The rewards that generate the highest investments tend to be those through which the artists give more of themselves through personal appearances and engagements, often in small scale or intimate settings. For example, two fans paid $10,000 for an "art-sitting" and dinner with Palmer (Lindvall 2012). Anecdotal evidence suggests that artists find these quite challenging, due to the high level of social and cultural capital required to manage them, and the potential unpredictability of the event. As we outlined earlier in this chapter, direct interaction with fans in person and even via social media requires considerable emotional labour as they seek to cultivate and build relationships that might be economically sustaining (Morris 2014). In this regard, such investments may be seen as more complicated exchanges that take on elements of the gift in as much as they have long-lasting social obligations and implications and lack the degree of separation that traditionally accompanies transactions based on exchange.

One might interpret these developments in rather different ways. They might be viewed as part of a new technological democracy which allows for more public deliberation on products and services and, indeed, more input into their design, funding and realization. Like democracy, this does not mean that everyone participates, or participates equally. Some consumers want to build, drive, and even fund the communities into which they are hooked and are orbiting around in tighter circuits and at faster speeds; this is the deep end of fandom. As we have noted, recent technological developments have enabled them to do this more fully, controlled by the extent to which individuals have disposable income for such investment. Other consumers want a fleeting encounter according to the circumstances in which they find themselves. Alternatively, one might see crowdfunding as a costless incubator site for record companies, which provides a proof-of-concept test and brings new talent to the market, which they can then sign and channel recordings to streaming sites in which the record companies are heavily invested and divert little money back to artists. In other words, the creative commons that some commentators want to see may be simply a new form of ownership, little more than the latest phase in the commodification of consumer desire. This is a way in which capitalism can extract value from resources that are more or less free and easily accessible; moreover, it is difficult to describe such value extraction as exploitation, if such resources are not only given freely but also with enthusiasm.

O'Dair and Owen (2019) offer a cautionary note about the potential of crowdfunding, arguing that it is not as promising for emerging artists as is sometimes suggested. The success of Amanda Palmer, as described above is, they argue, unusual; they note that as of January 2018, only just under half (49.45 per cent) of the music projects on Kickstarter had been successfully funded, and the sums raised significantly lower than the sort of figure raised by Palmer. Palmer's success, they suggest, was underpinned by the fact that she already had a significant fan base from her time in Dresden Dolls. Gamble *et al.* (2017), in their qualitative analysis of crowdfunding in music, also note how the benefits for the financial models of independent artists are dependent on fanbase demographic variables relating to age group, due to a "sustained apprehension from younger audiences" (2017: 33). Subsequently, O'Dair and Owen (2019) argue that for many new artists it is likely that they will be unable to "break out of their local market, in which they may be known through live performance, or from an equally small online market developed through posting recorded music that is consumed for free" (2019: 11). Thus, they go on to argue, "for musicians, and emerging musicians in particular, the DIY potential of the digital era is being restricted by a lack of access to capital – and traditional crowdfunding has not proved a viable alternative" (2019: 11). Moreover, from an analysis of the use of Kickstarter by Canadian musicians, Bannerman (2020) argues that claims for its democratizing potential have validity up to a point, in as much as it "does make economic capital and financial resources more accessible to debut musicians and to those musicians who do not have the social capital (connections) to win a grant or music label support" while also benefitting musicians "working in small cities, who may not have robust networks of support, [but who] can access funds through Kickstarter" (Bannerman 2020: 258). However, these access gains are, Bannerman argues, ultimately modest given that they disproportionately benefit white male musicians. Bannerman notes that in return for such limited gains "the owners of Kickstarter collect significant profits, appropriate the social capital brought to the site by its users, and capitalize on the success, prestige, and cultural capital of their users" (Bannerman 2020: 259).

Towards decentralized musical economies: the case of blockchain

More recently, developments around Web 3.0,[7] the blockchain and the Metaverse, are allowing new innovations and more equitable forms of artist funding to be explored. Potts and Rennie (2019) suggest that one way to view blockchain is as an institutional or governance technology that forms an economic infrastructure for creative industries that increase capabilities and productivity while at the same time disrupting markets, business models and organizational forms by bringing about a radical process of reintermediation, reducing the need for established intermediaries necessary for trust and validation (such as lawyers and auditors for example). Potts and Rennie identify two types of specific effects. The first relates to a new institutional infrastructure in terms of money and finance, consisting of tokens[8] and digital registries for identifying assets, including intellectual property using smart contracts[9] and various other organizational infrastructure built on the new technology of shared ledgers. The second effect relates to creative production and consumption. In this context, Potts and Rennie argue, "blockchain technology suggests a technical prospect (which may or may not be realized) to facilitate broader and lower-cost opportunities for collaborative production, and of more direct (P2P) relationships between artistic producers and fans" (2019: 96).

For O'Dair *et al.* (2016: 14), "blockchain technology could have a significant effect on crowdfunding, with artists issuing their own shares or tokens and smart contracts guaranteeing that pledge contributions would be returned were funding targets not met". The emergence of non-fungible tokens (NFTs) – unique digital assets represented by tokens (strings of text) encoded on a share accounting ledger (underpinned by blockchain technologies) – represent perhaps the most widely recognized application of blockchain within the creative

---

7   "Web 3.0" is a term used to describe uses of the World Wide Web which incorporate concepts such as decentralization, blockchain technologies, and token-based economics. This is often contrasted with "Web 2.0" in which data and content are typically centralized in a small group of companies referred to as Big Tech.

8   A digital token is a digital representation of an asset, value, or utility. It can be used for various purposes, such as accessing services, participating in decentralized applications or representing ownership in an asset.

9   A smart contract is a piece of software run on a distributed ledger enabling the automatic execution of activities based on pre-set contingent rules (Borgogno & Martino 2024).

industries, providing a means by which fans can directly support musicians[10] in a range of musical activities including composition and music making, live performance and merchandising. Pointing to NFT-related trends, Turchet (2023) argues that we are now seeing a: "profound (and likely lasting) change in how musicians create music and engage with their audiences and fans. Essentially, we are witnessing a new fan-artist relationship, where the fan not only acts as a direct patron, but can also get revenues from the support provided to the artist" (Turchet 2023: 1817).

More broadly, Turchet argues, blockchain technologies have the potential for novel forms of revenue streams to arise. These centre around fans directly supporting musicians through a variety of different means (without passing through any intermediary), such as, for example, buying merchandise in the form of digital assets (for example, NFTs), or the purchase of the rights of a musical composition with blockchain tracking ownership. Most existing strategies for crowdfunding for music projects operate, as noted above, via a reward model, which does little to offer funders a return on their investment, and as such musicians raising money in this way rely on supporters that are both committed and at least partly philanthropic. Recent developments in crowdfunding platforms have sought to address this issue by offering fans the opportunity to take financial shares in the recording projects they are supporting. The Swedish MusicTech start-up Corite, for example, operates a platform whereby artists create fan campaigns to obtain support for activities around the production and distribution of music (recording and promotional activities, for example), with backing provided up-front by fans in return for a share of the streaming revenues following release. Should the release meet a pre-defined target for number of streams across MSPs, supporters see the return of their original investment, and should the release exceed this streaming goal, supporters begin to make a profit on their investment, based on the size of their contribution. Thus, such as model is seen as a win-win for both musicians and their supporters, albeit with the inherent risk that comes with any such investment that money will be lost with no financial reward (although fans may still feel compensated through the non-financial rewards associated with the philanthropic backing of emerging artists). Since its launch in 2020, Corite has promoted almost three hundred artist-led crowdfunding campaigns across a range of genres, all of which have been funded to their target goals, although no data

---

10 However, the values of NFTs have proved to be highly volatile, as they are highly reactive to variations in the price of cryptocurrencies (Ante 2021). This suggests this would be an unreliable source of income for musicians or other creative workers, notwithstanding other concerns about protecting the intellectual property rights of NTFs against infringement in the form of unauthorized minting and duplication.

is available on what proportion of fans profit from, or even recoup, their initial investment.

We are now also witnessing new developments related to the convergence of blockchain technologies and the Metaverse, where connected users will be able to virtually interact within each other, through the form of avatars, in a shared virtual environment whilst working, collaborating, playing, selling and purchasing. Turchet (2023) argues that contemporary audiences are seeking more engaging musical experiences and closer interactions with performers, and that development in the Metaverse bring new opportunities to cater to these demands. Turchet points to the emergence of a "Musical Metaverse", dedicated to musical activities from composing and music making to performing and experiencing virtual live concerts, while at the same time music is crossing over into other Metaverse spaces. The online game platform and game creation system ROBLOX, for example, has hosted virtual concerts from high profile artists such as Lil Nas X, David Guetta, Mariah Carey and George Ezra, while the online game platform Fortnite has hosted exclusive virtual musical performances from artists such Travis Scott and Ariana Grande. Both of these platforms generate revenue through in-game sales of their virtual currencies – Robux and V-bucks respectively – which are exchanged for exclusive content and experiences. In the case of virtual concerts, fans are able to attend and interact with concertgoers via their in-game avatars in ways that familiar in gameplay, with light shows and special effects of the kind found at physical concerts. In 2021, Sony Music Entertainment announced a strategic partnership to bring Sony Music recording artists into the Roblox Metaverse, and to work together to develop innovative music experiences for the Roblox community and offer a range of new commercial opportunities for Sony Music artists to reach new audiences and generate new revenue streams around virtual entertainment. Indeed, Sony have been very much at the forefront of developments in the Musical Metaverse; in 2022 Sony Music acquired Prism Project, a virtual-talent initiative launching "vTubers" (virtual YouTubers) with their associated avatars/animated characters. Upon its closure in March 2024, the programme had eighteen managed artists, who subsequently became independent (i.e. they were not signed) once the programme ended. The reason for the closure of the programme was cited as being the considerable staff resources required to sustain and then grow the brand (Dredge 2024b).

The Musical Metaverse offers the potential for fans to have new ways of connecting with music, their favourite artists, and to each other, creating "an enriched range of music interaction modalities that ultimately are expected to greatly benefit a large variety of music stakeholders" (Turchet 2023: 1824). Indeed, several MusicTech start-ups are making headway with developments in the Music Metaverse as part of what is being termed a "decentralized" or "distributed" creator economy. In 2022, the MusicTech firm Melodity, for example, announced that it was developing a Web 3.0 monetization infrastructure that enables play-to-earn (P2E, where users can earn cryptocurrency via playing games), listen-to-earn (L2E, where users can earn cryptocurrency by listening to music or other audio content) and Metaverse opportunties based on a proprietary blockchain. Melodity claims it plans for artists to keep 90 per cent of revenue from their art, a rate they hope will become a new benchmark. Their platform has three elements: DoMeta, a music-centric Metaverse in which artists fans can play, learn, create and participate in live events together, combining blockchain, NFTs and play-to-earn; DoDuet a platform revolving around contests and gamifying music, offering listen-to-earn opportunities; and DoMart, an NFT marketplace for the platform, offering music distribution and the sale and licensing of composite music NFTS. The platform operates its own cryptocurrency: the Melodity token ($MELD).

Such models are reflective of a wider shift from more traditional platform economics towards a new decentralized token economy (Voshmgir 2020) or "tokenomics". In its most straightforward application to music, "tokenization" refers to a process whereby the ownership of each piece of digital music is distributed into many parts, which can then be exchanged for monetary investment from a large number of investors. In this regard, platforms may use tokenization to facilitate direct investment and ownership by fans in the success of creative careers and outputs, and from which they may take a share. Yet, such platforms also utilize tokenized economies to monetize the data, content and engagement of platform users. They do so by creating their ecosystems in collaboration with the community in ways that are much more open than traditional platform models, enabling new forms of value co-creation and exchange beyond those associated with the dominant "attention economy" of Web 2.0 (Elsden *et al.* 2024). This could include, for example allowing users to earn tokens for their interactions, such as liking, sharing, or commenting on posts, or sharing particular forms of data with the platform. These tokens can then be traded or redeemed for rewards, creating a new layer of engagement and participation.

Such strategies are particularly used where the platform's primary objective is the exchange of information – for example, social networks, content distribution, and video streaming (Lage *et al.* 2022) – information which can subsequently be sold to third parties, such as data collection companies, for purposes such as targeted advertisements, generating profits for the platform. The previously mentioned crowdfunding start-up Corite, for example, recently launched "missions" where users can earn "fan power" (in the form of digital tokens, called "CO tokens") by engaging in a variety of tasks linked to the platform and the artists on the platform. In its first iteration, as the platform looks to build users, these missions involve fans completing profiles on the platform, connecting their Discord account, following the social media and Spotify accounts of the platform, and inviting friends to the platform, for all of which these receive fan power tokens. These tokens can be collected and then in theory later be redeemed towards rewards such as access to exclusive content as the platform develops. Users can also connect their cryptocurrency wallets to the platform in order to receive pay-outs from investments in releases in cryptocurrency. In essence, for such music platforms, the use of tokenomics is aimed at incentivizing fans to consume and engage with content and activities on the platform, building an engaged user base from which not only artists but also the platform itself can subsequently benefit through various strategies for monetization, including the monetization of user data.

Platform developers such as those mentioned above, along with many industry commentators, describe such developments as creating decentralized or distributed creator economies that empower creators to monetize their work and take control of their intellectual property rights. The building of systems that run on code are attractive in that they offer up the possibility of a radical form of reintermediation that removes the requirement for all manner of costly intermediaries charging for their services (Borgono & Martino 2024). But such platforms are in fact positioning themselves as key intermediaries between artist and audience. As such, this brings into question the notion that such developments truly represent decentralization, subject as they are to the underlying economic logics of platforms. As Elsden *et al.* (2024: 184) note, an underlying concern amongst creative communities in relation to contemporary internet platforms is the scope or the platform to "unilaterally extract (and abuse) the value co-created laboriously" between artists and their audiences. In this respect, a more radical vision of blockchain-enabled decentralization has come to the fore in recent years: the decentralized autonomous organization (DAO).

DAOs are forms of internet-based organizations which are collectively owned, and member managed. In their essence, DAOs are complex blockchain smart contracts which allow token holders to participate directly in decision making processes and decentralized entrepreneurial activities (Borgogno & Martino 2024). By offering a form of decentralization, the DAO also offers up the potential to bring about considerable efficiencies through reintermediation. In the most common structure of a DAO, everyone in the organization contributes to decision-making through a system of proposals and voting (Catlow & Rafferty 2022). Some DAOs give members the right to a portion of an organization's profits (or losses) while others provide their members with the right to access or manage the resources or services within the DAO, abiding by and trusting the software and the smart contracts underpinning the DAO rather than relying on legal formalities (Borgogno & Martino 2024). However, more than this, from a radical perspective they also represent mechanisms for technologically formalizing artistic (and often geographically dispersed) friendships, collaborations and network structures, creating "resilient and mutable systems for scale-free interdependence and mutual aid" (Catlow & Rafferty 2022: 27). DAOs allow communities of artists to develop their own instruments for self-and-community realization, create the distribution cultures, platforms and channels to share ideas, practices and insights, and own a stake in their mutual future prosperity *(ibid.)*. For example, Friends with Benefits is a DAO that was established in 2020. Wanting to "redefine the cultural industries", the DAO operates as "an artist's collective that uses blockchain tokens to unlock access, manage payments, and collectively vote on group investments" (O'Dwyer 2023: 233, 235). As O'Dwyer describes:

> Friends with Benefits is not the first example of its kind ... but it received the most mainstream attention, with over 6,000 members including musicians Azelia Banks and Erykah Badu. It was like a virtual club ... only instead of premises, the collective runs on multiple Discord channels dedicated to fashion, music, art and live-streamed event content. Users must buy into the FWB token to become a member of the collective. (O'Dwyer 2023: 234)

While markets alone, Catlow and Rafferty (2022) argue, produce inequality, monopoly and fragility, diverse ecologies produce resilience. In theory at least, DAOs offer the potential to decentralize the ownership, governance and value capture of platforms, shifting the balance of power from platforms and the market to creators and their audiences. First, they allow for the realization through distributed ledger technologies of new and more direct opportunties for audiences and fellow artists alike to invest in and take ownership of the success of creative careers and outputs. At the heart of a DOA sits the digital token, and that token has a price, enabling particular forms of monetization and value, and (collective) saving and investment. However, as Schneider (2022: 20) contends with regards to DOA members, "the benefits they care most about are not financial: like any friendship, a DOA will not survive long if its heart can only pump transactions". Second, then, DOAs crucially offer new opportunities for collectivity and solidarity amongst artists through shared membership and decision making in new decentralized organizational forms.

Given the above, DAOs might be seen as aligning with a broader "cypherpunk" ethos, a term that refers to "social movements, individuals, institutions, technologies, and political actions that, with a decentralized approach, defend, support, offer, code, or rely on strong encryption systems in order to re-shape social, political, or economic asymmetries" (Ramiro & Queiroz 2022: no pagination). Jirásek (2023), however, questions just how decentralized DAOs are in reality, arguing that many DAOs are decentralized in name only. He points, for example, to issues such as power asymmetries whereby major token holders have a disproportionate say in organizational voting, low community participation in developing and voting in proposals, and the use of off-chain voting. Such issues can result in DAOs not being authentically decentralized which in turn has significant implications for their radical social and economic potential in a cultural field such as music. Moreover, O'Dwyer questions how radical they really are, given that in 2021 the Friends with Benefits DAO was the beneficiary of a $10 million investment from Andreessen Horowitz, one of Silicon Valley's largest venture capital firms, for which it was expecting a significant return on the investment:

> Friends with Benefits did not just tokenize art – it tokenized prestige, vibes, bragging rights, membership with the in crowd. People were buying in in the hope that they would belong, but also make money. Kind of like art, honestly. (O'Dwyer 2023: 236)

Conclusion

Optimistic discourses have emerged around social media platforms as a means for artists to reach new global audiences, monetize fan bases and facilitate more stable, financially self-sustaining independent careers. For independent artists, a large social media following may be key to gaining a recording contract with a record label, as it presents a mechanism through which artists can demonstrate an already established fan base. Increasingly A&R staff at labels are looking for such indicators that an artist has an existing and sizeable audience for their music to inform their decision-making (Arditi 2020). In turn, a recording contract may be key in allowing an artist to develop a financially sustainable career. Yet, it seems clear that that developing and maintaining an online presence involves an entrepreneurial approach to self-marketing and brings new (and often invisible and unpaid) demands in the shape of relational labour. Furthermore, the matter of artists being able to monetize the "attention" they are being paid online is far from straightforward, given that successful media campaigns are exceptionally labour intensive. It is also made more difficult by the viral nature of music promotion in the social media age. Without connections to formal music industries institutions, artists encounter significant limits in trying reach broader audiences (Sargent 2009). In their research into young musicians in the Netherlands, Leenders *et al.* (2015) find that, while social media platforms provide some benefits for independent artists, access to most old and new media platforms is largely resource dependent and that "some level of fame, success and marketing support is needed before these media offer a significant opportunity for young artists" (2015: 1813). Therefore, they found that the most successful artists in their sample were represented by a record company, who both control access to mass media and are able to use new media effectively as part of their bundling strategies.

Given the above, in this chapter we have subsequently highlighted the growing importance of what we have termed "mobilizing fan enthusiasm", and in particular how crowdfunding platforms are filling a venture gap in the music industries where money to fund the emergence of new music is increasingly the responsibility of musicians. Crowdfunding, we have argued, through leveraging the power of affect and emotion, has the potential for some to provide the investment needed to develop new music and establish musical careers. However, some commentators have argued that that crowdfunding failed to prove it is a viable alternative to "traditional" record label funding mechanisms, leaving the potential of many artists in the digital era restricted by a lack of access to capital (O'Dair & Owen 2019). Taken together, social media and crowdfunding form part of the contemporary "promotional universe" that surrounds artists and which "exhorts them to participate" (Klein *et al.* 2017: 231). But the "systematic difficulties" surrounding music under capitalism (Hesmondhalgh 2020) continue to make it extremely difficult for smaller independent artists to develop financially self-sustaining independent careers despite the possibilities and affordances of these platforms. In this regard, in this chapter we have also considered some of the more radical decentralized social and economic alternatives offered by blockchain technologies, and in particular DAOs, which represent possibly profound change in the ways in which musicians engage with each other, their audiences and fans, and make money from their creative labour. Or, as O'Dwyer (2023) argues, possibly more of the same, but in a new guise. Building on this, in the next chapter, we move on to consider the opportunities for innovation, audience engagement and revenue generation associated with live streaming platforms, set in the context of live performance to the music industries. We reflect in particular on the complexities of monetizing music through live streaming.

Before closing this chapter, however, it is important to recognize that it is highly likely that both the major record labels and the MSPs will themselves seek to further exploit the monetization of fan enthusiasm and explore more decentralized platform models. With regards to music streaming, a recent article by the American investment bank Goldman Sachs (2023) suggested that there is a $4.2 billion market opportunity for "superfan monetization". They point to the fact that with revenues per stream currently falling, one way to boost revenue is through "superfan segmentation". Current streaming models do not distinguish among users, charging each the same flat monthly fee. This, they argue, fails to recognize the different levels of engagement customers have with streaming platforms and artists, neglecting the value that may be created by a specific artist or song. In doing so, they project that monetization of superfans could add \$2 billion of incremental revenue for streaming platforms by 2027 and \$4 billion by 2030, representing a 16 per cent boost to paid streaming revenues.[11] Accordingly, they argue, the structure of payments between streaming services and music labels will need change to distinguish "premium content". They also point to the option of a user-centric model that distributes pay-outs from each user's subscription based directly on the user's listening habits, or the option of a more flexible artist-centric model that seeks to distribute payouts based on the value an artist creates and provides for the platform. With regards to crowdfunding, Gamble *et al.* (2017) note, major labels are currently using crowdfunding to various degrees on account of its compatibility with the pre-sell aspect; that is, enabling the creation of a buzz amongst fans and making them feel invested in a particular artist or project, while at the same time gaining a sense of fan interest in projects and helping the labels to financially de-risk. The adoption of crowdfunding, they argue, could also affect other aspects of the major's financial models, such as the "prospect of incorporating crowdfunding into mini subscription services to the artist in the lead up to an album release" (Gamble *et al.* 2017: 34). As they suggest, the majors are displaying clear signs of innovative approaches to integrating crowdfunding into various configurations of their business models.

---

11 Although for some artists, there are clearly downsides to the rise of superfans. In addition to the dangers of some fans reacting badly to perceptions of being let down, as discussed in Chapter 1 in the case of Chappel Roan, some artists have in turn reacted badly to what they perceive is the predictability of response that occurs when groups of fans attend several live performances in a single tour and crowd out local attendees. For example, in 2024 Chrissie Hynde of The Pretenders used social media to communicate directly to such superfans: "When we go on tour, the whole point of it for the band is that we are playing to a different audience every night. That's why we go on tour! ... So if we're in Edinburgh (like we are tonight), we look forward to seeing local faces. This is what makes it new for us every night. We appreciate those of you who follow us and buy tickets for multiple nights, so please don't be offended if we request you to move out of the front row ... All we are asking is that you give the local fans a chance. This is what keeps it new for us ... especially after being on tour for so many months" (cited in Singh 2024). Such was the negative reaction from their most loyal – and most lucrative – fan base that by the end of the year Hynde had at least qualified her comments as part of a more general apology to fans who she criticized during live shows for using smart phones to film and record performances (Mensah 2024).

6
LIVE MUSIC, LIVE STREAMING

Introduction

In 2024, the music company Music Ally, which provides a range of services for the music industries such as news feeds, marketing, training and events, released another of its "how-to" Sandbox guides for practitioners, which in this case focused on the "superfan" (Gorman 2024). Building on the kinds of developments outlined in the last two chapters – such as the mobilization both of data and techniques of engagement that might better exploit fandom and affect across social media – the guide offers tips to music industries professionals on the best ways of "building, nurturing, and monetizing the most enthusiastic and supportive followers of an artist" (Gorman 2024; no pagination). The ideas for engagement suggested in the guide are designed to make fans feel they were gaining unusual levels of engagement with artists by manufacturing episodes of "exclusivity", while at the same time creating opportunities for the artists and their representatives to extract income from their followers by creating "opportunities" through which they might express their "loyalty" through various acts of expenditure. Aware that such strategies might appear too nakedly instrumental and coldly calculative in an environment driven by affect and emotion, the Music Ally guide notes the importance of doing this in "an authentic way ... at different budget points" (Gorman 2024; no pagination). As well as a helpful checklist for artists and managers, the guide offers a set of exemplar case studies of the ways in which some artists have used technologies and innovative methods of engagement to create a sense of both community and exclusivity for their most committed fans, while all the time giving these fans further opportunities to spend money on the objects of their affection.

Such fan engagement strategies are seen as invaluable for artists in an environment where income from recorded music is much reduced and where popular music struggles to gain attention among an audience demographic that that is likely to spend time using varied forms of digital entertainment across various social media platforms (Leyshon 2014). From the case studies provided by Music Ally, it appears that one of the key spaces in which to enact these strategies is a performance or event of some kind. An example provided in the guide is that of a "listening event", where fans are given access to a limited number of place-specific opportunities to listen to a new recording by an artist, with a case study drawing on the experiences of vocalist and guitarist Adrianne Lenker. The organization of her programme of listening events was outlined to Music Ally by the head of marketing at her record company: "... we did 12 listening events worldwide with hi-fi audio, limited edition lyric books illustrated by Adrianne that were only available there, for free, for everybody. We premiered a video that's not coming out for a couple of months, people brought T-shirts and tote bags, and we did free screen printing with a drawing by Adrianne. Basically trying this experience with us" (quoted in Gorman 2024: 6).

While a listening party may be a new kind of event (Riom 2023), musical performance has been a key part of the wider musical economy since the development of an economic market for live music in the nineteenth century, and this remained the dominant form of income within the emergent music industries until the development of sound recording and the creation of a broader market for such recordings (Attali 1985). Thereafter, performance assumed a secondary but complementary role to the market for recorded music.

However, as a crisis raged through the music industries in the early twenty-first century, live performance was revalued, and the observations in 2002 of one long-established superstar artist, David Bowie, proved to be both perceptive and prescient, when he claimed that the live event would be a way of generating revenues that would be more or less immune to the damage being done to royalty income through the advance of MP3s and P2P networks:

> Music itself is going to become like running water or electricity ... so it's like, just take advantage of these last few years [of royalty income] because none of this is ever going to happen again. You'd better be prepared for doing a lot of touring because that's really the only unique situation that's going to be left. It's terribly exciting. But on the other hand it doesn't matter if you think it's exciting or not; it's what's going to happen. (Quoted in Parales 2002).

While some of his other predications made in the interview provided to be less than accurate,[1] his observations about the importance of live performance were strong enough for economist Alan Krueger to translate this insight into a

---

1   For example, Bowie confidently predicted the end of copyright within a decade and that record companies would no longer be key agents in the music distribution system of the near future (Parales 2002).

conceptual understanding of change in the music industries – which he named the Bowie Theory – to explain "a technology-induced erosion of the complementarity between record sales and concert tickets" (Krueger 2005: 27). Drawing on US data for 1996–2003, Krueger illustrated that the average price of concert tickets had increased by 82 per cent over this period, while the equivalent figure for the Consumer Price Index, a background measure of inflation, had increased by only 17 per cent. Before the rise of MP3 and file sharing, recorded music and live performance were indeed complementary, in that the demand for both were positively influenced by one another. However, as the demand for recorded music fell – at least in the form of legal purchases – there was an increased demand for live performance, which was reflected in a sharp increase in the prices that artists were able to charge for tickets, which changed the relationship between records and concerts.

Whereas many artists used to treat concerts and touring as a loss leader for promoting record sales, the inversion of this business model meant that for many artists new recordings became less a way of generating income but, rather, a source of new musical material and media interest which could then be exploited through the sale of concert tickets and related merchandise. By the end of the 2010s, even those artists that were responsible for large volumes of streams on MSPs, that in turn ensured that they captured the majority of the MSP revenue pools, were also generating a large proportion of their income from live performance. According to Krueger, the top 48 musicians who toured in 2017 earned, on average, as much as 80 per cent of their total income from live performances (through sales of both tickets and merchandise), with the balance made up by recorded music (15 per cent) and publishing fees (5 per cent) (Krueger, 2019; 40). Even allowing for the impact of inflation, it is no surprise that the highest grossing tours in popular music history have taken place in the last 20 years (see Table 6.1).

Indeed, by the mid-2020s the musical event reached new levels of economic power, as Taylor Swift in 2023 embarked on an 18-month tour schedule which consisted of more than 150 shows across six continents. By the end of 2023, despite having played less than 50 per cent of the planned performances, the Eras Tour had already become the highest grossing tour in history, with ticket sales of more than $1 billion, surpassing that of the previous highest earning tour, that of Elton John's "farewell" performances, which consisted of more than twice as many shows over five years either side of the Covid-19 pandemic[2] (Barnes 2024).

---

2 Although in revenues standardized to 2006 prices, the date of the earliest tour on the list in Table 6.1, Swift's earnings were roughly equivalent to that earned by U2 in their 2009–11 tour. However, by the time of its conclusion, the Eras Tour will have comfortably surpassed that of U2's 360° Tour both in absolute and relative prices.

Table 6.1 Top 10 music tours by gross income, as of October 2023

Rank	Artist	Tour	Date	Performances	Attendance (m)	Gross Income ($m)	Gross Income ($m) (2006 prices)	Rank (Gross Income ($m) (2006 prices)
1	Elton John	Farewell Yellow Brick Road Tour	2018–20, 2022–23	330	6.0	939	621	2
2	Ed Sheeran	The ÷ (Divide) Tour	2017–19	258	8.9	776	612	3
3	U2	U2 360° Tour	2009–11	110	7.3	736	660	1
4	Coldplay	Music of the Spheres World Tour	2022–23	107	6.3	618	409	8
5	Harry Styles	Love on Tour	2021–23	169	5.0	617	408	9
6	Guns N' Roses	Not in This Lifetime … Tour	2016–19	158	5.4	584	461	5
7	Beyonce	Renaissance World Tour	2023	56	2.8	580	384	10
8	The Rolling Stones	A Bigger Bang Tour	2005–06	111	3.5	558	558	4
9	The Rolling Stones	No Filter Tour	2017–19	58	2.9	547	431	6
10	Coldplay	A Head Full of Dreams Tour	2016–17	115	5.4	524	431	6

Source: Frankenberg (2023).

The scale of the Eras Tour was such that it had significant economic impacts on the locations at which the performances took place, with many venues reporting record attendances. An average of 54,000 fans attended each Taylor Swift concert in 2023 (Mitra 2024), and it was estimated that in addition to the ticket price each person spent around $1,300 per performance on items such as travel, accommodation, subsistence and merchandise (Barnes 2024). The US Travel Association calculated that the impact of the US section of the tour generated as much as $10 billion in both direct and indirect spending at and around the events (Mitra 2024). As the Tour moved to Europe in 2024, the impact of just eight concerts on spending in the UK services sector was attributed by at least one economic commentator to an economic surge in the economy significant enough to mean the Bank of England missed one of its monthly inflation targets (Elliot 2024). For musicians less successful than Taylor Swift, live performance is also critical, although it may account for a lower proportion of their total income than it does for top artists, not least because earnings derived from performing often needs to be supplemented by non-musical work in order make ends meet. Nevertheless, Kruger estimates that on average US musicians earn over two thirds of their income from performances of some kind (including giving music lessons, for example), with a median overall salary in 2016 of $20,000, compared to $35,00 for the workforce as a whole (Krueger 2019: 54–5).

The large reduction in revenues received from recorded music meant that live music necessarily became an important alternative source of income for musicians. But the fact that live music was able to provide at least some financial compensation was in part because recorded music had become more accessible not ubiquitous, first through illegal downloading and then through the rise of MSPs. In the past, the cost of making and storing physical recordings, in the form of vinyl, cassette or CD, created their own scarcity, and had an impact on the budgets of those who consumed music in its various formats and who also made up the potential audiences for live performances. As recorded music became abundant and available at a low cost, so the live event underwent a process of revaluation as a unique and memorable event. Indeed, as Power and Hallencreutz (2002) note, as the recorded music industry proved unable to enforce copyright in the face of the widespread use of MP3s in the early twenty-first century, so it increasingly began to take on features long established within the Jamaican musical economy, which had risen to prominence in the 1960s and 1970s through the success of genres such as calypso, ska and reggae (Blackwell & Morley 2023). In Jamaica, the weakness of civil society meant that musical creativity unfolded in an environment with ineffectual intellectual property rights. This ensured that a "lax attitude to musical ownership and property rights, by the standards of copyrighters, was not only a part of the current general cultural norms that operate in the Kingston scene ... [but] thought of as central to musical expression" (Power & Hallencreutz 2002: 1848–9). As a result, the absence of copyright enforcement meant that royalty income was unreliable, and live performance became an essential form of revenue generation in the Jamaican music industries. The Jamaican model, which for most of its existence seemed an aberration despite the international significance of its musical output, had become the norm, at least for a while.

By 2020 the pivotal role that live performance played in the reproduction of the music industries meant that the advent of the Covid-19 pandemic presented something of an existential crisis both to musicians and to the live music industry more broadly. Entertainment venues across the world were closed as part of broader lockdown protocols to prevent close contact between audience members might encourage the transmission of the virus. In the UK, the scale of the problem was laid out in evidence presented to the House of Commons Digital, Culture, Media and Sport Committee during the first few months of the pandemic, which depicted an industry that had, not surprisingly, all but ground to a halt:

> The Music Venue Trust estimates that 93% of the grassroots venue network faces permanent closure, with 86% of venues reporting that their core threat stems from an inability to meet commercial rent demands ... The National Arenas Association projects that the 23 UK arenas it represents will lose almost £235 million worth of ticket sales over a six-month period ... The UK's thriving festival and live events sector has been particularly badly hit ... the Association of Independent Festivals says that 92% of its members face permanent collapse ... cancellations over spring and summer mean a complete loss of income for the year ahead, which could have devastating consequences for the SMEs and self-employed workers in the live events supply chain.
>
> (House of Commons Digital, Culture, Media and
> Sport Committee 2020: 22–3)

Moreover, the crisis was acute for many working in the music industries given the preponderance within it of self-employment. In the UK, it was estimated that up to 40 per cent of all musicians were eligible for neither the Coronavirus Job Retention Scheme ("furlough") nor the Self-Employed Income Support Scheme (Musicians' Union 2020). Nevertheless, in the midst of this, some musicians were able to devise a way of earning income by turning to digital platforms that facilitated live streaming and that hitherto had mostly been used by the game playing community.

During the pandemic, an increasing number of record labels, promoters and artists working in the creative sector began to explore live streaming and, in so doing, find new ways of generating income. The remainder of this chapter focuses on this novel use of platforms within the contemporary music industries. The discussion is organized into three main parts. First, we outline the rise of live streaming and the role played by the dominant platform, Twitch, and the way in which it has enabled artists to earn money from platform-intermediated performances. Second, we draw on our research findings to reveal the opportunities, but also the challenges, of using live streaming as a means of revenue generation within the music industries. Third, and finally, we provide some concluding comments and observations.

The rise of live streaming

As van Es (2017) has observed, describing an event as "live" frequently involves some degree of conceptual flexibility, particularly when performances are technologically intermediated. The Covid-19 pandemic necessarily forced music artists and businesses to innovate with new digital ways of showcasing, promoting and distributing music. Following the closure of live music venues and the associated loss of live music incomes, the use of live streaming platforms during the pandemic to meet audience demand created a new paradigm of engagement (Frenneaux & Bennett 2021) for artists socially distanced from their audiences, opening up a range of opportunities and consequences for artists, listeners and platforms (Zhang & Negus 2021). Many high-profile major label artists began using new streaming platforms developed by innovative MusicTech start-ups to sell tickets for, and to facilitate the performance of, exclusive online shows with high-end production values and audio quality. In December 2021, for example, Oasis lead singer Liam Gallagher performed live on a barge travelling down the River Thames. The show lacked a physical audience but was livestreamed globally via the Melody VR platform at the cost of £16.50 per ticket. For smaller labels and artists live streaming was a far more modest affair, largely enabled by the live-streaming capacities of the major social media platforms, such as Facebook and Instagram Live. One interviewee explained how: "There was an initial panic, this is the end of the world and everything ... and then sort of a stage of camaraderie where people tried to get a bit creative ... zoom gigs and split screen performances where people played instruments" (label manager, independent record label, Liverpool).

These performances were not necessarily merely about generating direct income from ticket sales *per se*. Rather, they were about allowing bands and labels to stay active and to keep audiences engaged and creating social media content with the hope of further driving sales of recorded music and keeping audiences "warm" for the return of physical gigs. While many interviewees noted that there were some initial positive experiences and a good reaction from audiences to live streams, there was also a consensus that the livestream space became quickly saturated and audience interest quickly tailed off as the pandemic progressed:

> We did one live streamed event ourselves. It went pretty well. And a few bands on the label did … "live from lockdown". And they were done pretty well as well. It gave us stuff to be able to put on social media as well, and just get active. The downside of that, though, was that everyone was putting out stuff on social media and everyone was doing live performances during lockdown, and it just got a bit saturated after a bit.
> (Label manager, independent record label, West Yorkshire)

Despite the positives of live streaming for many musicians and music businesses during the pandemic, the consensus amongst our research participants was that live streams did not provide a suitable replacement for live music shows in physical spaces as they lacked the atmosphere, artist-audience interactions, and sociality of live music proper. Yet, given the scale of the adoption of live stream technologies and formats, as the pandemic eased there was a sense that livestreaming might be a permanent feature of the music industries, especially in a hybrid-format where live performances in physical spaces with an audience were also streamed for a wider audience viewing online. Pre-empting this, many venues began to invest in livestreaming technologies ahead of the return of live music, in an attempt to maximize revenues post-pandemic. Yet here again experiences of trying to innovate in this hybrid space were mixed:

> At that point we were all thinking, gosh, is livestreaming here to stay? And loads of venues were buying equipment … So, I wanted to experiment with hybrid live shows to see what audiences were doing, to see whether it could be sustainable … We put on 15 shows, and we also turned them into virtual showcases. It was a flop. I don't think it works … none of the live streams pulled in an audience big enough to cover the actual costs of the filming. So, I am now convinced the hybrid and live streaming gigs of the kind of quality we were going for just were not the right thing. And now you've got all these venues, all this fancy camera equipment and nothing to do with it.
> (Chief executive, talent development and music export organization, Manchester)

Elsewhere, innovation and experimentation in the use of streaming technologies successfully developed sufficient online audiences during the pandemic such that hybridity continued to be successful post-pandemic. Innovations continue to happen in the live streaming space to the benefit of smaller record labels and independent artists. The online music distribution platform Bandcamp, for example, has recently launched the Bandcamp Live streaming and listening party service, building on some of the online innovations around monetization, gifting and live chat first seen in platforms such as Twitch. One interviewee described how: "We are doing some live stream stuff, now that Bandcamp has introduced a live streaming platform that's really good because it integrates with their sales platform as well, so you can do really cool launch party events and that sort of thing, and all the sales channels are integrated into it, so it's quite a good way of shifting units as well" (label manager, independent record label, West Yorkshire).

While Twitch has played a role in enabling these hybrid performances, its ability to do so was in part a result of the role it offered as an essential safety net for musicians reliant on money from live performance but who were suddenly denied opportunities to work, while in many cases, for reasons outlined earlier, also being excluded from accessing government support during the pandemic. Twitch offered musicians an established and accessible platform, having grown rapidly as a result of hosting a form of live performance that was best mediated through a digital platform: live streamed computer gaming. This activity attracted large and enthusiastic audiences, and the platform gradually developed its own system of payments and rewards that enabled some streamers to earn sizeable incomes through their game playing and hosting skills. Musicians had begun to explore the opportunities of using Twitch to tap alternative ways of earning money from performance prior to the emergence of the Covid-19 virus, but the numbers doing so during the pandemic increased sharply as it offered a vital source of income in the absence of alternatives. By April 2020, music had emerged as a distinct and growing channel on Twitch such that the platform appointed its first head of product and engineering for music.

Twitch

The Covid-19 pandemic accelerated the adoption of digital platform technologies across large sections of economy and society, as remote at-a-distance transactions and communications helped to reduce the amount of face-to-face contact in order to slow the transmission of the virus (Davies *et al.* 2022; Leyshon 2023; Tooze 2021). While a great deal of attention was focused on the boost that the pandemic was having for online distributors such as Amazon, online streaming services like Netflix, or meeting and communication software providers like Zoom and Microsoft Teams, less attention was paid to developments in the music industries where a main beneficiary was Twitch. Exploited for many years by computer gamer players who used the affordances of the platform to generate income streams by developing supportive audiences willing to offer money as a form of steady income, after 2020 Twitch attracted growing numbers of musicians to follow the paths paved by gamers.

The origins of Twitch can be traced to the mid-2000s phenomenon of "social cam" websites, where the growing availability of webcams encouraged people to set up their own websites to broadcast ostensibly mundane and trivial activities, but which nevertheless managed over time to gain audiences. Early social cam websites were modest in their ambitions, "typically hosting people simply streaming their everyday lives via webcams, offering amateur talk shows or even mundane 'puppycam' channels where viewers watch litters of sleeping newborn dogs" (Taylor 2018: 3). One such site was Justin.tv, a live streaming platform founded in 2007, which allowed anyone to broadcast their own live video content to the internet. It bore some resemblance to the far bigger and more popular YouTube, but Justin.tv was distinctive in that enabled real-time broadcasts. As the platform gathered more viewers, it increased its focus on gaming and esports, which in 2011 encouraged the firm to create Twitch as a distinctive offshoot platform dedicated to live streams of electronic game playing. The popularity of the platform prompted Amazon to purchase it for $1 billion in 2014, which gave Twitch access to Amazon's digital infrastructure and tools, which both stabilized the platform and turned it into an "extendable platform", using its application programming interface (API) to encourage innovation by third-party developers (Taylor 2018).

By the time the pandemic arrived, Twitch had drawn on the financial backing of Amazon and its distributed developer base to establish itself as one of the leading live streaming platforms globally, with millions of monthly active users and an active community of streamers and viewers across a range of genres. As Taylor notes, the achievement of Twitch is that it is an assemblage, that brings together a range of human and technological actors to create an event:

> Live streaming is a rich illustration of the assemblage of play, whereby a variety of actors (human and nonhuman), infrastructures, institutions, and interrelations make play, performance, and work possible. Producing a successful broadcast involves a great deal of cultivation. Balancing the audience and forms of engagement with the content, deploying a complex array of material and infrastructural components, and managing a variety of relationships on- and offline (including economic ones) all become part of the work of streaming play.
>
> (Taylor 2018: 80)

In the wake of Taylor's pioneering work in this area, a growing body of work has explored the multifaceted ecosystem of live streaming on Twitch, highlighting its transformative impact on cultural practices, audience engagement, labour dynamics and, critically for our argument here, its monetization strategies. In essence, Twitch is an intermediary that seeks the attention of users, which it can monetize through exposing users and viewers to advertisements, for a fee:

> At a base level, the Twitch platform is organized around ad revenue, with commercials running on streams and the proceeds going to Twitch. This changes, however, if a streamer becomes an official Twitch partner or affiliate – an opaque process that is based on content, average concurrent viewership, and broadcast regularity. Once admitted to one of these programs, the streamer gets a share of the ad revenue, which Twitch – though not disclosing figures – has publicly defined as an "industry-leading CPM".
> (Taylor 2018: 116)

CPM is an acronym of cost per *mille*, or the rate that an advertiser pays for 1,000 impressions of their ad online, and this is what drives the competition for audience attention. As audiences scale, so do the number of ad impressions, so driving up the revenues that can be shared by Twitch with performers.

As Twitch has pioneered the building of new monetisable audiences, so it has also created the possibility of new kinds of performances. It has facilitated new entanglements between affective and economic processes as a growing body of academic work has begun to reveal. For example, Mark Johnson and Jamie Woodcock have, across a number of contributions, explored the affective labour of Twitch streamers, emphasizing the emotional and performative aspects of what they do, arguing that streaming involves a complex interplay of work and play, driven by what they describe as a "neoliberal subjectivity" that values constant performance (Johnson & Woodcock 2019a, 2019b; Woodcock & Johnson 2019). The economic pressures to build an audience and monetize content through various means take an emotional toll on streamers, who need to mobilize "the entrepreneurship of the self, equating success as the result of hard work via the volume of hours streamed per week" (Woodcock & Johnson 2019: 820).

Effort is turned into income through the ways in which the platform enables streamers to monetize audience attention, through a gamification of monetary support. Audiences can be mobilized as sources of income in direct and indirect ways. Audiences can provide money directly to streamers through regular, recurring subscriptions, which are often set at different tiers with varying price points. Twitch receives 50 per cent of the subscription fee, with streamers receiving the other 50 per cent. They can also provide money to streamers through irregular donations or "tips" that can be both in monetary form as well in special in-platform currency. Indeed, across the wider platform economy, virtual tipping is emerging as the next iteration of strategies to "mobilize fan enthusiasm" (see Chapter 5), with established and emerging platforms alike encouraging virtual tipping. Twitch was one of the first platforms to allow tips directly through its own currency system, "Bits", with which viewers can "cheer" streamers during live streams. Twitch takes a cut from the value of bits, with streamers receiving approximately 70 per cent of the value spent using the cheer option. Platforms such as YouTube, Instagram, and TikTok have now developed their own tipping systems for live broadcasts, while in April 2020 Spotify announced the launch of Artist Fundraising Pick, where fans can directly donate money to an artist, or to a good cause selected by the artist.[3]

Such monetization strategies are often enhanced and encouraged by the setting of "targets" or goals by streamers, designed to incentivize donations so that performers can achieve certain levels of income to meet planned expenditures. These goals can range from buying new equipment to improve the quality of the stream, to simply meeting monthly rental income, for example. Audiences are also the source of indirect income, as streamers can earn income from advertisers using their channel to target adverts at certain demographics, while some streamers also benefit from sponsorships offered by companies who can provide free products or promotion "for highlighting their wares during particular broadcasts" (Johnson & Woodcock 2019b: 1). The affordances of the Twitch platform have, over time, been subject to a process of innovation and experimentation by streamers that has settled down into more or less de-facto standards that facilitate monetization and income production, albeit that this is highly variable and highly time consuming in ways that often blur the lines between paid work and leisure (Sjöblom *et al.* 2019).

By the end of the 2010s, Twitch was able to report that it had over 100 million regular viewers. The scale of use meant that the practice of video game streaming on the platform was even beginning to have feedback effects on the video game industry itself, in terms of game visibility, game lifespan and game development (Johnson & Woodcock 2019a). Its success encouraged the growth of live streaming in other areas, notably in esports (e.g., Mao 2022). But with the advent of the Covid-19 pandemic and the subsequent global lockdowns, Twitch attracted a host of new users, as the platform became a refuge for musicians who were reliant upon live performances for income, but also for audiences deprived of a highly valued form of musical consumption. To date, only limited research has been undertaken on the migration of musical performers and audiences to Twitch during the pandemic. Vandenburg (2022) is a rare exception in this regard, having examined the growth of live-stream music concerts on Twitch to determine the extent to which streams succeed as "interaction rituals", arguing

---

3 Spotify claims not to take any of the money donated through this feature.

that the platform is best suited to small-scale performances. This is because virtual concerts cannot provide the same level of emotional energy and collective engagement as physical concerts due to the absence of physical co-presence and the limitations of the online platform. Nevertheless, the online concerts hosted during the episodes of social isolation caused by lockdowns were positive experiences for many. Live performances on platforms such as Twitch helped to maintain social ties and provide a sense of belonging during periods of isolation (Vandenberg *et al.* 2021). So, while live streamed musical performance may not fully replicate the collective energy and solidarity found in physical gatherings, livestreamed performances offered a sense of community and shared experience.[4] Therefore, while live-streamed performances could not compete with their analogues in physical spaces, during the pandemic they did not have to, and so were able to successfully gather audiences. As a result, musicians, echoing the earlier behaviour of video game players, were able to turn to Twitch during the Covid-19 pandemic to monetize live performances. For example, Rendell (2021), undertook a study of three examples of what he described as "portal shows" during the pandemic and illustrated how they were able to offer alternative revenue sources for artists in the absence of physical venues. This was in part through traditional means, such as ticket sales and merchandise purchases, but also through donations and tips, in the ways pioneered by video live streamers. Moreover, some artists were also able to take advantage of advertising and sponsorship. However, Rendell acknowledged that while these strategies provided alternative revenue streams for musicians, they often benefited established artists more, raising questions about access and equity.

Platform performances in a pandemic: monetizing music through Twitch

> Every musician that's on Twitch is kind of ahead of the curve. And we're hoping that we can stay ahead of the curve. (Rachel May, interview)

The objective of our research with musicians using the Twitch platform was to better understand the trade-offs between two interrelated forms of labour undertaken by musicians in using such platforms: on the one hand, relational online labour – the building of relationships and communities with fans and other musicians – and, on the other, transactional labour – labour undertaken

---

4   Vanderberg and her colleagues draw attention to the potential of music livestreams as a tool for enhancing mental health, combating loneliness, and contributing to collective consciousness and community resilience in times of crisis (Vandenberg *et al.* 2021).

to facilitate the monetization of music. More specifically, the research sought to explore how musicians build their online profiles and balanced undertaking the relational labour needed to cultivate and engage an online fan base (Baym 2018) with the more "transactional" activities required to monetize their fan base, to generate income on Twitch and, in some cases, other online platforms.

Recency bias meant that at the outset of the research we tacitly expected that the majority of musicians we studied on the Twitch platform would have been motivated to join the platform in response to the closure of live venues during Covid-19 lockdowns. For some musicians, this was indeed the case. For example, David Griffiths, a UK-based professional musician who had once been signed to a record label, had toured internationally and, in recent years, had pursued a successful career as a "gigging musician", found his main source of income curtailed by the pandemic:

> I was running a function/corporate band ... working ... small events, from ... pubs to clubs, to larger ... corporate events, the sort of bigger companies ... we were very, very busy and really very fortunate ... it was every weekend I was gigging ... with a few of my musical friends. And then, of course ... Covid happened which was really, really difficult for the likes of me to ... really get over.   (David Griffiths, interview)

This had a serious financial impact on him and his girlfriend, also a musician, and with whom he cohabited: "our livelihoods, were either just gone entirely, or [were now] just insignificant". Similar impacts were experienced internationally. Beth Mallin, a US based artist, found her plans to raise money to fund the recording of a new album upended by the pandemic:

> I was about to launch the Kickstarter for my new album ... I launched it two days prior to the Oval Office announcement about Covid. So ... a lot of musicians got right on [Twitch], you know, and streamed right away and just like switched gears. And I wasn't one of them! I didn't do anything for eight months. I went on unemployment. I was one of the people who ... doesn't handle trauma by leaping into action, first of all. And also, I kept thinking like, "Oh, just a few more weeks" and like, "Oh my, next month?" And, you know, so I didn't – I couldn't – play shows. I didn't do anything for income at all. I was just on unemployment waiting to see what happened. And then around October [2020] I started to feel like maybe I should figure something out. (Beth Mallin, interview)

Other regular live performers also faced the dilemma of whether to wait or seek alternative ways of working. One UK-based performer who had developed a career as a DJ while also holding down a regular "day job" recounted the sense of statis and financial stress:

> ... it was really weird at first because I just assumed it would be like, "Oh, maybe a couple of weeks' stuff, a big step forward and then it will ... be OK" ... I mean, obviously, it just went on and on ... Yeah, it was kind of a bit of a kick really with it. When it first happened ... you're just so used to doing stuff most weekends ... it was a strange adjustment ... I was furloughed for a whole year, basically ... money wise, I ... did notice it. Yeah, it was a bit of a heavy blow. (Chris Smith, interview)

Another professional musician, a singer-songwriter who normally performed over 250 gigs each year, candidly went through his tax records during our interview to reveal the precipitous decline in his post-pandemic earnings: "In the tax year from April 2019 ... up to ... April 5th [2020 earnings were] ... £30,087 just from doing that covers work. That was revenue. The next tax year [it was] £740! ... all you can do is laugh about it, that's all you can do about it, because there was nothing we could do" (George Boyd, interview). Faced with such a crisis, all these musicians made the decision to start streaming on Twitch to explore a new way of making revenues. In doing so, they followed a path that had in fact already been taken by numerous others over the proceeding decade, many of whom had not been gigging musicians prior to the pandemic but had joined the Twitch platform as music began to become more visible on the platform and was seen as a way of generating an audience, and a little income. These early adopters were often talented musicians but may not have had the necessary confidence or the opportunity to perform at venues but, by using Twitch, discovered that they were able to build a following through alternative means.

Whether they had newly arrived on the platform or were more established musicians that had been using Twitch for years, most of our interviewees placed significant emphasis and effort on the importance of the relational labour that was required to build and maintain an audience. This was judged to be important in terms of both monetary and non-monetary rewards. Indeed, for many musicians it was the sense of a supportive online community where much of the value of the platform lay, giving the musicians a sense of creative fulfilment and a much more intimate connection to an audience than was possible in traditional live music performance. Non-monetary rewards were afforded high importance by musicians continuing to stream on the platform, and their audiences – or "community" as they were usually described – provided both social and emotional support. Yet, at the same time, musicians recognized that the majority of their income from the platform – scheduled subscriptions, gift subscriptions (or "subs"), virtual tips and donations – emanated from a small number of generous fans within their communities. But balancing the relational labour of building and engaging an online fan base with the "transactional" relations of monetizing their fans and followers involved difficult and uncomfortable judgements. All of the musicians we interviewed had some degree of reluctance to "push" or cajole their audiences to directly request money through subscriptions, denotations and tips:

> You play music and then you are balancing that with chat and then I guess I have to balance that with pushing people toward subscription, pushing people toward goals, and maybe I don't want to put people off by kind of pushing those things too hard.   (Zach Stanley, interview)

> I don't want to ask people for money. I'm not saying it's wrong, but I don't know, I just feel like that's always been the tone of the streams. And I know that people have told me that they appreciate that, they feel like most others push that a lot more. But I don't think that means I make that much less.   (Katalia Ingles, interview)

Nevertheless, most artists had developed a sense of how explicit they could be in directly asking fans to give them money, and how such requests could be coded and framed in ways that they considered would be acceptable to their communities. Most artists expressed gratitude when subs and donations were received but did not actively request or demand money for the performances they were providing. Rather, it was commonplace for streamers to set up "donation goals", which would be graphically represented on screen during a stream, the aim of which was to raise funds to support the channel in some way (for example, to buy new equipment or instruments that would improve the streaming experience for their followers) or for new creative projects (for example, requesting money to enable the artist to record original material). Streamers felt more comfortable asking for donations towards such creative goals and projects. In one case, a musician had set up an explicit donation target simply to pay rent, but this artist was an exception rather than the rule. Others set more coded income targets, such as those that would allow the musician to remain full-time for example, but one US-based musician cautioned aspiring musicians about the amount of revenue that could be made from streaming live music:

> I always tell this to people. You cannot go ... into streaming thinking that you're going to make money. You have to go into streaming thinking that you're going to have fun and you're going to do what you love to do. But the donations and all the income and the subscriptions, that's secondary. You cannot go ... there thinking that "Yeah, I'm going to get

donations". No, that's not the mentality that you need to have. So that's one thing that I tell people … if you want to stream, do it because you love it, because you are enjoying yourself and you're playing an instrument that you love and you're making friends online.

(Wanda Clark, interview)

Such caution flowed from a keen awareness among streamers about the negative implications of this form of labour, despite the largely positive and grateful response to the opportunities that Twitch had provided in terms of the rewards that could be gleaned from the platform. There was a recognition of the need to constantly "give" of oneself in return for the continued engagement, support and financial contribution from audiences. Streaming often requires difficult decisions around relational labour. Some streamers emphasized the need for authenticity, honesty and sharing to build support from audiences, feeling they were more likely to support them financially. Others were keen to set boundaries between themselves and their audiences, or in various ways felt they needed to "perform" as primarily an entertainer – positive, confident, polished, hiding emotions and the personal elements of their lives. Such a dilemma was expressed by one interviewee: "Sometimes I feel like I'm trying to manipulate how they will see me, so that way they can donate more or subscribe more. If I say something, like the wrong thing, I feel like maybe people start thinking like, 'Oh, she doesn't need donations, doesn't need subscribers". (Bailey French, interview)

Time spent live streaming represented simply the "surface" of relational and creative labour that also included significant additional time spent on Discord – the primary platform through which streamers engage with their community away from the live stream – as well as practicing their music and addressing ongoing technological issues, such as upgrading technologies, software and equipment to improve the quality of the stream, particularly in relation to what was perceived to be the background expectations of audiences. This technical learning was often, necessarily, auto didactic in nature. For all of the streamers we interviewed, this work and the associated relational labour around streaming was experienced in home spaces, and many reported exhaustion when their streams finished yet found it difficult to wind-down in the same spaces in which they stream. Furthermore, many participants felt an obligation to stream to their specified schedule, which was posted in advance on their Twitch home page, feeling that to do otherwise would let down their audience, or even lose members of the audience that they had worked to build. This led to many musicians streaming when they felt unwell and/or feeling that they were unable to take extended breaks away from the platform or from using related social media, for fear that interest in them would fade in their absence, with implications for their ability to derive income:

If streaming is your main income, it is sometimes a difficult decision in terms of you think, "Well, does that mean I'm going to lose money tonight or lose my audience?" It's worrying for two reasons. It's obviously the income side of things, but it's also audience attention because, you know, audiences online are fickle … my kind of mindset has always been, you know, if you're not live or you're not posting somewhere, you're not really visible. And that's a lot of pressure, really, and it's quite overwhelming when you say it like that, but it's definitely the truth.

(Emily Males, interview)

The sense of precarity and uncertainty about the viability of Twitch as a revenue platform for artists was summed up by Rachel May, as US-based musician, who had previously been a gigging artist before discovering Twitch a few years prior to the pandemic. She welcomed the way it helped overcome her reservations about life on the road and the misogyny and sense of danger that she often experienced living a peripatetic life moving from gig to gig. Yet, despite these compensations, earning a sustainable income as a professional musician on Twitch was far from assured:

[T]here's months like where the more you stream, the better you do. So, there's months where … I'm like, "Oh, great, this is cool". Like this is … enough, to just do Twitch. And there's months where you're like, "Nah, that's not going to work" … I would really like for Twitch to be my primary source of income. My goal is to get this many subs … to make this much money per stream, or to make … my hourly goal … in order for me to feel like I'm not just doing this for fun. By the end of the stream, I want to have made this much per hour. And that's and that's kind of how I judge that. (Rachel May, interview)

Unfortunately, the levels of income to be derived from Twitch were, for the majority of our informants, low, precarious, and highly unpredictable, with the returns often justified as "better than nothing". In some cases it was considered a form of subsidized practice which enabled them to improve their musical craft, which might be better rewarded in the future. This was the case with Zach Rose, a Canada-based classical guitarist:

[I]n terms of like a minimum wage job, it would be like very, very a very poor income. But for me, … I don't really think of it as like I'm making like $1 per hour or something, I think of it more like I am practising. And I just happened to get a great boon while practising. But I guess for a general figure, first three months I made like almost nothing. And

then I got my first pay out on like the fourth month of like one hundred dollars. And then it got to a point where it was like $100 every two months and then every month and then $200 a month, $300 a month, something like that. And that kind of right now fluctuates anywhere between like $300 to $1,000 per month randomly depending on I guess, pure chance chaos theory ... there's a few times ... where I would just be practising and then a person who's never been in the chat before, never viewed it, never done anything, would just donate like $500 randomly. And it's like, "OK, well thank you". It's very appreciative but very random.
                                                                              (Zach Rose, interview)

While interviewees felt that the Twitch music community was positive and supportive, with occasional generous financial donations such as the example above, all steamers had been exposed to criticism of their music or performances through audience members who engaged in abusive or insulating comments – commonly referred to as "trolling". This was especially acute for several female streamers who related experiences of criticism regarding their appearance as well as unwelcome sexualized attention: "Putting women down in the music community happens a lot ... comments are really quite crude and are incredibly sexist. Like, why are you coming here? If you have nothing to say that's nice and positive, then why say anything?" (Wanda Clark, interview).

To counter this behaviour, all the artists who we interviewed employed moderators, or "mods", from their most dedicated followers, who were given the authority by the artist to control audience entry and to expel any participants who made what were deemed to be inappropriate comments. This was seen to be highly effective by most artists. Indeed, some female artists said the policing of their audiences by mods created a "safe space" for performances. Some interviewees even said that Twitch was preferable to their experiences of live gigs, which often required negotiating inappropriate attention and in-person judgements and criticisms of musicianship, equipment choices, etc. But such activities added another layer of stress and anxiety to that of the precarious and volatile revenues.

In summary, the research identified at least three main categories of musicians using Twitch live streaming platform. First, gigging musicians who were on the platform to replace some of the income lost from live music (which to some degree subsequently returned); second, those who considered streaming as a secondary/hobby activity alongside other work; and third, and finally, those who were able to pursue streaming on a full-time basis. Income from streaming via subscriptions, tips and donations is, by its very nature, inherently variable, resulting in significant income precarity. The interviews revealed several social dimensions related to the ability to pursue streaming full time, with some

interviewees able to choose to pursue streaming full time and cope with its inherent precarity only because of certain social and economic advantages and
support mechanisms, such as continuing to live at home with parents, or in
properties owned by relatives, or being financially supported by a partner with a
"traditional" and better paid job. In interviews conducted later in the pandemic,
as lockdowns eased, we found that some musicians were beginning to transition
back into live music. Some interviewees at this stage were hoping to be able
to maintain their streaming activities alongside gigging at performance venues,
which suggests a possible durable legacy from the pandemic. However, many
were grappling with how they might be able to balance the two activities, often
alongside a "day job" which was normally non-musical in orientation.

Conclusion

The chapter has explored the importance of live performance to the music industries, with a focus on the impact of live streaming and its emergence as a
mechanism for performance and income generation during the Covid-19 pandemic. It has discussed how live streaming has influenced artists, highlighting
the adaptability of musicians in the face of pandemic restrictions. We have reflected on the complexities of monetizing music through live streaming, drawing on original research to reveal the diverse experiences of musicians and the
challenges they face in balancing relational and transactional labour. Following
Taylor (2018), we have sought to demonstrate how streamers balance musical
performance with relational labour as part of "complex negotiations between
system self, and others ... between freedom and constraint, self-direction and
obligation to oneself or community" (Taylor 2018: 261). Live streaming represents a form of live performance in which platform mechanisms privilege
presenteeism and the development of intimate connections with audiences.
Combined with precarity as a result of significant variability and uncertainty
with regards to incomes, online labour is highly intensive and demands constant
presence and engagement, which our findings suggest often result in exhaustion
and negative impacts upon mental health. This precarity also means that the
ability to pursue streaming as full-time career has class dimensions (affordability, stability), while experiences of online labour are highly gendered.

Overall, the chapter has sought to underscore the transformative potential
of live streaming in shaping the future of music performance and distribution,
highlighting opportunities for innovation, audience engagement and revenue
generation, while also addressing challenges such as income precarity and platform sustainability. In the next chapter, we explore further the ability of musicians to respond to, and benefit from the growing platformization of the music

industries, though a focus on the politics of platforms, and an examination of the relationship between digital literacy, data and broader processes of participation and democratization.

7
DIGITAL LITERACY, DATA AND DEMOCRATIZATION

Introduction

For many commentators, the process of platformization brings with it the promise of democratization. This has certainly been the case with music, where platforms have been held up as ways to diminish the power of traditional gatekeepers that police who has access to the means of production and participation in the music industries. For Hesmondhalgh (1997), fundamental to a democratic media system are the notions of *participation* and *access*. In the case of music, it has been argued that such a democratization is taking place driven by a decentralization in media technologies, with new platforms and other digital technologies resulting in lower entry costs across the music industries value chain, making it easier to access and participate in music production, distribution and consumption. In theory, the growing ubiquity of digital technologies and online access has allowed for anyone anywhere to make it in music, regardless of their economic or sociocultural background (Kiberg 2023). Yet, other commentators have remained critical of claims regarding democratization through digitalization in general, and platformization in particular. As we have previously argued, contemporary musicians and other music industries professionals alike work in a business ecology in which large digital platforms own, develop, steer and – critically – monetize several of the most influential music industries distribution channels (Frenneaux 2023). MSPs especially have become key new gatekeepers within the music industries and, as argued in earlier chapters, through both their control of the key musical distribution channels and their relationship of interdependency with the major corporations, carry forward elements of traditional music industries hegemony into the platformized era. For example, while platform mechanisms affect all musicians, those signed to big record companies stand to gain more exposure and income due to the larger marketing budgets, better expertise and greater reach of these companies. Most self-releasing musicians, on the other hand, seek greater control over creation, copyrights, cooperation and curation, only to experience new "platformized constraints", which is to say the need to produce particular forms of music or other creative content or undertake particular activities in response to the algorithmic environments of particular platforms (Frenneaux 2023; Qu *et al.* 2022). In this chapter, we discuss some of the responses from musicians to these consequences of platformization.

During this process of evolution, new skills have been developed by many artists, which have enabled and empowered them within this digital context. One important example has been the growing affordability of professional standard home-studio production technologies which, through their ease of use, have been widely adopted and so lowered the entry barriers to music production. Independent digital music production has been extensively examined in the academic literature (e.g., Watson 2014; Bell 2015, 2018; Walzer 2017; Chambers 2022). However, as Frenneaux (2023) observes, the development of skills beyond mere musical aptitude and creativity is essential for contemporary musicians and music producers. The declining cost and ease of use of recording technologies means that musicians can opt to circumvent the need to use professional recording studios. Professional studios are expensive due to their overheads, which include dedicated acoustic spaces, recording equipment and specialized labour (Watson 2016). However, even though these home recording technologies are affordable, musicians still must learn how to use them. In addition, musicians need to be accomplished across the forms of entrepreneurial and digital skill sets explored in Chapters 5 and 6, which are required to successfully use the variety of platforms necessary for promotion, online audience building and engagement, live performance and monetization.

In this chapter, we build upon the recognition of new skills and competencies to consider a broader concept of "digital literacy", a term which we deploy to encompass a wider set of knowledges and skills as they relate to the ability to draw benefits from platformization. Digital literacy here is centred on a knowledge or awareness of platforms and their purpose, as well as the necessary skills and competencies required to exploit the affordances they provide. These skills and competencies include, for example, an ability to gather, interpret and act upon the data provided by platforms, or to respond to the creative possibilities and constraints of platforms. Such skills are, of course, not just required by musicians and music producers, but by all music industries professionals working within the platform music industries, including record label staff and those providing other intermediary services such as music publishers and distributors and artist managers.

Our consideration of data literacy in this chapter is set within a critical framework that explores the relationship between platforms and democratization in the music industries and assesses the extent to which they have facilitated greater levels of access and participation. Specifically, we shall argue that data literacy, and more broadly the ability of individuals or companies to understand let alone determine how to capitalize upon processes of digitalization in the music industries, is dependent upon the wider distribution of various human and financial resources, such as individual digital and data know how, and the capability to access or employ individuals (or indeed as we shall see in the case of the major corporations, teams of individuals) with the required digital and data know-how. The unequal distribution of these resources across individuals and firms in the music industries, we argue, means that the rise of platform music industries has significant social equity implications.

In the first section of the chapter, we consider digital literacy in the context of data and metrics, illustrating the growing importance of data to creative and strategic decision making. At the same time, data is creating new divides between the data literate and those who lack the requisite knowledge, skills and financial resources to effectively utilize platforms and leverage the metrics that they provide. We then consider the importance and implications of the algorithmic recommendation and curation systems operated by MSPs. In particular we consider two possible consequences of these systems: first, that the curatorial power of MSPs might be exercised with bias to give preferential visibility to the major corporations, and; second, that attempts can be made to "game" song recommender systems included within MSPs (such as Discover Weekly on Spotify or New Music Mix on Apple Music, for example) through the creative process and by making music more "algorithmically attractive". In the final section of the chapter, we move on to consider how, for small independent record labels and other intermediaries, platformization is resulting in new ways of working, new business models and opportunities, and new challenges.

Data, metrics and digital literacy

As we have argued in earlier chapters, alongside the major corporations, MSPs and other platforms such as social media play a central and crucial role in shaping the dynamics of the music industries. However, while much of the debate concerning platforms has focused on payments to artists (Chapter 2), facets of platforms often overlooked are the related technologies of data tracking and collection, and how these are impacting both upon artists and other music industries actors. As Baym *et al.* (2021) argue, these technologies have fundamentally altered how media industries gather data, and have resulted in data becoming "more plentiful, detailed and networked" and measuring "many more aspects of audiences then before" (2021: 3419). MSPs capture immense amounts of granular data on audiences, some of which are then delivered back to creators, managers and other users. This data includes such information as streamer and follower numbers, the location of audiences, listener demographics (such as age and gender), the times and days songs are played, how many playlists on which artists feature, and even information on the point in songs at which listeners press skip (Hodgson 2021). Data insights are also provided to listeners to engage them. The most well-known of these data-driven engagement mechanisms is Spotify's Wrapped, a viral marketing campaign which at the end of each year presents Spotify users with a compilation of data about their activity on the platform over the past year and invites them to share it on social media. This includes information on songs and artists most streamed, and how this compares to the listening habits of other users, including spatial representations of this data (see Figure 7.1). In this regard, Maasø and Hagen argue that the true power of the MSPs reside in: "... the way in which they have become central information hubs, with links and feedback loops to all of the other stakeholders in the music business – either directly, through the interfaces and algorithms they control, or indirectly, through data gathered from partners and intermediaries" (Maasø & Hagen 2020: 29).

Recent research on the music industries and datafication has begun to consider how professionals in the music industries approach, understand and deploy metrics in their work. Hagen (2022), for example, argues that the ability to analyse metrics from online platforms is beneficial to new participants in the music industries, as it enables new means of participating, competing, and positioning oneself in the field. Similarly, Jones (2021) argues that metrics allow for new kinds of direct comparability. For both artists and record labels, for

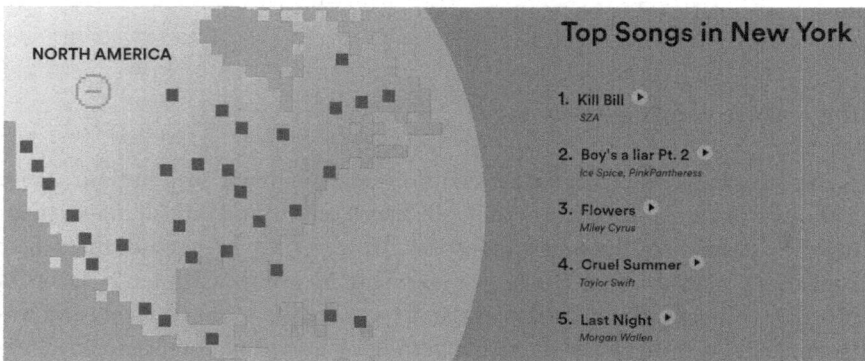

Figure 7.1 Spotify "Wrapped" interactive map of most streamed songs in 2023 by US City

Source: https://newsroom.spotify.com/2023-11-29/wrapped-top-songs-worldwide-map/ (accessed 20 May 2024).

example, data is becoming essential to everyday decision making and strategic planning: "… datafication and metrics are becoming more central to a range of activities *outside* of the steaming services and are of growing importance in the strategic planning and execution of efficient music distribution among various other stakeholders in the music industry" (Maasø & Hagen 2020: 19; emphasis in original).

Maasø and Hagen argue further that data has become "decisive for strategic and relational planning, communication, cooperation, and the execution of music launches, marketing, publishing, audience targeting, and approaches to new and emerging markets" (2020: 23). Similarly, Baym *et al.* (2021), in their study of the use of metrics by professionals in the music industries, found that label managers increasingly use platform data and other third-party sources to decide whether to sign an artist, to determine the audiences to whom the artist should be marketed and at what intensity, and which songs should be selected for release as singles (2021). Baym and her colleagues identify two main ways in which metrics are used by music industries workers. First, data are used internally, being selectively appropriated to guide decisions in risky environments; such as, for example, whether to provide additional marketing budgets for particular releases, to organize tours in particular locations, or indeed to reduce the support being given to a particular release or artist. Second, data are used in an externally facing manner, to develop persuasive stories to achieve goals when communicating across the music industries; such as, for example, indicators of sales success or buzz around a release or artists can be highly valuable when seeking to promote artists to journalistic outlets, live music promoters, radio pluggers and music supervisors (2021).[1]

Research in this area suggests that real-time data and up-to-the-moment metrics are those most valued by music professionals, allowing for some assessment of success or management of risk in the short-term. This includes, for example, monitoring market responses, streams, sales and interest from various sources, especially in regard to spikes or sudden changes. Strategic decisions can then be made from such data, such as, for example, whether additional marketing and promotion may be beneficial, or if a tour should be organized. Baym *et al.* (2021) argue that locational data is particularly important in this regard, in an attempt to find where the best listenership is located, and subsequently to focus promotional efforts towards locations where there may be a promotional or sales opportunity, such as where organizing a tour might prove to be worthwhile (or conversely, to focus promotional efforts towards locations where listenership is low). Such metrics are not only internally useful, but as noted, allow labels

---

1   A music supervisor oversees the music related aspects of film, television, advertising, video games and other existing or emerging visual media platforms.

to craft external narratives around artists, aimed for example at such interme-diaries as booking agents in particular locations. As Baym *et al.* (2021) argue, underlying much of this work is an effort to use metrics to find "real" fans who will spend money on artists, rather than more passive listeners who may not. In our own research, we found examples amongst record labels of geographical lis-tener metrics being used to inform strategic decisions. The following transcript is taken from an interview with a label manager of an independent record label based in Liverpool, UK, who describes how the label identified and subsequently signed a dance track breaking out from clubs in a particular region of the UK, and then how geographical data and metrics provided by the platform Shazam[2] (see Figure 7.2) informed strategic marketing decisions:

> It was 100% organic, you know, there was no label attachment, no pro-motion, no marketing, nothing. Liverpool and Dublin were the first two hot beds, and quickly the DJs in the clubs … picked up on it and were starting to support it. We then quickly traced it back, found the SoundCloud that it was coming from. So, our A&R guy in Liverpool reached out to him via SoundCloud. Quickly within a week the mo-mentum really took off. Several DJs started playing it heavily on their [radio] shows.
>
> At the same time we were making efforts to sign it. There's always that A&R thing where as soon as you hear something that, you know, there's something about it that's right for you … if all the DJs are playing it and they're saying it's working on the dance floor and radio shows, it was the right thing to go for. A couple of viral videos appeared at the same time of night-clubs in Dublin, and there was the crowd, singing it. So it had already embedded itself in a few Dublin hot spots as well as Liverpool. [But] with any record you're taking a punt, you're having a gamble. We felt confident that we could have success to our level with it. We signed it and by the next week, in the Shazam chart, he's already in the Top 200.
>
> For a first play you would always reach out to a key champion [radio DJ]. This was different. Somehow it came naturally from the clubs. Then a few regional specialist DJs. Then we registered it with Shazam and straight away it went in the Top 200. Suddenly, everyone's paying attention. You know it's such a vital tool now, Shazam. On your mobile device you have Shazam Explore so you can zoom in on the areas. We could zoom in straight away and see the real time reactions to the spot

---

2   Shazam is an application that can identify music based on a short sample played using the microphone on the device.

plays on Juice FM. He was getting real heavy Shazam traffic. Liverpool, North West, Merseyside, a bit of Lancashire, a bit of Cheshire, a bit of North Wales – Boom! It came out of there. It just collected. Capital FM Radio [then] jumped on him early. They championed the record and, you know, again straight away suddenly the Shazam action kind of multiplied. Then, suddenly, you were seeing it was coming out of the South East, out of London and all the suburbs, heating up off the Capital FM support.

This record came far quicker than a conventional record ... Ideally, we'd have planned to release it at the end of January but because everyone just went, "We're going to playlist it because it's massive in Shazam" ... we didn't get a usual campaign going.

(Label manager, independent record label, Liverpool)

An example such as this is indicative of how, for artists, label executives, managers and a range of other intermediaries, algorithms and data from MSPs and

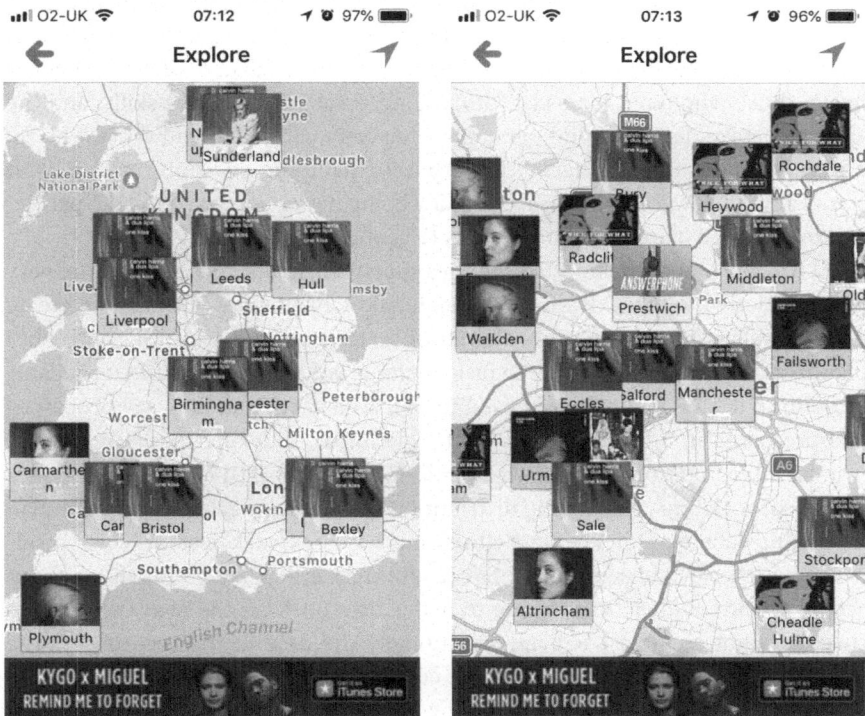

Figure 7.2 Example maps of Shazam activity in the UK

Source: Shazam App (accessed 10 May 2018).

other music platforms present significant opportunities. Yet, at the same time, datafication also presents significant challenges. As Baym *et al.* (2021) point out:

> The sheer range of potential data available represents a considerable challenge for many people working in the music industries. Metrics provide openings for those who are prepared to invest time and energy in collecting, interpreting, and framing them to gain advantages. But of course, this requires time, expertise, resources, and most importantly access to the data. The best resourced and most powerful actors continue to be able to use metrics most effectively. (Baym *et al.* 2021: 3437)

Not only does the sheer amount of data present a challenge in terms of the resources and time needed to analyse it, but also the skillsets required to interpret and use data and metrics are becoming more advanced. New skills are demanded to understand the ways in which music circulates, and how these dynamics can be better understood and accommodated through data (Hagen 2022). As such, Baym *et al.* (2021) argue, it would be mistaken to think of the increasing availability of data and metrics as a form of democratization or a means for greater transparency. Rather, they note a significant degree of inequality between those who have access to data, the necessary interpretive skills, and the ability to make decisions and persuade effectively with data, and those who do not. Inequalities in data literacy underpin inequality in decision-making, with actors able to develop skills-based literacy being better equipped to take part in, and make sense of, new business logics (Hagen 2022).

At the one end of the music industries spectrum, major record labels are very well positioned to take advantage of datafication, having the resources to create large global analytics teams. Through licence agreements with MSPs and other platforms, major labels are able to procure large volumes of data, often available to them in a "raw" form (as opposed to pre-visualized, that is to say processed and presented in a form decided by the platform), thus offering more control over its interpretation (Baym *et al.* 2021). As Arsenault (2017) argues, for major media corporations, controlling distribution mechanisms is less important than leveraging data to predict which delivery mechanisms work best for which product at which particular moment. Successful marketing, she contends, is about access to data. Rather than having to hedge bets on what the next commercial success might be – as has been traditionally the case in the recorded music industry – amassing data allows music corporations to develop a better picture of who audiences are, who is consuming what, on what platform, when and for how long, and to make more reliable predictions as to what they want before the audiences are themselves cognisant of it. Predictive analytics are thus driving the further conflation of production, distribution and marketing functions within corporations, allowing for new economies of scale and synergy, as well as new complementary connections between music corporations, platforms and BigTech corporations (Arsenault, 2017).

Meanwhile, at the other end of the music industries spectrum, are a host of small independent labels and artists. While small labels will at least get some interpretable data (albeit significantly more constrained compared to that provided through the preferential arrangements that the majors have with the MSPs, which give them access to the more detailed raw datasets as described previously), artists have traditionally had to rely on the basic metrics that all users of the platform can see. In addition to this, there are likely to be limits on the interpretation of data that come from limited expertise, or through a lack of time or motivation. As Baym (2018) has argued, while datafication can be powerful, it can also remain out of reach for artists working on their own or with limited resources. Given the importance of independent artists to the MSPs, however, there have been recent developments that seek to empower artists to access and interpret data. The Spotify for Artists platform, for example, which originally launched in 2013, now offers a variety of ways for artists to access data insights on their audience (albeit in ways previsualized by the platform), as well as suggesting actions for artists to develop their fanbases. As services such as Spotify for Artists demonstrate, in the platform music industries, digital literacy has become a vital skill that empowers artists to: effectively utilize diverse digital tools, software and platforms; to manage their online presence and connect with audiences, and; to obtain and interpret the data and metrics provided by them. They must then subsequently make data-informed decisions about their creative direction and promotional strategies based on audience behaviours and preferences (Kirui 2024). Artists who enter the music industries without this literacy, it is argued, will have a lower chance of success. However, even assuming data literacy, if no plans or resources are in place to execute a marketing strategy, then this data cannot be adequately instrumentalized or acted upon (Jones 2021).

Baym (2018) also suggests that for some artists it can appear too difficult – or simply too uninteresting – to develop the critical analytical skills required to interpret the numbers that digital metrics and digital analytics provide. Hagen (2022) found a significant amount of disinterest in data amongst creatives, whereby datafication was seen by artists as being more relevant to administrative and strategic tasks in the commercial marketplace. Similarly, Frenneaux (2023) found that while commercial success metrics are important, creative freedom remains the most significant factor for many artists, with intermediaries tending to be much more active with data than artists. Yet, conversely, in their study of musicians in Latin America, Siles *et al.* (2022) found that metrics sit at the core of musicians' sense of artistic validation. Metrics, they found, were often checked regularly – in their case, the data provided by their Spotify for Artists profile, about the practices of listeners – and this often took an emotional toll on artists. In a study of the use of the Spotify for Artists platform by musicians in Australia, Freeman *et al.* (2023) found that artists often obsessively monitored metrics, and that these metrics often elicited emotional responses, especially where listener numbers were not as hoped. This represents not only a matter of artistic validation: musicians often feel pressure to increase listener numbers due to the fact that these are key to spotting the opportunities that might be available to successful artists, including the potential for getting signed by a label or to work with a particular manager or intermediary (Morrow 2018). As Jones (2021) argues, the data and metrics made available by platforms contribute to a growing pressure on artists to think in terms of enterprise, and this is often the case even if they are not actually seeking to make a living from music. In keeping with the spirit of this "enterprise discourse", he argues, platform data "shows users the rewards on offer for conformity but leaves the actual work of self-governance up to individuals" (Jones 2021: 108).

Given the above, from the perspective of democratization the datafication trend seems to be no guarantee of greater equality. Findings reported in the literature suggest that those that possess the greatest resources are more likely to be successful in the music industries. Datafication, it seems, is simply creating a new divide between those who are data literate, and those who do not have the knowledge, skills, software or technology to effectively utilize platforms and leverage the metrics that they provide (Baym *et al.* 2021). As D'Ignazio (2017) observes in relation to data inequality in society more broadly, the collection, storage and processing of large amounts of data creates a situation of asymmetry and inequality because the actors who collect, store and process the data – in our case, the MSPs – are very different from those whose data are collected, stored and processed, and who subsequently might seek to make use of this data – in our case, musicians and songwriters. The solution for this inequality, she argues, is in cultivating data literacy for empowerment in non-technical audiences. Yet, even if some artists and other music industries professionals do find themselves to be better informed through data, they are also at the same time likely to be become increasingly reliant on data and the platforms that supply them (Hagen 2022). While one must take care not to portray these actors as "victims" of datafication, given that many find meaningful insights in data that they can use or leverage in self-promotional efforts (Freeman *et al.* 2023), ultimately, as Hagen (2022) has argued, the provision of information produced by platforms to copyright owners and music creators strengthens the latter's ongoing platform dependency. At the same time increased data literacy across the music industries tends to legitimize the surveillance and data-driven business models that predominantly benefit platforms and data owners.

Responding to algorithmic recommender systems

Even where some level of data literacy exists among music professionals, the benefits of data access are tempered by the power asymmetries and lack of transparency associated with processes of algorithmic recommendation and curation that leave independent musicians and smaller labels almost entirely reliant on MSPs and other platforms for their online visibility (Freeman *et al.* 2023). This is having at least two consequences, each of which requires critical consideration considering debates as to whether digitalization is resulting in greater democratization within the platform music industries. First, it is commonly believed that major corporations and larger labels draw on their connections with MSPs to push to have music added to playlists and receive invitations to prioritized playlists (Maasø & Hagen 2020). Indeed, significant concerns have been raised within the independent music industries that the curatorial power of MSPs might be exercised with bias, in order to give preferential visibility to the major corporations as major catalogue holders, and in the case of Spotify, part owners of the platform (Aguiar *et al.* 2021). In his research with MSP and record label employees, Hodgson (2021) finds that as part of an "obsession" with playlisting, major labels are increasingly employing large teams of staff whose job is exclusively focused on ensuring that the label's artists are featured in the popular-algorithmically determined playlists. This is something they have done with significant success. For example, a study published by consultancy firm Music Tomorrow found that in a four-year period up to 2022, major labels accounted for nearly 70 per cent of the music featured on Spotify's New Music Friday, of which 30 per cent was UMG content, 19 per cent was Warner content and a further 19 per cent Sony content (King 2022). For certain other playlists, the study found, major labels accounted for as much as 87 per cent of the content.

Their ability to achieve this is partly a case of having "insider access" to the MSPs; that is direct connections to the relevant editors, together with a level of influence that comes from the relations between the MSPs and the majors as both key rentiers and shareholders in the platform. But it is also a reflection of the ability of corporate marketing and data teams to provide compelling metrics (for example, radio play, social medial presence, tour success) that appeal to editors when deciding what to include in playlists. Such resource investments from the major labels reflects the fact that playlists are seen as the primary method to ensure artists reach larger audiences and increase royalty incomes from the platforms. However, independent musicians and smaller labels do not have insider access to, nor the power to influence, tastemakers at MSPs, and as such can find themselves "out of the loop" of algorithmic-driven recommendation systems.[3] This has potentially significant consequences; as one of our own in-terviewees, argued, "it's not an exaggeration to say that one big Spotify feature could get an artist a [contract with a] major ... it could be the tipping point between an artist getting a deal or not" (label manager, independent record label, Manchester). One strategy that can be adopted by musicians in this respect is to work with particular intermediaries – for example digital distributors or artists management companies – who are in a position to influence MSP curators to get their songs included on playlists (Morrow 2018; Sun 2019). Yet again, how-ever, resource inequalities come into play here, given firstly that artists often have to put significant labour into building personal relationships with these intermediaries such that they will preferentially "push" their music to the MSPs (Siles *et al.* 2022), and secondly that such intermediaries are themselves becom-ing more reactive to metrics in terms of selecting which artists they work with or push to MSPs (Morrow 2018).

Second, as Hodgson (2021) argues, attempts to game the song recommender systems seem to be widespread, with artists and record labels vying to make their music more "algorithmically attractive", such that music becomes both more visible and more commercially successful on the MSPs. The manipulation of these systems, he argues, offers potential access to large audiences and finan-cial reward for their labour, but at the same time results in forms of "creative ambivalence" due to the way in which gaming algorithms tends to be a creatively constrictive rather than empowering process. A small but emerging body of lit-erature has begun to consider the ways in which artists and other music creators negotiate with different platform logics when producing music, recognizing that platforms offer both creative possibilities and "creativity constraints" (Kiberg 2023). One example of this is the need to "hook" listeners on to a track with the first few seconds of it playing. Currently, most MSPs only register a royalty payment for a song if it is streamed for at least 30 seconds. Therefore, through the process of creating and editing music to ensure that the hook comes more quickly, artists and record labels can game the system to decrease the chances of listeners skipping the track so missing out on royalty payments whilst also increasing the likelihood of tracks being chosen by the algorithmic system for playlists (Hodgson 2021). Indeed, as Kiberg (2023) points out, the need to capture and relate to audiences as immediately as possible is a tendency which short-form video reels on platforms such as TikTok is driving even further.

---

3   The Spotify for Artists platforms does offer opportunities for "playlist pitching" whereby artists can share contextual information on upcoming tracks with Spotify editors. However, given that this service is free and available to all artists, the extent to which this enables artists to cut through the "noise" and catch the attention of these key tastemakers is questionable.

Through interviews with artists, Siles *et al.* (2022) explored several other ways in which playlisting is impacting upon musical creativity. First, they found a perception amongst artists that streaming had diminished the importance of albums and foregrounded singles, resulting in a shifting in song writing from album development to the creation of independent musical units targeted at playlist inclusion. Second, they found that a consequence of this shift was a demand on artists to constantly release new songs, whilst also creating a perception that artists who failed to meet this expectation might be excluded from playlists in the future. Finally, they found that some artists had playlists in mind when writing songs, for example shortening songs to improve chances of being playlisted, producing catchy melodies, or writing songs for playlists with an emphasis on particular moods, events or "contextual cues" from listeners (Prey 2018). The latter reflects some of the pressure on musicians to fit their music into the pre-established musical categories being created by the MSPs through their playlists, which often differ significantly from the traditional genre categories and symbolic norms within which artists may be creating music. Other strategies include exploiting the low barriers to distribution through MSPs by focusing on quantity, and adding large quantities of short, quickly recorded songs. For example, in 2024 *The New York Times* reported on the exploits of Matt Farley, who claims to have written a cumulative total of 24,000 songs and has released music on Spotify under 80 different pseudonyms with the objective of generating streams not through the quality of the music, but through user searches. His song titles often approximate those of well-known songs (the titles of which cannot be copyrighted), people's names and various scatological terms. This approach, while time consuming, was financially rewarding; in 2023 the number of streams were sufficient to generate Farley an income of nearly $200,000 (Martin 2024).

Such strategies represent tactics for what Morris *et al.* (2021) term "sonic optimization". Alongside this, there is evidence of musicians and record labels seeking to game algorithmic systems by means of what they term "metadata optimization", that is to say artists seeking to optimize their discographies for maximum discovery and profit using metadata. Metadata is identifying data embedded in a music file, detailing everything from the artist's name and the song's release date to associated genres and songwriters credits. Optimizing such data can make music more discoverable via platforms and increase the likelihood of it being picked up by algorithmic recommender systems. Here, once again, new forms of digital literacy are required by musicians and other music industries actors. As Morris argues, such techniques for standing out are becoming: "... increasingly computational and rely on an intermingling of code and content in ways that push musicians, labels, and other stakeholders to think more like data curators: experts at optimizing content, code, and metadata in a quest for a platform ready product" (Morris 2020: 3). This, Morris argues, adds pressure on musicians and producers to treat their music not just as songs that need to reach listeners, but as an "intermingling of sonic content and coded metadata that needs to be prepared and readied for discovery" (Morris 2020: 2). More broadly, Morris *et al.* refer to this as "cultural optimization", a process of "... measuring, engineering, altering, and designing elements (e.g., interfaces, metadata, features, functions, etc.) of digital cultural goods (i.e., music, games, apps, podcasts, etc.) to make them more searchable, discoverable, usable, and valuable in both economic and cultural senses" (Morris *et al.* 2021: 162–3). This cultural optimization, they suggest, involves seeing cultural products as datafied content, and producing cultural products in ways that will be specifically visible to the myriads of discovery engines and interfaces that content must circulate through on contemporary digital platforms.

Yet, as Hodgson (2021) points out, artists can often find themselves torn between their creative impulses on the one hand, and the financial incentives of optimizing music for playlisting on the other. As such, he argues:

> ... the way musicians and labels position themselves creatively towards recommender systems is varied and complex. Musicians – whether independent artists or those signed to a record label – are not absorbed wholly into the democratizing worldview of streaming platforms; they think about creativity strategically in response to these algorithmic regimes in a variety of context-dependent ways.   (Hodgson 2021: 12)

In his research in Norway, for example, Kiberg (2023) finds varying degrees of willingness amongst musicians to allow themselves to be "formatted" by these influences. Some claimed to have adapted willingly, while others tried to oppose the compositional trends being imposed by platforms. Some held an optimistic view of the creative possibilities that platforms possess, while others were critical of the creative limitations that platforms provide. And yet others held an intermediate position, one where negotiations between platforms structures and creative autonomy is played out – which Kiberg terms as "creative platform negotiations" – and where musicians look for ways to create innovative expressions that take both economic and artistic motivations into consideration. Similarly, Polak and Schaap (2024) find that musicians actively strike a balance between creative autonomy and commercial viability, as offered by streaming and social media platforms, where autonomous creativity and attention for metrics can both have a place. Optimization, they contend, "is not simply a binary switch, but a consciously considered potential ingredient to the production process that varies in included amount, based on contextual variations" (Polak & Schaap 2024: 13). In the platform music industries, platforms bring together the often-conflicting agendas and motivations of the MSPs, musicians and other music producers, record labels and listeners into the same space, resulting in a dynamic and constantly adapting set of practices and relationships (Morris 2020).

Independent music companies, Covid-19 and the digital transition

In the discussion above, we considered some of the implications of the emergence of MSPs for artists and music industries companies, with a specific focus on data and metrics, and its implications for musical creativity. However, it is important to recognize that while the most demonstrable impact of platformization and digitalization is the emergence of the MSPs as the dominant vehicles for music distribution, platformization also is driving a broader digital transformation across all aspects of the music industries. The rise of a host of platforms and services across music production and consumption has brought about new ways of working, new business models, new opportunities, and new challenges. The emergence of digital artist and repertoire (A&R) – A&R activities undertaken online rather than in person at live music venues – artist promotion via social media, the ubiquity of digital distribution, and the rise of live streaming technologies are offering music companies – and in particular small independent music companies – the potential to reach across geographical space to garner artists, audiences and business connections in ways that were previously not possible given their limited financial and human resources. Similar positive narratives regarding democratization and empowerment to those developed in the context of unsigned artists have also often been applied to independent record labels and other intermediaries, suggesting a step change in their ability to compete for market share against larger record labels. Yet our research with small regional independent music companies immediately following the Covid-19 pandemic found that the limited resources and capabilities – both human and financial – of such firms meant that they face significant barriers to being able to realize emergent digital opportunities. These barriers cast doubt over those narratives that confidently anticipate the democratizing and liberating power of digital technologies within the music industries. As is set out below, these barriers are non-trivial and persistent.

The Covid-19 pandemic presented a unique opportunity to study the impacts of platformization and digitalization on the music industries, in two specific areas. First, with the closure of retail outlets, pressing plants and live music venues, the pandemic unevenly impacted on physical formats for music distribution and performance, upon which many small independent companies significantly rely. Our findings suggested that an association could be broadly drawn between the impact of the pandemic on independent music companies and the proportion of revenue they received from streaming platforms and other digital music distribution strategies. For those labels and publishers that derived a large share of their revenues from digital music, the impacts of the pandemic on other non-digital revenue streams were offset to some degree by an increase in digital revenues, which protected their overall revenues. As one interviewee noted, "I think we were really lucky in our business ... we are very digital focused and so we were very, very fortunate in that regard that we were able to just carry on regardless" (director, independent record label, Manchester). For many small regional labels, however, the greatest share of their income is generated by physical products – and especially vinyl records – not digital music. When the Covid-19 pandemic struck, together with Brexit-related impacts on the availability of labour and supply chains, there were significant supply chain problems, specifically the delivery of materials to pressing plants and the onward shipping of goods, creating production and distribution delays. Second, the pandemic presented a unique opportunity to study the platformization and digitalization of the music industries in regard to the way in which the pandemic encouraged music businesses to innovate with new digital ways of presenting, promoting and distributing music. Chapter 6 gave an account of how, for example, following the closure of live music venues and the associated loss of live music incomes during the pandemic, many artists who were socially distanced from their audiences made use of live streaming platforms to meet audience demand, sometimes with but often without record company support. As noted, these platforms opened up a range of opportunities and consequences for artists, listeners and platforms (Zhang & Negus 2021), some of which we explored earlier with specific reference to the live streaming platform Twitch.

However, while such digital platforms and innovations offered opportunities for independent music companies, there remain fundamental challenges to running a music company which make these digital opportunities difficult to capitalize upon. Many of these challenges centre on the limited capacities, capabilities and know-how at the level of the individual and the company. Generally, digital platforms were considered by research participants in positive terms, offering new possibilities for promotion, marketing and audience engagement online. In part, such a positive view was informed by pandemic experiences, when traditional mechanisms for marketing and distribution were disrupted. As noted, the pandemic encouraged or forced music businesses to engage and, in some cases, collaboratively innovate with a variety of platforms. Participants recognized the importance of developing digital "literacy" in this regard; that is, being aware of what platforms and digital services were available or becoming available, and how to take best advantage of the affordances these platforms provided. As discussed earlier, for example, livestreaming is a case in point here.

Developing these skills often involved word of mouth within social networks and observing what others were doing, and a significant amount of self-learning and experimentation. Many interviewees noted the importance of recognizing their own limitations in knowledge and skills and being honest with musicians as to what they could provide. It was often the case that musicians had better digital literacy than the staff working at labels and intermediaries, and took the initiative for promotion, marketing and audience engagement, something that is becoming increasingly common within the independent sector. Indeed, during our research we discovered programmes being run by talent development organizations that sought to develop independent artists' digital skills, while no such schemes existed for those working in or running independent music companies.

Yet, while recognizing the importance of digital literacy, our interviewees placed a greater importance on getting support with the development of a set of broader "business skills" related to running a business in the music industries, skills which would enable them and their businesses to develop a stable and sustainable basis from which to subsequently innovate. The most extensively and intensively discussed of these support needs was the need for mentorship. Especially for those who had founded their own businesses and had experienced the early stages of business operation, mentorship was seen as a mechanism for learning both general business management, and the specific facets of operating a business in the music industries – including, for example, legal issues around recording contracts and music rights: "Maybe we should be considering mentorship schemes for people that would like to set up labels, what you have got to learn in the early days, how to do releases … how to how to do a deal with somebody, how to fill in your tax return, you know, those sorts of things" (label manager, independent record label, Liverpool). For the majority of those running their own businesses, there had been a significant degree of learning-on-the-job. This inevitably resulted in decisions being taken which, in retrospect, were viewed as mistakes. These mistakes often had financial implications or been otherwise detrimental to the development of the business. As one interviewee described: "There were a lot of mistakes during that planning process, which, you know, it would have been quite nice not to make, some of them quite expensive. So, yeah … mentorship would have been good" (label manager, independent record label, West Yorkshire).

However, while recognizing the benefits of, and need for, a broader mentorship programme, interviewees questioned how this could work in practice. Two key issues were raised. The first was pay and reward for mentors. Many who have experience within the music industries undertake mentoring on an informal basis out of good will. Yet it was recognized that if this was to be formalized, mentors must be remunerated: "there should be a financial incentive for the mentor. Their value needs to be reflected. I think we've got to be financially rewarded because it's time consuming and people have enough to do" (label manager, independent record label, Leeds). Another noted that: "I think a lot of the time in the music industry that there's an expectation that people do a lot out of goodwill because they love to support music and so on ... that's all well and good, but you need to find a mechanism to reward people for doing it" (label manager, independent record label, Liverpool).

The second issue is the availability of sufficient people with the requisite experience to provide meaningful mentorship to those starting out. The above interviewee posed the question, "Who do you get that's got the experience? The success not just to mentor artists, of course, but ... for people who would like to set up labels" (label manager, independent record label, Liverpool). At the same time, the same interviewee noted the need for mentors to have not only experience, but also to have maintained their love and enthusiasm for their work: "So it's having the balance of those with experience giving actual guidance but also, keep them enthusiastic about their dream. You don't want people putting people off by telling them it's too difficult". All of this suggests issues of experience, capacity and personality in creating programmes of mentorship. Notwithstanding the above, important mentorship can be obtained from outside the music industries: "We're getting business support from a local manager ... getting that kind of advice, if it's something that you don't know anything about, it can be invaluable, you know ... For us, we've been doing it for a while, so it's reinforcing some ideas and just helping us think a little bit more about where we need to grow and how to develop" (director and producer, music production company, Manchester). Interviewees expressed a need to better connect music businesses with wider business support mechanisms. Key issues mentioned in this respect included the skills necessary to be self-employed, such as keeping accounts and understanding associated tax implications. In short, there was a need to support music industries businesses as *businesses*.

The second most commonly raised requirement for support centred on the need for financial support. This was most acute in the initial stages of business start-up. For record labels especially, small business loans are usually not an option because of the levels of risk to both the lender and borrower associated with investing in music artists who may not be commercially successful. Rather, for most small labels, there is an investment of a very modest amount of personal capital into the company to fund initial deals. The money recouped from initial releases is then used to fund subsequent releases. However, money can take a significant amount of time to recoup, and there is the significant risk that initial releases will not generate enough money to fund later releases, at which point the label fails, or more personal capital is required. This places most start-up labels in an extremely precarious financial position. As one interviewee explained:

"What would have really helped is basically like a kind of an interest free loan or getting a business loan to get a record pressed. Because as soon as you get one record pressed, you can start selling them, keep the money for the next" (label manager, independent record label, Manchester).

Moreover, a lack of sufficient finances significantly limits the extent the release can be supported and promoted. Interviewees noted that even a small loan, or more preferably a non-repayable grant to remove the risk of not being able to repay, would enable them to give their full support to early releases, increasing potential commercial success: "You've got a great band there ... it's going to need some seed funding to propel parts of the project. You don't need three or four grand ... you need £250 for a photoshoot and another £400 for a press campaign. You just need these little bits to propel it, because at some point it's going to sustain itself" (managing director, music management company, Manchester).

If the development of new financial support mechanisms was seen as a good thing, discussions regarding the possible benefits of financial support were often also couched in the need for mentorship and understanding how financial support can be most productively utilized: "I think I would have said money, but then money's great, if you don't know what you do with it, it's not going to make a difference" (label manager, independent record label, Leeds). Several interviewees noted that often business and artists in the music industries are not aware of the funding mechanisms that already exist: "just awareness of those kinds of pots of money and how you apply for them ... and support to apply for them as well" (director, independent record label, Manchester), while another noted that "a lot of people don't even know what the Arts Council is. Or even like ... the EMI [Sound] Foundation" (label manager, independent record label and promoter, Manchester). Here, mentors or other forms of creative business-focused support fulfil a vital role in linking businesses with available sources of funding.

While a significant body of literature has developed examining the economic precarity of musicians in the contemporary music industries (see, e.g., Morgan & Wood 2014; Umney & Kretsos 2015; Hoedemaekers 2018; Threadgold 2018; Nørholm Lundin 2023), there have been few attempts to consider the impacts of financial precarity and other resource limitations (skills, time) in relation to small independent music businesses. As Patrickson (2021: 586) argues: "The vast majority of people working in the creative industries worldwide tend to be either working solo or in small teams with limited time and resources available to help them manage the administrative and legal aspects of their business, let alone research and develop innovations, or even acquire the skills required in a fast-changing digital ecology". These are of course long-standing issues that predate the emergence of the platform music industries, but which saw an exacerbation in the context of the digital transition and Covid-19. While discussions of digital engagement and innovation prompted interesting discussions regarding future business models and promotional strategies for small independent music businesses, it was clear from participants that ideally innovations require the creation of a stable and self-sustaining businesses with aesthetic autonomy, that is to say their ability to make independent creative decisions.

Conclusion

In this chapter, we have focused on independent musicians and music businesses to consider their ability to respond to, and benefit from, the broader platformization of the music industries. Moving beyond discussions of financial remuneration (Chapter 2), we have considered the conditions under which these key actors access and participate in platform economies – key tenets of what has been considered to be an emerging process of democratization under digitalization. In particular, we have centred our discussion around "digital literacy", which we take to refer to a set of knowledges and skills that facilitate an ability to draw benefits from platformization, including a knowledge and awareness of platforms and their purpose, and the related skills needed to exploit the opportunities they provide. We have considered how and why such data literacy has become important, with a particular focus on data and metrics; creative responses to the algorithmic recommendation and curation systems operated by the MSPs, and finally; the opportunities and challenges that platformization and digitalization present to independent music businesses. Set in relation to broader debates regarding platforms and democratization in the music industries, we have argued that digital literacy, and more broadly the ability of individuals or companies to extract benefits from digitalization, is dependent upon a wider set of human and financial resources, and that this brings into question overly positive narratives regarding democratization.

More recent developments with blockchain and Metaverse technologies, as discussed in Chapter 5, suggest that digital literacy is likely to become more important in the immediate future, and especially so when it comes to the matter of democratization, decentralization and the hegemony of the MSPs and major record labels. Jones (2021) argues that in order challenge digital platforms' monopoly of attention, musicians should seek to adopt new strategies of resourcefulness that might include "building alternative distribution networks, bringing forms of cooperative and collective ownership that are already present office onto social media, and taking *control of 'code'* in order to emphasize the materiality of resistance online" (Jones 2021: 144; emphasis added). As we have discussed, blockchain technologies appear to hold significant potential in the context of both online and offline music scenes, being considered by many as a mechanism for empowering cultural activities and communities, enhancing the common good, and enabling the creation of alternative and more horizontally structured market economies (Semezin 2023) – for example, through decentralized autonomous organizations (DAOs). These goals align closely with notions of participation, access, and creative autonomy, all central tenets of the development of more democratic media systems (Hesmondhalgh 1997).

However, such perspectives must be balanced by the reality that "taking control of code" requires advanced digital literacy skills, and this represents yet another set of barriers for independent musicians and music industries companies to overcome. Furthermore, as Kirui (2024) argues, navigating these changes involves not only understanding the technical aspects of technologies such as blockchain, but also being able to grasp their implications on revenue streams and user engagement (Kirui 2024). Although the burden of developing such digital literacy may be eased by independent artists, music businesses and intermediaries working together, as Jones (2021) recognizes, platforms and their related algorithms and metrics encourage and reward individualistic competition in ways that might undermine efforts to collectivize production and distribution. Furthermore, Jones points to the lack of interest in "coding as resistance" (see, for example, Moody 2001 and Weber 2004, on open-source coding), even in DIY communities, mirroring the disinterest we highlighted earlier in the chapter amongst many musicians to metrics. In the end, such factors mean that for those left working alone with limited human, financial and social network resources, digital literacy often remains a significant barrier to access and participation in the platform music industries. This being said, very recent advances in the DAO technical ecosystem around accessible interfaces, financial tools, and voting and community management systems, mean that it is now possible for non-technical experts to start to experiment with blockchain and blockchain-based DAOs. Such tools offer the possibility of extending the decentralizing and democratizing potential of such technologies beyond the technical classes (Catlow & Rafferty 2022).

8
CONCLUSION

The rise of the platform music industries

While digital platforms are now ubiquitous across large parts of the economy, the underpinning motivation for writing this book has been our argument that the music industries have served as *frontier industries* for processes of platformization that have subsequently been rolled out elsewhere. Indeed, commentaries in both popular and specialist media have frequently described the music industries as the "canary in the coal mine" for a series of digital disruptions, ranging from the advent of streaming, through the emergence of an internet of things (IOT), to virtual reality and blockchain, in ways that have guided subsequent developments in a host of other industries (Howard 2015, 2018). Subsequently, musicians have in turn been held up as the "canaries" for the future of employment practices in an economy dominated by platforms, including the removal of employment rights and even basic remuneration. This has been reflected in the very high-profile and often heated debates that continue to take place around the MSPs and remuneration of artists, set in the context of broader aesthetic and moral arguments about the value of music and the ability of artists to make a living from their profession. It is also reflected in the emerging body of literature on the mental health of musicians in relation to the intensified demands around entrepreneurship and relational labour being placed upon them (Gross & Musgrave 2020; Loveday *et al.* 2023; Musgrave 2023a, 2023b).

More broadly, we have sought to demonstrate the ways in which the music industries position as a bellwether sector has occurred in the context of the development of a new and *distinctive form of platformization* that reaches beyond shifts in the technologies of distribution and consumption to a wider condition in which platformization and platform (re-)intermediation have permeated the entire musical economy. Adopting a platform political economy perspective – that is, seeing the contemporary music industries as being *increasingly constituted through the logics and logistics of platforms* – has enabled us to attempt a holistic and systematic evaluation of how processes of platformization are shaping and having an impact on the music industries. Throughout the book we have emphasized the impacts that platformization has had on a range of activities, from the management of music rights to digital innovation, to marketing and promotion, to financing, and to live performance. We have also drawn out the complex dynamics, conflicts and inequalities that arise from platformization as they impact upon a range of key actors across the various music industries, and the conditions under which these key actors access and participate in platform economies. Taken together, we have argued that platformization in the music industries has brought together the often-conflicting agendas and motivations of the MSPs, musicians and other music producers, record labels and listeners in ways which are dynamic and are resulting in a constantly adapting set of practices and relationships.

One of the key characteristics of the distinctive form of platformization that we are witnessing in the music industries is the unfolding of new types of relations between incumbents and platforms. Some early accounts of platformization that took root in the populist end of the business literature suggested that digital platforms would lay waste to powerful incumbent firms across a host of economic sectors. But despite the three waves of platform reintermediation outlined in this book, the music industries not only remain highly oligopolistic, but incumbent corporations are arguably even more powerful than before. There are two factors which are particularly notable here. First, we have argued that the MSPs are digital platforms that have their own dynamics of economic transformation that encourage capital concentration and centralization. As with all platforms, they embody a number of familiar capitalist developments including consolidation, economies of scale, rent-seeking, and uneven distribution of power (Andersson Schwarz 2017; Nieborg & Poel 2018). They also, we suggest, both reflect existing structural inequalities and amplify them in new ways. Through the complex relations of interdependencies that have developed between the MSPs and the music industries' major corporations, MSPs have served to reinforce the power structures of the traditional musical economy, whilst also adding new dynamics based on a winner-takes-all sensibility. We see this, for example, in the way in which the allocation of revenue from MSPs takes place on a proportional basis related to an artist's share of total streams, rather than a pre-determined per stream rate for all artists.

Second, and relatedly, a copyright-enabled system of rent extraction has developed which has encouraged the formation of an enormously powerful oligopoly in the market for musical intellectual property. For large music corporations in the digital era, huge back catalogues of copyrighted music are significant assets with regards to generating income. Major labels have responded to recent technological changes by shifting their efforts away from the discovery of "new-to-the-world" talent in favour of a focus on leveraging previously successful artists. As we have argued this is reflective of one of the broader characteristics of rentier capitalism whereby rent-based asset incomes are associated with the extraction rather than creation of value – or, put another way, primarily focus on the "sweating of assets". The control of these assets through the strict enforcement of copyright, we have demonstrated, positions the major corporations as the key rentiers in the networks of the music industries. The ways in which these key actors have become bound together in a very particular system of *rent extraction* (Meier & Manzerolle 2019) is, we would argue, the key determining factor in shaping the nature of relations between the major corporations, MSPs, and artists, which in turn are shaping the distinctive form of platformization that we are witnessing across all sectors and levels of the music industries.

The ongoing concentration of power amongst a small number of corporations, together with these new dynamics of rent extraction, has important implications in relation to debates around democratization. If one considers the twin pillars of *participation* and *access* as being fundamental to the development of democratic media systems (Hesmondhalgh 1997), then platformization might be considered to bring with it the promise of democratization in the music industries. This is particularly the case with regards to the production of music and the subsequent economic and cultural participation of musicians and music producers in the music industries. Platforms and other digital technologies offer the promise of lower entry costs across the music industries value chain, making it easier for musicians to access and participate in music production, distribution and consumption regardless of economic, network-based or sociocultural background. For consumers, it could be argued that media consumption has also been democratized in some respects, given the abundance and convenience of content on streaming services. Yet, as we have sought to demonstrate, contemporary musicians and other music industries professionals alike work in a business ecology in which large digital platforms own, develop, steer and, critically, *monet*ize several of the most influential music industries distribution channels (Frenneaux 2023). Given the interdependent relations that have developed between the MSPs and the music industries' major corporations, the system of rights and ownership underpinning the music industries are arguably now more deeply embedded in technological systems and more removed from democratic debate than ever (Hesmondhalgh 2019). In this way, the particular processes of platformization and political economy at work in the contemporary music industries problematize claims regarding the disruptive, disintermediating and democratizing potential of platforms more generally.

Alongside of our treatment of major corporations, we have also sought to outline the implications of platformization on the musicians and other independent music industry practitioners who now find themselves at the "sharp end" (Haynes & Marshall 2018) of the platform music industries, and how these actors have developed strategies and tactics to respond to these changes. As outlined earlier, the impacts of the file-sharing crisis of the early 2000s on the industries' major corporations have since resulted in a sustained period of reduced capital flow, smaller artist rosters, substantially reduced record label budgets, and new forms of disintermediation. The consequence of this is that we have witnessed the demise of what might be described the "welfare function" of record labels, which has resulted in a marked increase in the number of independent self-releasing artists, many of whom operate in conditions of precarity with unpredictable levels of income generation (Mulligan & Jopling 2019). While arguably such independence from the corporate system allows for more opportunities for artists to realize more variable kinds of musical and related outputs, with more agency over both the form and process of their musical creation and production, many of the tasks previously performed by music label representatives (for example, promotion, marketing and distribution) now fall to artists (Kribs 2017). Thus, artists find themselves in a situation which poses new challenges in achieving sustained success and may need help generating income from their work (Frenneaux 2023). Subsequently we are witnessing a new round of reintermediation as MusicTech start-ups and various new intermediary firms – such as administrative music publishers, as just one example – look to develop platforms and services that respond the needs of independent artists for a range of intermediary services.

As we have also argued, platforms and their related technologies have distinctive affordances, many of which would seem to promise musicians greater control over creation, copyrights, collaboration, marketing and promotion, distribution and monetization. New forms of intermediary music services and platforms, together with the plethora of social media, live streaming and crowdfunding platforms, appear to offer new independent artists and self-releasing musicians the opportunity to build, reach and monetize audiences in ways which will allow them to thrive alongside more established acts. In our research into how musicians use the Twitch live streaming platform, for example, we demonstrated how during the Covid-19 pandemic, the affordances of the platform allowed some independent musicians to make money from online live music performances when physical live music spaces were closed. Others were "platform-only" musicians who had never performed live in a physical space but were encouraged on to the platform by the opportunities it offered for performance, community-building and generating income.

Yet, in much the same way as signed musicians necessarily subject themselves to the control of firms – under the aegis of intellectual property and contract law regimes – in return for potential financial reward (Stahl 2013), the MSPs and other platforms used by independent musicians, whilst providing potentially beneficial affordances, seek to commodify outputs in ways that blur the separation between creativity and business (Qu *et al.* 2023). The autonomy of independent musicians, for example, is brought into question by the "unpredictable algorithmic environment" (Frenneaux 2023) within which they operate and to which they seek to respond to gain agency and advantage. In this book, we have drawn attention to the ways in which some musicians seek to "game" song recommender systems as they vie to make their music more "algorithmically attractive", and how data and digital literacy have become fundamental skills for contemporary musicians, music companies and intermediaries. We have also argued that data creates new divides between the data literate and those who lack the knowledge, skills and financial resources to effectively utilize platforms and leverage the metrics that they provide.

Furthermore, amongst a heightened level of market *noise*, there is a proliferation of modalities and platforms that must be engaged concurrently as musicians seek to identify the market *signal* that will enable them to gain momentum and progress (Frenneaux 2023). At the same time, through our accounts of musicians' use of social media and live streaming platforms, we have emphasized how self-promotion through such platforms places particular requirements and demands on artists and musicians to adopt entrepreneurial approaches to promotion and perform online relational and emotional labour. There is now significant pressure on musicians to build relationships across social media to advance their careers and a growing sense that their livelihood depends on how well they self-brand, self-promote and connect (Baym 2018). Yet, even so, as Haynes and Marshall (2018) note, online success does not easily translate into material sustainability: "offline inequalities" in the field of music, such as an individual's economic resources or social networks, are not easily undone via online resources (Verboord & van Noord 2016).

Where next?

One of the inherent risks in authoring a book about the music industries and technology is how quickly it might become outdated as the music industries pass into the next phase of technological disruption and/or crisis. The rate of change has been particularly rapid over the past two and a half decades as the music industries have experienced the three distinct waves of platform reintermediation outlined earlier, rendering some academic accounts of the music industries as pieces of historical reflection almost immediately as they were published. However, given the stabilization that we have witnessed around streaming as the primary mechanism for the distribution of music, and the lack of any replacement technology on the near horizon, together with the ongoing embedding of the platform business model throughout the value chains of the musical economy, we have good reason to believe that this book will act as a basis for further evaluations of the music industries in coming years.

This is not to suggest of course that the music industries and related technologies will stand still. Far from it. Throughout the book, we have pointed to different areas of nascent technological innovation, along with their attendant social and economic practices, which we anticipate could be particularly important in the future. Many of these technologies sit at the intersection of production and consumption, connecting musicians and fans together in more engaging and intimate ways. This is something which, given the present dynamics of the music industries, is only likely to be become more important with regards to musicians making at least some kind of living from their music. In particular, the potential of what have been termed as decentralized or distributed creator economies is being recognized both in the context of music and beyond. Web 3.0 offers opportunities for creator economy platforms and their users to leverage emerging technologies such as augmented reality, blockchain, cryptocurrencies and NFTs, and Metaverse technologies, to alter the economics of the creator economy in ways that facilitate further reintermediation and the cultivation of closer relationships between content creators and fans, and perhaps, in turn, the promise of greater creative autonomy. In this book, we have pointed to some examples of where these innovations are already underway.

Yet, if the growing body of literature on platform capitalism tells us anything, it is that the tendency of platforms towards consolidation and control works counter to aspirations of decentralization and (re)distribution. Furthermore, recent literature on the sharing economy, whilst outlining its potential for creating a decentralized, equitable and sustainable economy (Bradley & Pargman 2017), points to how the type of altruistic, non-profit and community-orientated activities characterizing "true" and transformative non-market forms of sharing (Belk 2014) sit in opposition to the logics of the platform economy whereby the commodification of "sharing" introduces market relations into all aspects of everyday life in a "nightmarish form of neoliberal capitalism" (Martin 2016: 149). Therefore, aspirations around platform-enabled decentralization and distributed creator economies are only likely to be realized if the platforms and related technologies themselves (for example, management of rights and financial elements through the blockchain) are, if not controlled, then at least more strongly influenced by, musicians and other creatives. We have discussed DAOs as one potential organizational form in which this could be realized. Along similar lines, Hardjono and Pentland (2019) argue the need for "data cooperatives" for artists and musicians, allowing the community to share IT resources – such as data storage, analytics processing, blockchains and distributed ledgers – and apply smart contracts to remedy some of the various challenges currently facing the industry, such as licence tracking management. However, as discussed previously, for this to happen would require attendant demands on musicians and other intermediaries to engage critically with data and to become digitally literate, while at the same time acquiring understanding the requirements of successful entrepreneurship.

A technological development that we have identified as having potentially significant impacts upon the future of the music industries is artificial intelligence (AI). As we have argued, new developments in machine learning and generative AI, together with increased computing power, have led to notable improvements in the quality of the music generated by AI (Drott: 2021). This has produced concerns that generative AI technologies may in time replace artists and musicians within the creative process, while also raising anxieties around the attribution of copyright and authorship. In particular, there are fears that there is the potential of significant amounts of AI-generated music to flood on to MSPs, which while financially beneficial to platforms with regards to royalty payments, would likely undercut the market for human-composed music and therefore displace the work of musicians at a time when making a living for music is increasingly problematic. It is difficult to predict at this point just how significant an issue this is likely to be, although the streaming platform Deezer very recently announced, following the launch of a new AI-detection tool, that 10,000 AI-generated tracks were being uploaded to the platform every day, which amounts to roughly 10 per cent of the daily content delivered to the platform. Deezer also announced that the company plans to exclude fully AI-generated tracks from algorithmic and editorial recommendation (Tencer 2025).

Clearly, a major determining factor with regards to the impact of AI will be the adequacy of existing copyright regimes when applied to AI music, the ability of rights holders (specifically the major corporations) to defend these rights, and whether re-evaluation of these regimes happens in the near future in ways that directly target AI-generated products (Sturm *et al.* 2019). Perhaps inevitably, early proposals with regards to AI-related changes to copyright law are proving to be controversial. At the time of writing, for example, the UK government is consulting on proposals that would allow AI companies to use material that is available online without respecting copyright if they are using it for text or data mining. While proposals would give artists or creators the ability to opt out – termed a "rights reservation" – critics have argued that is not possible for an individual writer or artist to notify thousands of different AI service providers that they do not want their content used in that way, or to monitor what has happened to their work across the whole internet. In response, an alternative proposal was being put forward whereby artists opt in to give their permission for their content (Kuenssberg 2025). At the same time, however – assuming copyright regimes that are favourable towards artists rather than technology per se – positive narratives have sought to emphasize the creative potential of AI. As such computational tools become increasingly central to artistic practice, co-creative spaces can become zones of community interaction and engagement, within which the creative potential of technologies is developed, expanded, critiqued and challenged. Such spaces, it has been argued, can encourage the stretching of the boundaries of (human) imagination to spark creativity across new imaginative terrains (Stark & Crawford 2019; Lundman & Nordström 2023).

And it is here, as in other areas, that a critical examination of the music industries has value for considering implications for the creative economy, and the wider economy more generally. As we have argued, the music industries have been an important testing ground for platform technologies, which have now become pervasive. While AI has already advanced in the music industries in music production (for example in assisting or even automating tasks such as mixing and mastering) a key watershed moment will be when it becomes possible to create music with AI that manages to successfully register affect and approval among audiences, which in turn will make it a viable revenue generating strategy. While the use of AI tools might, in theory, lower barriers to entry, enabling those with ideas but perhaps not the technical skills to create music in ways that would not otherwise be possible, such developments are more likely to favour those with deeper pockets and greater capital reserves. AI generated music, in combination with a narrow band of MSPs and an even smaller group of rights owning organizations, would see the idea of creative economy as a powerful and perhaps impenetrable and insurmountable oligopsony. Such a development it is likely to increase income polarization by flooding MSPs with new music, increasing levels of competition for listening attention, and making earning a living in the music industries an ever more difficult achievement. The progress of AI in the music industries, as with platform technologies, will provide a preview of how automation, creative collaboration, and algorithmic data-driven personalization and recommendation could reshape the economy more widely.

ACKNOWLEDGEMENTS

In some of chapters in this book we draw on primary data collected with the financial support of research funders, which we acknowledge here. We thank both the funders and the research participants for their roles in supporting the research underpinning this book. Chapter 4 draws on qualitative interviews with MusicTech start-ups and a range of related actors and organizations based in London and Stockholm, undertaken as part of research supported by Loughborough University. Chapter 5 analyses primary qualitative data on artist royalty earnings and social media platforms, collected and analysed as part of a Knowledge Transfer Partnership funded by the AHRC and ESRC through Innovate UK. Chapter 6 draws on qualitative interviews with musicians utilizing live streaming platforms, collected as part of a research project funded by the British Academy. Chapter 7 draws on qualitative interviews with record labels and a range of other local music industry companies and intermediaries based in the North West of England, collected as part of a research project funded by the Creative Industries Policy and Evidence Centre (AHRC).

Throughout the book we reproduce, rework, update and extend text from our previously published work, as detailed below. We wish here to recognize the contribution of our co-authors to these publications, and therefore to the research that informs this book. "User as asset, music as liability: the moral economy of the 'value gap' in a platform musical economy" by Andrew Leyshon and Allan Watson, in P. McDonald (ed.), *The Routledge Companion to Media Industries* (2022). Reproduced by permission of Taylor and Francis Group, LLC, a division of Informa plc (Chapter 2). "Negotiating platformisation: MusicTech, intellectual property rights and third wave platform reintermediation in the music industry" by Allan Watson and Andrew Leyshon, *Journal of Cultural Economy* 15:3 (2022), © Academy of Criminal Justice Sciences 2022, reprinted by permission of Taylor & Francis Ltd on behalf of Academy of Criminal Justice Sciences (Chapters 3 and 4). "Tech start-up capitalisation in an oligopolistic copyright industry: the case of the contemporary music industry" by Allan Watson, Andrew Leyshon and George Windsor, *Cultural Trends* 33:5 (2023), © Informa UK Ltd, trading as

Taylor & Francis Group 2023, reprinted by permission of Taylor & Francis Ltd (Chapter 4). "Does social media pay for music artists? Quantitative evidence on the co-evolution of social media, streaming and live music" by Allan Watson, Joseph B. Watson and Lou Tompkins, *Journal of Cultural Economy* 16:1 (2022), © Academy of Criminal Justice Sciences 2022, reprinted by permission of Taylor & Francis Ltd on behalf of Academy of Criminal Justice Sciences (Chapter 5). © 2016 From "Leveraging affect: mobilizing enthusiasm and the co-production of the musical economy" by Andrew Leyshon, Nigel Thrift, Louise Crewe, Shaun French and Pete Webb, in B. Hracs, M. Seman & T. Virani (eds), *The Production and Consumption of Music in the Digital Age*. Reproduced by permission of Taylor and Francis Group, LLC, a division of Informa plc (Chapter 5). "Supporting regional music production clusters in the post-pandemic era: placing business support at the heart of local cultural policy" by Allan Watson, *International Journal of Cultural Policy* 30:5 (2024), © Informa UK Limited, trading as Taylor & Francis Group 2023, reprinted by permission of Taylor & Francis Ltd (Chapter 7).

Finally, we wish to extend our thanks to Camilla Erskine and Steven Gerrard of Agenda Publishing for their encouragement, support and guidance from the book's commission through to its completion.

REFERENCES

Abercrombie, N. & B. Longhurst (1998). *Audiences: A Sociological Theory of Performance and Imagination*. Thousand Oaks, CA: Sage.

Aguiar, L., J. Waldfogel & S. Waldfogel (2021). "Playlisting Favorites: Measuring Platform Bias in the Music Industry". *International Journal of Industrial Organization* 78 (Sep):102765. https://doi.org/10.1016/j.ijindorg.2021.102765.

Alberti, A. (2011). "Kobalt Music Group: Redefining Music Publishing". *Music Business Journal* (blog). https://www.thembj.org/2011/12/kobalt-music-group-redefining-the-role-of-a-music-publisher/.

Allen, D. (2013). "Why David Byrne Is Wrong About Spotify". *The Guardian*, 16 October. www.theguardian.com/commentisfree/2013/oct/16/why-david-byrne-wrong-spotify-thom-yorke.

Andersen, B., R. Kozul-Wright & Z. Kozul-Wright (2007). "Rents, Rights N'Rhythm: Cooperation, Conflict and Capabilities in the Music Industry". *Industry & Innovation* 14(5): 513–40. https://doi.org/10.1080/13662710701524106.

Anderson, C. (2006). *The Long Tail: Why the Future of Business Is Selling Less of More*. New York: Hyperion.

Andersson Schwarz, J. (2017). "Platform Logic: An Interdisciplinary Approach to the Platform-Based Economy". *Policy & Internet* 9(4): 374–94. https://doi.org/10.1002/poi3.159.

Ante, L. (2021). "The Non-Fungible Token (NFT) Market and Its Relationship with Bitcoin and Ethereum". *SSRN Electronic Journal*. https://doi.org/10.2139/ssrn.3861106.

Arditi, D. (2014). "iTunes: Breaking Barriers and Building Walls". *Popular Music and Society* 37(4): 408–24. https://doi.org/10.1080/03007766.2013.810849.

Arditi, D. (2015). *iTake-over: The Recording Industry in the Digital Era*. Lanham, MD: Rowman & Littlefield.

Arditi, D. (2019). "Music Everywhere: Setting a Digital Music Trap". *Critical Sociology* 45(4/5): 617–30. https://doi.org/10.1177/0896920517729192.

Arditi, D. (2020). *Getting Signed: Record Contracts, Musicians, and Power in Society*. Cham, CH: Palgrave Macmillan.

Arsenault, A. (2017). "The Datafication of Media: Big Data and the Media Industries". *International Journal of Media & Cultural Politics* 13(1): 7–24. https://doi.org/10.1386/macp.13.1-2.7_1.

Attali, J. (1985). *Noise: The Political Economy of Music*. Minneapolis, MN: University of Minnesota Press.

Bachtiar, P., P. Vandenburg & H. Sawiji (2022). "City-Level Tech Startup Ecosystems and Talent Development in Indonesia". Asian Development Bank. https://doi.org/10.22617/BRF220512-2.

Banks, M. (2007). *The Politics of Cultural Work*. Basingstoke: Palgrave Macmillan.

Bannerman, S. (2020). "Crowdfunding Music and the Democratization of Economic and Social Capital". *Canadian Journal of Communication* 45(2): 241–63. https://doi.org/10.22230/cjc.2020v45n2a3469.

Barnes, K. (2024). "The Taylor Swift Effect: 8 Ways the Eras Tour Broke Records and Shattered Sales". Grammy Awards blog, 14 March. https://www.grammy.com/news/taylor-swift-eras-tour-records-movie-disney-plus-stream.

Barr, K. (2013). "Theorizing Music Streaming: Preliminary Investigations". *Scottish Music Review* 3: 1–20.

Baym, N. (2015). "Connect With Your Audience! The Relational Labor of Connection". *The Communication Review* 18(1): 14–22. https://doi.org/10.1080/10714421.2015.996401.

Baym, N. (2018). *Playing to the Crowd: Musicians, Audiences, and the Intimate Work of Connection*. New York: New York University Press.

Baym, N. *et al.* (2021). "Making Sense of Metrics in the Music Industries". *International Journal of Communication* 15: 3418–41.

Baym, N., L. Swartz & A. Alarcon (2019). "Convening Technologies: Blockchain and the Music Industry". *International Journal of Communication* 13: 402–21.

Beeching, A. (2020). *Beyond Talent: Creating a Successful Career in Music*. Third edition. New York: Oxford University Press.

Beer, D. (2008). "Making Friends with Jarvis Cocker: Music Culture in the Context of Web 2.0". *Cultural Sociology* 2(2): 222–41. https://doi.org/10.1177/1749975508091034.

Belk, R. (2014). "You Are What You Can Access: Sharing and Collaborative Consumption Online". *Journal of Business Research* 67(8): 1595–600. https://doi.org/10.1016/j.jbusres.2013.10.001.

Bell, A. (2015). "DAW Democracy? The Dearth of Diversity in 'Playing the Studio'". *Journal of Music, Technology & Education* 8(2): 129–46. https://doi.org/10.1386/jmte.8.2.129_1.

Bell, A. (2018). *Dawn of the DAW: The Studio as Musical Instrument*. Vol. 1. Oxford: Oxford University Press.

Benkler, Y. (2006). *The Wealth of Networks: How Social Production Transforms Markets and Freedom*. New Haven, CT: Yale University Press.

Benner, M. & J. Waldfogel (2016). "The Song Remains the Same? Technological Change and Positioning in the Recorded Music Industry". *Strategy Science* 1(3): 129–47. https://doi.org/10.1287/stsc.2016.0012.

Bennett, L., B. Chin & B. Jones (2015). "Crowdfunding: A *New Media & Society* Special Issue". *New Media & Society* 17(2): 141–8. https://doi.org/10.1177/1461444814558906.

Berger, V. (2024). "Why Major Labels Are Suing AI Music Startups Udio And Suno For Mass Copyright Infringement". *Forbes*, 27 June. https://www.forbes.com/sites/virginieberger/2024/06/27/why-major-labels-are-suing-ai-music-startups-udio-and-suno-for-mass-copyright-infringement/.

Bhattacharjee, S. *et al.* (2006). "Impact of Legal Threats on Online Music Sharing Activity: An Analysis of Music Industry Legal Actions". *Journal of Law and Economics* 49(1): 91–114. https://doi.org/10.1086/501085.

Blackwell, C. & P. Morley (2023). *The Islander: My Life in Music and Beyond.* London: Nine Eight Books.

Bleier, A., B. Fossen & M. Shapira (2024). "On the Role of Social Media Platforms in the Creator Economy". *International Journal of Research in Marketing* 41(3): 411–26. https://doi.org/10.1016/j.ijresmar.2024.06.006.

Bloom, M. (2024). "Hipgnosis Sells to Blackstone for $1.6 Billion". Pitchfork blog, 9 July 2024. https://pitchfork.com/news/hipgnosis-sells-to-blackstone-for-dollar 16-billion/.

Boldrin, M. & D. Levine (2002). "The Case against Intellectual Property". *American Economic Review* 92(2): 209–12.

Bonini, T, & A. Gandini (2019). "'First Week Is Editorial, Second Week Is Algorithmic'": Platform Gatekeepers and the Platformization of Music Curation". *Social Media + Society* 5(4): 205630511988000. https://doi.org/10.1177/2056305119880006.

Bonini, T. & P. Magaudda (2024). *Platformed! How Streaming, Algorithms and Artificial Intelligence Are Shaping Music Cultures.* Cham, CH: Palgrave Macmillan.

Borgogno, O. & E. Martino (2024). "Decentralised autonomous organisations: targeting the potential beyond the hype". *Law, Innovation and Technology* 16(2); 392–431. https://doi.org/10.1080/17579961.2024.2392933.

Born, G. (2005). "On Musical Mediation: Ontology, Technology and Creativity". *Twentieth-Century Music* 2(1): 7–36. https://doi.org/10.1017/S147857220500023X.

Bradley, K. & D. Pargman (2017). "The Sharing Economy as the Commons of the 21st Century". *Cambridge Journal of Regions, Economy and Society* 10(2): 231–47. https://doi.org/10.1093/cjres/rsx001.

Briot, J.-P. & F. Pachet (2020). "Deep Learning for Music Generation: Challenges and Directions". *Neural Computing and Applications* 32(4): 981–93. https://doi.org/10.1007/s00521-018-3813-6.

Brown, E. & D. Piroska (2022). "Governing Fintech and Fintech as Governance: The Regulatory Sandbox, Riskwashing, and Disruptive Social Classification". *New Political Economy* 27(1): 19–32. https://doi.org/10.1080/13563467.2021.1910645.

Bucher, T. & A. Helmond (2017). "The Affordances of Social Media Platforms". In J. Burgess, T. Poell & A. Marwick (eds), *The SAGE Handbook of Social Media*, 233–53. London: Sage.

Bustinza, O. *et al.* (2013). "Music Business Models and Piracy". *Industrial Management & Data Systems* 113(1): 4–22. https://doi.org/10.1108/02635571311289638.

Carter, E. (2024). "Poverty among Riches: Understanding the Contracted Economy for Recorded Music and Its Impact on Market Actors". *Journal of Cultural Economy*, January, 1–15. https://doi.org/10.1080/17530350.2024.2302152.

Catlow, R. & P. Rafferty (eds) (2022) *Radical Friends: Decentralised Autonomous Organisations & the Arts.* Torgue Editions.

Chambers, P. (2022). "Producing the Self: Digitisation, Music-Making and Subjectivity". *Journal of Sociology* 58(4): 554–69. https://doi.org/10.1177/14407833211009317.

Charlton, C. *et al.* (2020). "MLwin version 3.05". Centre for Multilevel Modelling, University of Bristol.

Chen, H. (2000). "Don't Sell Out, Sell Bonds: The Pullman Group's Securitization of the Music Industry". *Vanderbilt Journal of Entertainment and Technology Law* 2(2): 161–9.

Chen, Y. & R. Hassink (2022). "The Geography of the Emergence of Online Peer-to-Peer Lending Platforms in China: An Evolutionary Economic Geography Perspective". *International Journal of Urban Sciences* 26(2): 351–71. https://doi.org/10.1080/12265934.2021.1879664.

Chen, S. (2021). "Flying with Two Wings or Coming of Age of Copyrightisation? A Historical and Socio-legal Analysis of Copyright and Business Models and Developments in the Chinese Music Industry". *Global Media China* 6(2): 191–206. https://doi.org/10.1177/2059436421998466.

Choi, D. & A. Perez (2007). "Online Piracy, Innovation, and Legitimate Business Models". *Technovation* 27(4): 168–78. https://doi.org/10.1016/j.technovation.2006.09.004.

Choi, H. & B. Burnes (2013). "The Internet and Value Co-Creation: The Case of the Popular Music Industry". *Prometheus* 31(1). https://doi.org/10.1080/08109028.2013.774595.

Choi, H. & B. Burnes (2017). "Bonding and Spreading: Co-Creative Relationships and Interaction with Consumers in South Korea"s Indie Music Industry". *Management Decision* 55(9): 1905–23. https://doi.org/10.1108/MD-10-2016-0691.

Christophers, B. (2020). *Rentier Capitalism: Who Owns the Economy, and Who Pays for It?* London: Verso.

Christophers, B. (2022). "Mind the Rent Gap: Blackstone, Housing Investment and the Reordering of Urban Rent Surfaces". *Urban Studies* 59(4): 698–716. https://doi.org/10.1177/00420980211026466.

CISAC (2019). "Creators' Royalties Shift to Digital as CISAC Global Collections Hit Record €9.7 Billion". https://www.cisac.org/Newsroom/news-releases/creators-royalties-shift-digital-cisac-global-collections-hit-record-eu97.

Clancy, M. (2022). "Law – You Can Call Me Hal: AI and Music IP". In M. Clancy (ed.), *Artificial Intelligence and Music Ecosystem*. Abingdon: Focal Press.

Cockerell, C. (2024). "Kate Nash and Lily Allen on OnlyFans should be a wakeup call for the music industry". *The Standard*, 24 November. https://www.standard.co.uk/lifestyle/kate-nash-lily-allen-onlyfans-music-industry-b1195961.html.

Conti, A., M. Thursby & F. Rothaermel (2013). "Show Me the Right Stuff: Signals for High-Tech Startups". *Journal of Economics & Management Strategy* 22(2): 341–64. https://doi.org/10.1111/jems.12012.

Cooke, C. (2020). *Dissecting the Digital Dollar*. Third edition. London: Music Managers Forum.

Crittenden, A., V. Crittenden & W. Crittenden (2019). "The Digitalization Triumvirate: How Incumbents Survive". *Business Horizons* 62(2): 259–66. https://doi.org/10.1016/j.bushor.2018.11.005.

Curran, P., K. Obeidat & D. Losardo (2010). "Twelve Frequently Asked Questions About Growth Curve Modeling". *Journal of Cognition and Development* 11(2): 121–36. https://doi.org/10.1080/15248371003699969.

Cusumano, M., A. Gawer & D. Yoffie (2019). *The Business of Platforms: Strategy in the Age of Digital Competition, Innovation, and Power*. New York: Harper Business.

Daellenbach, K., R. Kusel & M. Rod (2015). "The Ties That Bind? Online Musicians and Their Fans". *Asia Pacific Journal of Marketing and Logistics* 27(2): 168–90. https://doi.org/10.1108/APJML-08-2013-0095.

Dailey, H. (2024). "Chappell Roan Drops Out of All Things Go Day Before the Festival: 'Things Have Gotten Overwhelming'". *Billboard*, 27 September. https://ca.billboard.com/music/music-news/chappell-roan-cancels-all-things-go-festival-set-1235787117/.

David, M. (2010). *Peer to Peer and the Music Industry: The Criminalization of Sharing*. London: Sage.

Davies, W. *et al.* (2022). *Unprecedented? How Covid-19 Exposed the Politics of Our Economy*. London: Goldsmiths Press.

Davis, C., T. Creutzberg & D. Arthurs (2009). "Applying an Innovation Cluster Framework to a Creative Industry: The Case of Screen-Based Media in Ontario". *Innovation* 11(2): 201–14. https://doi.org/10.5172/impp.11.2.201.

De Groote, J. & J. Backmann (2020). "Initiating Open Innovation Collaborations between Incumbents and Startups: How Can David and Goliath Get Along?" *International Journal of Innovation Management* 24(2): 2050011. https://doi.org/10.1142/S1363919620500115.

Deltorn, J.-M. & F. Macrez (2021). "Authorship in the Age of Machine Learning and Artificial Intelligence". In S. O'Connor (ed.), *Oxford Handbook of Music Law and Policy*. Oxford: Oxford University Press.

Department of International Trade (UK) (2018). "British Music Innovation: Hitting the Right Notes for the Future." London: Department for International Trade.

Dhar, V. & E. Chang (2009). "Does Chatter Matter? The Impact of User-Generated Content on Music Sales". *Journal of Interactive Marketing* 23(4): 300–307. https://doi.org/10.1016/j.intmar.2009.07.004.

D'Ignazio, C. (2017). "Creative Data Literacy: Bridging the Gap between the Data-Haves and Data-Have Nots". *Information Design Journal* 23(1): 6–18. https://doi.org/10.1075/idj.23.1.03dig.

Dijck, J. van. (2013). *The Culture of Connectivity: A Critical History of Social Media*. Oxford: Oxford University Press.

Dredge, S. (2020). "What Are User-Centric Music Streaming Payouts? Start Here …". MusicAlly blog, 13 May. https://musically.com/2020/05/13/what-are-user-centric-music-streaming-payouts/.

Dredge, S. (2023). "Music & Copyright Publishes Its Market Share Analysis for 2022". MusicAlly blog, 26 April. https://musically.com/2023/04/26/music-copyright-publishes-its-market-share-analysis-for-2022/.

Dredge, S. (2024a). "Billboard Reveals UMG TikTok Takedowns Impact on Most Popular Songs". MusicAlly blog, 4 March. https://musically.com/2024/03/04/billboard-reveals-umg-tiktok-takedowns-impact-on-most-popular-songs/.

Dredge, S. (2024b). "Sony Music Shuts down Its Prism Project Virtual-Talent Brand". MusicAlly blog, 5 March. https://musically.com/2024/03/05/sony-music-shuts-down-its-prism-project-virtual-talent-brand/.

Dredge, S. (2024c). "Spotify Paid More than $9bn to the Music Industry in 2023". MusicAlly blog, 2 August. https://musically.com/2024/02/08/spotify-paid-more-than-9bn-to-the-music-industry-in-2023/.

Dredge, S. (2024d). "Spotify Q3 2024 financial results reveal record operating profit". MusicAlly blog, 12 November. https://musically.com/2024/11/12/spotify-q3-2024-financial-results-reveal-record-operating-profit/.

Drott, E. (2018). "Why the Next Song Matters: Streaming, Recommendation, Scarcity". *Twentieth-Century Music* 15(3): 325–57. https://doi.org/10.1017/S1478572218000245.

Drott, E. (2021). "Copyright, Compensation, and Commons in the Music AI Industry". *Creative Industries Journal* 14(2): 190–207. https://doi.org/10.1080/17510694.2020.1839702.

Drott, E. (2024). *Streaming Music, Streaming Capital*. Durham, NC: Duke University Press.

Duffett, M. (2013). *Understanding Fandom: An Introduction to the Study of Media Fan Culture*. New York: Bloomsbury.

Duffy, B., T. Poell & D. Nieborg (2019). "Platform Practices in the Cultural Industries: Creativity, Labor, and Citizenship". *Social Media + Society* 5(4): 205630511987967. https://doi.org/10.1177/2056305119879672.

Dumbreck, A. & G. McPherson (eds) (2016). *Music Entrepreneurship*. London: Bloomsbury.

Durand, C. & W. Milberg (2020). "Intellectual Monopoly in Global Value Chains". *Review of International Political Economy* 27(2): 404–29. https://doi.org/10.1080/09692290.2019.1660703.

Edlom, J. & J. Karlsson (2021a). "Hang with Me – Exploring Fandom, Brandom, and the Experiences and Motivations for Value Co-Creation in a Music Fan Community". *International Journal of Music Business Research* 10(1): 17–31. https://doi.org/10.2478/ijmbr-2021-0003.

Edlom, J. & J. Karlsson (2021b). "Keep the Fire Burning: Exploring the Hierarchies of Music Fandom and the Motivations of Superfans". *Media and Communication* 9(3): 123–32. https://doi.org/10.17645/mac.v9i3.4013.

Eisenmann, T., G. Parker & M. Van Alstyne (2011). "Platform Envelopment". *Strategic Management Journal* 32(12): 1270–85. https://doi.org/10.1002/smj.935.

Elkin-Koren, N., Y. Nahmias & M. Perel (2020). "Is It Time to Abolish Safe Harbor? When Rhetoric Clouds Policy Goals". *Stanford Law & Policy Review* 31(1): 1–50.

Elliot, L. (2024). "Taylor Swift Hotel Demand Helps Keep UK Inflation at 2%". *The Guardian*, 17 July. https://www.theguardian.com/business/article/2024/jul/17/uk-headline-inflation-rate-remains-unchanged-at-2.

Elsden, C., C. Speed & D. Murray-Rust (2024). "Decentralised Creative Economies and Transactional Creative Communities". In: M. Terras *et al.* (eds), *Data-Driven Innovation in the Creative Industries*, 176–95. Abingdon: Routledge.

Eriksson, M. *et al.* (2019). *Spotify Teardown: Inside the Black Box of Streaming Music*. Cambridge, MA: MIT Press.

Es, K. van (2017). *The Future of Live*. Cambridge: Polity.

Fairchild, C. (2015). "Crowds, Clouds, and Idols: New Dynamics and Old Agendas in the Music Industry, 1982–2012". *American Music* 33(4): 441–76. https://doi.org/10.5406/americanmusic.33.4.0441.

Forde, E. (2016). "Anatomy of a Catastrophe: The Fall of Crowdmix". MusicAlly blog. https://musically.com/2016/08/05/anatomy-of-a-catastrophe-the-fall-of-crowdmix/.

Forde, E. (2024). *1999: The Year the Record Industry Lost Control*. London: Omnibus.

Frankenberg, E. (2023). "Billboard Boxscore Top 10 Tours of All Time: Beyonce Breaks Ground". Billboard blog, 13 October. https://www.billboard.com/lists/billboard-boxscore-top-10-tours-all-time-elton-john-harry-styles/coldplay-a-head-full-of-dreams-tour-2016-17/.

Freeman, S., M. Gibbs & B. Nansen (2023). "Stories and Data: Australian Musicians Navigating the *Spotify for Artists* Platform". *Popular Music and Society*, November, 1–23. https://doi.org/10.1080/03007766.2023.2286569.

Frenette, A. 2016. "'Working at the Candy Factory': The Limits of Nonmonetary Rewards in Record Industry Careers". In B. Hracs, M. Seaman & T. Virani (eds), *The Production and Consumption of Music in the Digital Age*, 85–98. Abingdon: Routledge.

Frenneaux, R. (2023). "The Rise of Independent Artists and the Paradox of Democratisation in the Digital Age: Challenges Faced by Music Artists in the New Music Industry". *DIY, Alternative Cultures & Society* 1(2): 125–37. https://doi.org/10.1177/27538702231174200.

Frenneaux, R. & A. Bennett (2021). "A New Paradigm of Engagement for the Socially Distanced Artist". *Rock Music Studies* 8(1): 65–75. https://doi.org/10.1080/19401159.2020.1852770.

Fuchs, C. (2015). *Culture and Economy in the Age of Social Media*. New York: Routledge.

Fumagalli, A. *et al.* (2018). "Digital Labour in the Platform Economy: The Case of Facebook". *Sustainability* 10(6): 1757. https://doi.org/10.3390/su10061757.

Galuszka, P. & T. Legiedz (2024). "Financialization of Music: Song Management Firms and Fractionalized Copyright". *Information, Communication & Society*, 1–17. https://doi.org/10.1080/1369118X.2024.2317903.

Gamble, J., M. Brennan & R. McAdam (2017). "A Rewarding Experience? Exploring How Crowdfunding Is Affecting Music Industry Business Models". *Journal of Business Research* 70: 25–36. https://doi.org/10.1016/j.jbusres.2016.07.009.

Garofalo, R. (1999). "From Music Publishing to MP3: Music and Industry in the Twentieth Century". *American Music* 17(3): 318. https://doi.org/10.2307/3052666.

Gee, K. & P. Yeow (2021). "A Hard Day"s Night: Building Sustainable Careers for Musicians". *Cultural Trends* 30(4): 338–54. https://doi.org/10.1080/09548963.2021.1941776.

Gerken, T. (2024). "TikTok and Universal Settle Music Royalties Dispute". BBC News, 2 May. https://www.bbc.co.uk/news/articles/cll4ggr8re1o.

Geurts, A. & K. Cepa (2023). "Transforming the Music Industry: How Platformization Drives Business Ecosystem Envelopment". *Long Range Planning* 56(4): 102327. https://doi.org/10.1016/j.lrp.2023.102327.

Goldman Sachs (2023). "Music Streaming Services Are on the Cusp of Major Structural Change". 31 July. https://www.goldmansachs.com/intelligence/page/music-streaming-services-are-on-the-cusp-of-major-structural-change.html.

Gorman, F. (2024). "The Sandbox Guide to Marketing to Superfans". MusicAlly. https:// musically.com/wp-content/uploads/2023/01/Sandbox311-200402.pdf.

Graham, G. *et al.* (2004). "The Transformation of the Music Industry Supply Chain: A Major Label Perspective". *International Journal of Operations & Production Management* 24(11): 1087–1103. https://doi.org/10.1108/01443570410563241.

Gross, S.-A. & G. Musgrave (2020). *Can Music Make You Sick? Measuring the Price of Musical Ambition.* London: University of Westminster Press.

Gu, X., N. Domer & J. O'Connor (2020). "The Next Normal: Chinese Indie Music in a Post-COVID China". *Cultural Trends* 30(1): 63–74. https://doi.org/10.1080/09548963. 2020.1846122.

Guyer, J. (2016). *Legacies, Logics, Logistics: Essays in the Anthropology of the Platform Economy.* Chicago, IL: University of Chicago Press.

Hagen, A. (2022). "Datafication, Literacy, and Democratization in the Music Industry". *Popular Music and Society* 45(2): 184–201. https://doi.org/10.1080/03007766.2021. 1989558.

Halgamuge, M. & D. Guruge (2022). "Fair Rewarding Mechanism in Music Industry Using Smart Contracts on Public-Permissionless Blockchain". *Multimedia Tools and Applications* 81(2): 1523–44. https://doi.org/10.1007/s11042-021-11078-6.

Hardjono, Thomas and Alex Pentland. (2019). "Empowering artists, songwriters & musicians in a data cooperative through blockchains and smart contracts". arXiv:1911.10433. https://doi.org/10.48550/arXiv.1911.10433

Harrigan, P. *et al.* (2021). "Identifying Influencers on Social Media". *International Journal of Information Management* 56 (Feb): 102246. https://doi.org/10.1016/j.ijinfomgt. 2020.102246.

Harris, R. (2013). *Easy Money? The Definitive UK Guide to Funding Music Projects.* Remi Harris Consulting.

Haynes, J. & L. Marshall (2018). "Beats and Tweets: Social Media in the Careers of Independent Musicians". *New Media & Society* 20(5): 1973–93. https://doi.org/10. 1177/1461444817711404.

Hendrikse, R., D. Bassens & M. Van Meeteren (2018). "The Appleization of Finance: Charting Incumbent Finance's Embrace of FinTech". *Finance and Society* 4(2): 159–80. https://doi.org/10.2218/finsoc.v4i2.2870.

Hendrikse, R., M. Van Meeteren & D. Bassens (2020). "Strategic Coupling between Finance, Technology and the State: Cultivating a Fintech Ecosystem for Incumbent Finance". *Environment and Planning A: Economy and Space* 52(8): 1516–38. https:// doi.org/10.1177/0308518X19887967.

Hepworth, D. (2024). *Hope I Get Old Before I Die: Why Rock Stars Never Retire.* London: Penguin.

Herlihy, D. & Y. Zhang (2016). "Music industry and copyright protection in the United States and China". *Global Media and China* 1(4): 390–400. https://doi.org/ 10.1177/2059436417698061.

Hesmondhalgh, D. (1997). "Post-Punk's Attempt to Democratise the Music Industry: The Success and Failure of Rough Trade". *Popular Music* 16(3): 255–74. https://doi. org/10.1017/S0261143000008400.

Hesmondhalgh, D. (2019). "Have Digital Communication Technologies Democratized the Media Industries?" In J. Curran & D. Hesmondhalgh (eds), *Media and Society*, 101–20. London: Bloomsbury Academic.

Hesmondhalgh, D. (2021). "Is Music Streaming Bad for Musicians? Problems of Evidence and Argument". *New Media & Society* 23(12): 3593–615. https://doi.org/10.1177/1461444820953541.

Hesmondhalgh, D. & L. Meier (2018). "What the Digitalisation of Music Tells us about Capitalism, Culture and the Power of the Information Technology Sector". *Information, Communication & Society* 21(11): 1555–70. https://doi.org/10.1080/1369118X.2017.1340498.

Hesmondhalgh, D. *et al.* (2021). "Music Creators' Earnings in the Digital Era". Intellectual Property Office.

Hetherington, K. (1998). *Expressions of Identity: Space, Performance, Politics*. London: Sage.

Hochschild, A. (2012). *The Managed Heart: Commercialization of Human Feeling*. Updated edition. Berkeley, CA: University of California Press.

Hodgkinson, W. (2024). "Is There a Future for Bands? Why I Fear for Rock'n'roll, by Our Music Critic". *The Times*, 29 February. https://www.thetimes.co.uk/article/493648dc-766d-499e-b6c6-e4b5245c2394?shareToken=56bc2b6f44b21fb92e74b94d695ac5c0.

Hodgson, T. (2020). "Quantifying Music: Imagined Metrics in Digital Startup Culture". *Culture, Theory and Critique* 61(4): 424–39. https://doi.org/10.1080/14735784.2021.1894961.

Hodgson, T. (2021). "Spotify and the Democratisation of Music". *Popular Music* 40(1): 1–17. https://doi.org/10.1017/S0261143021000064.

Hoedemaekers, C. (2018). "Creative Work and Affect: Social, Political and Fantasmatic Dynamics in the Labour of Musicians". *Human Relations* 71(10): 1348–70. https://doi.org/10.1177/0018726717741355.

House of Commons Digital, Culture, Media and Sport Committee (2020). "Impact of COVID-19 on DCMS Sectors: First Report". London: House of Commons.

Howard, G. (2015). "Canary In A Coalmine: From Internet of Things to VR to Blockchain: How Music Guides Other Industries". *Forbes*, 31 December. https://www.forbes.com/sites/georgehoward/2015/12/31/canary-in-a-coalmine-from-internet-of-things-to-vr-to-blockchain-how-music-guides-other-industries/.

Howard, G. (2018). "Canary In A Coal Mine: How Streaming Music Presages The End Of Ownership ... Of Everything". *Forbes*, 8 March. https://www.forbes.com/sites/georgehoward/2018/03/08/canary-in-a-coal-mine-how-streaming-music-presages-the-end-of-ownership-of-everything/.

Hracs, B. (2015). "Cultural Intermediaries in the Digital Age: The Case of Independent Musicians and Managers in Toronto". *Regional Studies* 49(3): 461–75. https://doi.org/10.1080/00343404.2012.750425.

Hracs, B. & D. Leslie (2014). "Aesthetic Labour in Creative Industries: The Case of Independent Musicians in Toronto, Canada". *Area* 46(1): 66–73. https://doi.org/10.1111/area.12062.

Hracs, B. & J. Webster (2021). "From Selling Songs to Engineering Experiences: Exploring the Competitive Strategies of Music Streaming Platforms". *Journal of Cultural Economy* 14(2): 240–57. https://doi.org/10.1080/17530350.2020.1819374.

Hyrynsalmi, S., M. Rantanen & S. Hyrynsalmi (2021). "The War for Talent in Software Business – How Are Finnish Software Companies Perceiving and Coping with the Labor Shortage?" In *2021 IEEE International Conference on Engineering, Technology and Innovation (ICE/ITMC)*, 1–10. Cardiff: IEEE. https://doi.org/10.1109/ICE/ITMC52061.2021.9570207.

IFPI (2017). "Global Music Report 2017 – State of the Industry". https://www.musikindustrie.de/fileadmin/bvmi/upload/06_Publikationen/GMR/GMR2017_press.pdf.

IFPI (2018). "Joint Music Sector Statement – YouTube's Fact-Free Fear-Mongering". 21 November. https://www.ifpi.org/joint-music-sector-statement-youtubes-fact-free-fear-mongering/.

IFPI (2023). "Global Music Report 2023 – State of the Industry". https://ifpi-website-cms.s3.eu-west-2.amazonaws.com/GMR_2023_State_of_the_Industry_ee2ea600e2.pdf.

IFPI (2025). "Global Music Report". https://globalmusicreport.ifpi.org/.

Ingham, T. (2017). "Kobalt Capital Raises $600M Fund to Spend on Buying Music Copyrights". Music Business Worldwide blog, 6 November. https://www.musicbusinessworldwide.com/kobalt-capital-raises-600m-to-spend-on-buying-copyrights/.

Ingham, T. (2024). "Done Deal: Blackstone Is the New Owner of Hipgnosis Songs Fund, as Investment Giant's Bid Wins Shareholder Approval". Music Business Worldwide, 9 June. https://www.musicbusinessworldwide.com/done-deal-blackstone-the-new-owner-of-hipgnosis-songs-fund-as-investment-giants-bid-wins-shareholder-approval/.

Jirásek, M. (2023). "The Fallacy of Decentralised Autonomous Organisations: Decentralised in Name Only? *Internet Policy Review*, 13 March; no pagination.

Johnson, M. & J. Woodcock (2019a). "'And Today's Top Donator Is': How Live Streamers on Twitch.Tv Monetize and Gamify Their Broadcasts". *Social Media + Society* 5(4): 205630511988169. https://doi.org/10.1177/2056305119881694.

Johnson, Mark R, and Jamie Woodcock. (2019b). "The Impacts of Live Streaming and Twitch.Tv on the Video Game Industry". *Media, Culture & Society* 41 (5): 670–88. https://doi.org/10.1177/0163443718818363.

Jones, E. (2020). "What Does Facebook 'Afford' Do-It-Yourself Musicians? Considering Social Media Affordances as Sites of Contestation". *Media, Culture & Society* 42(2): 277–92. https://doi.org/10.1177/0163443719853498.

Jones, E. (2021). *DIY Music and the Politics of Social Media*. New York: Bloomsbury Academic.

Joven, J. (2018). "Measuring Attention on Spotify Playlists: Followers vs. Listeners". https://hmc.chartmetric.com/measuring-attention-on-spotify-playlists-followers-vs-listeners/#:~:text=That%2C%20very%20generally%20speaking%2C%20any,as%20a%20rule%20of%20thumb.

Kenney, M. & J. Zysman (2020). "COVID-19 and the Increasing Centrality and Power of Platforms in China, the US, and Beyond". *Management and Organization Review* 16(4): 747–52. https://doi.org/10.1017/mor.2020.48.

Kiberg, H. (2023). "(Plat)Formatted Creativity: Creating Music in the Age of Streaming". *Cultural Sociology* (Oct): 17499755231202055. https://doi.org/10.1177/17499 755231202055.

King, A. (2022). "A New Study Confirms the Obvious: Major Labels Control Spotify Playlists". Digital Music News blog, 4 May. https://www.digitalmusicnews.com/2022/ 05/04/spotify-playlist-study-major-labels/.

Kirui, A. (2024). "Digital Literacy for Musicians: Navigating Music Streaming Services for Independent Artists in Kenya". *Journal of Music and Creative Arts (JMCA)* 3(1): 10–22. https://doi.org/10.51317/jmca.v3i1.479.

Kiss, C. & M. Bichler (2008). "Identification of Influencers – Measuring Influence in Customer Networks". *Decision Support Systems* 46(1): 233–53. https://doi.org/10. 1016/j.dss.2008.06.007.

Kjus, Y. (2016). "Musical Exploration via Streaming Services: The Norwegian Experience". *Popular Communication* 14(3): 127–36. https://doi.org/10.1080/15405702.2016. 1193183.

Kjus, Y. (2022a). "License to Stream? A Study of How Rights-Holders Have Responded to Music Streaming Services in Norway". *International Journal of Cultural Policy* 28(1): 61–73. https://doi.org/10.1080/10286632.2021.1908276.

Kjus, Y. (2022b). "Twists and Turns in the 360 Deal: Spinning the Risks and Rewards of Artist–Label Relations in the Streaming Era". *European Journal of Cultural Studies* 25(2): 463–78. https://doi.org/10.1177/13675494211044731.

Klein, B., L. Meier & D. Powers (2017). "Selling Out: Musicians, Autonomy, and Compromise in the Digital Age". *Popular Music and Society* 40(2): 222–38. https:// doi.org/10.1080/03007766.2015.1120101.

Knopper, S. (2009). *Appetite for Self-Destruction: The Spectacular Crash of the Record Industry in the Digital Age*. London: Simon & Schuster.

Kobalt (2021). "Kobalt Capital Chooses KKR And Dundee Partners To Buy Fund II". 19 October. https://www.kobaltmusic.com/press/kkr-purchases-kobalt-capitals-fund-ii-music-rights-portfolio-for-approximately-11-billion/.

Kribs, K. (2017). "The Artist-as-Intermediary: Musician Labour in the Digitally Networked Era". *eTopia*, April. https://doi.org/10.25071/1718-4657.36768.

Krueger, A. (2005). "The Economics of Real Superstars: The Market for Rock Concerts in the Material World". *Journal of Labor Economics* 23(1): 1–30. https://doi.org/ 10.1086/425431.

Krueger, A. (2019). *Rockonomics: A Backstage Tour of What the Music Industry Can Teach Us about Economics and Life*. New York: Currency.

Kuenssberg, L. (2025). "Paul McCartney: Don't let AI rip off artists". BBC News, 25 January. https://www.bbc.co.uk/news/articles/c8xqv9g8442o.

Lage, O., M. Saiz-Santos & J. Manuel Zarzuelo (2022). "Decentralized Platform Economy: Emerging Blockchain-Based Decentralized Platform Business Models". *Electronic Markets* 32(3): 1707–23. https://doi.org/10.1007/s12525-022-00586-4.

Langley, P. & A. Leyshon (2017). "Platform Capitalism: The Intermediation and Capitalisation of Digital Economic Circulation". *Finance and Society* 3(1): 11–31. https://doi.org/10.2218/finsoc.v3i1.1936.

Langley, P. & A. Leyshon (2021). "The Platform Political Economy of FinTech: Reintermediation, Consolidation and Capitalisation". *New Political Economy* 26(3): 376–88. https://doi.org/10.1080/13563467.2020.1766432.

Lee, B. (2024). "Chappell Roan Cancels US Festival Appearance: 'Things Have Gotten Really Overwhelming'". *The Guardian*, 27 September. https://www.theguardian.com/music/2024/sep/27/chappell-roan-cancels-us-festival#:~:text=%E2%80%9CThings%20have%20gotten%20overwhelming%20over,Thank%20you%20for%20understanding.

Lee, P. (2022). "Enhancing the Innovative Capacity of Venture Capital". *Yale Journal of Law and Technology* 24: 611–705.

Leenders, M. *et al.* (2015). "How Are Young Music Artists Configuring Their Media and Sales Platforms in the Digital Age?" *Journal of Marketing Management* 31(17/18): 1799–817. https://doi.org/10.1080/0267257X.2015.1034158.

Leight, E. & C. Stutz (2023). "Everything to Know About Spotify's New Royalties Model: How Does It Work & Who Will It Impact?" Billboard, 20 November. https://www.billboard.com/business/streaming/spotify-new-royalties-model-explained-how-work-1235501887/.

Lewis, M. (2002). *Next: The Future Just Happened.* New York: Norton.

Leyshon, A. (2001). "Time–Space (and Digital) Compression: Software Formats, Musical Networks, and the Reorganisation of the Music Industry". *Environment and Planning A: Economy and Space* 33(1): 49–77. https://doi.org/10.1068/a3360.

Leyshon, A. (2003). "Scary Monsters? Software Formats, Peer-to-Peer Networks, and the Spectre of the Gift". *Environment and Planning D: Society and Space* 21(5): 533–58. https://doi.org/10.1068/d48j.

Leyshon, A. (2014). *Reformatted: Code, Networks, and the Transformation of the Music Industry.* Oxford: Oxford University Press.

Leyshon, A. (2023). "Economic Geography II: The Economic Geographies of the COVID-19 Pandemic". *Progress in Human Geography* 47(2): 353–64. https://doi.org/10.1177/03091325231156926.

Leyshon, A. & N. Thrift (2007). "The Capitalization of Almost Everything: The Future of Finance and Capitalism". *Theory, Culture & Society* 24(7/8): 97–115. https://doi.org/10.1177/0263276407084699.

Leyshon, A. *et al.* (2005). "On the Reproduction of the Musical Economy after the Internet". *Media, Culture & Society* 27(2): 177–209. https://doi.org/10.1177/0163443705050468.

Li, L. (2022). "Artificial Intelligence: An Earthquake in Copyright Protection of the Digital Music". In D. Bielicki (ed.), *Regulating Artificial Intelligence in Industry*. Abingdon: Routledge.

Liang, Y., J. Aroles & B. Brandl (2022). "Charting Platform Capitalism: Definitions, Concepts and Ideologies". *New Technology, Work and Employment* 37(2): 308–27. https://doi.org/10.1111/ntwe.12234.

Lindvall, H. (2012). "Amanda Palmer Raised $1.2m, but Is She Really 'the Future of Music'?" *The Guardian*, 26 September. http://www.theguardian.com/media/2012/sep/26/amanda-palmer-future-of-music.

Lotz, A. (2021). *Media Disrupted: Surviving Pirates, Cannibals, and Streaming Wars.* Cambridge, MA: MIT Press.

Loveday, C., G. Musgrave & S.-A. Gross (2023). "Predicting Anxiety, Depression, and Wellbeing in Professional and Nonprofessional Musicians". *Psychology of Music* 51(2): 508–22. https://doi.org/10.1177/03057356221096506.

Lundman, R. & P. Nordström (2023). "Creative Geographies in the Age of AI: Co-creative Spatiality and the Emerging Techno-material Relations Between Artists and Artificial Intelligence". *Transactions of the Institute of British Geographers* 48: 650–64. https://doi.org/10.1111/tran.12608.

Maasø, A. & A. Hagen (2020). "Metrics and Decision-Making in Music Streaming". *Popular Communication* 18(1): 18–31. https://doi.org/10.1080/15405702.2019.1701675.

Maffesoli, M. (1996). *The Time of the Tribes: The Decline of Individualism in Mass Society.* London: Sage.

Magaudda, P. & M. Solaroli (2021). "Platform Studies and Digital Cultural Industries". *Sociologica* 14(3): 267–93. https://doi.org/10.6092/ISSN.1971-8853/11957.

Mallaby, S. (2023). *Power Law: Venture Capital and the Art of Disruption.* London: Penguin.

Mao, E. (2022). "The Effectiveness of Event Marketing in an Attention Economy: Findings from Twitch Live-Stream Esports Tournament Events". *Journal of Media Economics* 34(3): 194–211. https://doi.org/10.1080/08997764.2022.2115503.

Marshall, L. (2013). "The 360 Deal and the 'New' Music Industry". *European Journal of Cultural Studies* 16(1): 77–99. https://doi.org/10.1177/1367549412457478.

Marshall, L. (2015). "'Let's Keep Music Special. F—Spotify': On-Demand Streaming and the Controversy over Artist Royalties". *Creative Industries Journal* 8(2): 177–89. https://doi.org/10.1080/17510694.2015.1096618.

Marshall, L. (2019). "Do People Value Recorded Music?" *Cultural Sociology* 13(2): 141–58. https://doi.org/10.1177/1749975519839524.

Marshall, L. & S. Frith (2004). *Music and Copyright.* Second edition. New York: Routledge.

Martin, B. (2024). "Why Did This Guy Put a Song about Me on Spotify?" *New York Times Magazine*, 31 March. https://www.nytimes.com/2024/03/31/magazine/spotify-matt-farley.html?smid=nytcore-ios-share&referringSource=articleShare&sgrp=c-cb.

Martin, C. (2016). "The Sharing Economy: A Pathway to Sustainability or a Nightmarish Form of Neoliberal Capitalism?" *Ecological Economics* 121 (Jan): 149–59. https://doi.org/10.1016/j.ecolecon.2015.11.027.

McCourt, T. & P. Burkart (2003). "When Creators, Corporations and Consumers Collide: Napster and the Development of On-Line Music Distribution". *Media, Culture & Society* 25(3): 333–50. https://doi.org/10.1177/0163443703025003003.

McCrum, D. (2016). "A Short History of the Bowie Bond". *Financial Times*, 11 January. https://www.ft.com/content/6b4839dd-0539-34c4-bb1d-0edf95255d72.

McIntyre, D. & A. Srinivasan (2017). "Networks, Platforms, and Strategy: Emerging Views and Next Steps". *Strategic Management Journal* 38(1): 141–60. https://doi.org/10.1002/smj.2596.

McIntyre, H. (2024). "Queen Makes History As They Sell Their Catalog For More Than $1 Billion". *Forbes*, 20 June. https://www.forbes.com/sites/hughmcintyre/2024/06/20/queen-makes-history-as-they-sell-their-catalog-for-more-than-1-billion/.

McLeod, K. (2005). "MP3s Are Killing Home Taping: The Rise of Internet Distribution and Its Challenge to the Major Label Music Monopoly". *Popular Music and Society* 28(4): 521–31. https://doi.org/10.1080/03007760500159062.

Meier, L. (2015). "Popular Music Making and Promotional Work inside the 'New' Music Industry". In K. Oakley & J. O'Connor (eds), *Routledge Companion to the Cultural Industries*, 402–12. Abingdon: Routledge.

Meier, L. & V. Manzerolle (2019). "Rising Tides? Data Capture, Platform Accumulation, and New Monopolies in the Digital Music Economy". *New Media & Society* 21(3): 543–61. https://doi.org/10.1177/1461444818800998.

Mensah, J. (2024) "The Pretenders' Chrissie Hynde apologises to fans over her smartphone gripes". Radio X, 19 December. https://www.radiox.co.uk/news/music/the-pretenders-chrissie-hynde-apologises-over-phones-front-row-gig-goers/.

Meyn, J. *et al.* (2023). "Consequences of Platforms' Remuneration Models for Digital Content: Initial Evidence and a Research Agenda for Streaming Services". *Journal of the Academy of Marketing Science* 51(1): 114–31. https://doi.org/10.1007/s11747-022-00875-6.

Mier, T. (2024). "Chappell Roan Cancels All Things Go Fest Shows to 'Prioritize My Health'". *Rolling Stone*, September. https://www.rollingstone.com/music/music-news/chappell-roan-cancels-all-things-go-shows-prioritize-health-1235114446/.

Mitra, M. (2024). "Swiftonomics: The Economic Influence of Taylor Swift". Investopedia, 8 March. https://www.investopedia.com/swiftonomics-definition-8601178.

Montgomery, L. & J. Potts (2009). "Does Weaker Copyright Mean Stronger Creative Industries? Some Lessons from China". *Creative Industries Journal* 1(3): 245–61. https://doi.org/10.1386/cij.1.3.245_1.

Moody, G. (2002). *The Rebel Code: The Inside Story of Linux and the Open Source Revolution*. Cambridge, MA: Perseus Publishing.

Morgan, G. & J. Wood (2014). "Creative Accommodations: The Fractured Transitions and Precarious Lives of Young Musicians". *Journal of Cultural Economy* 7(1): 64–78. https://doi.org/10.1080/17530350.2013.855646.

Morgan Stanley (2023). "Kobalt Partners with Morgan Stanley Tactical Value to Invest More Than $700 Million In Music Copyrights". 1 November. https://www.morganstanley.com/im/en-us/individual-investor/about-us/newsroom/press-release/kobalt-partners-with-mstv-to-invest-more-than-700-million-in-music-copyrights.html.

Morris, J. (2014). "Artists as Entrepreneurs, Fans as Workers". *Popular Music and Society* 37(3): 273–90. https://doi.org/10.1080/03007766.2013.778534.

Morris, J. (2015). *Selling Digital Music, Formatting Culture*. Oakland, CA: University of California Press.

Morris, J. (2020). "Music Platforms and the Optimization of Culture". *Social Media + Society* 6(3): 205630512094069. https://doi.org/10.1177/2056305120940690.

Morris, J., R. Prey & D. Nieborg (2021). "Engineering Culture: Logics of Optimization in Music, Games, and Apps". *Review of Communication* 21(2): 161–75. https://doi.org/10.1080/15358593.2021.1934522.

Morrow, G. (2018). "Distributed Agility: Artist Co-Management in the Music Attention Economy". *International Journal of Arts Management* 20(3): 38–48.

Morrow, G. & F. Li (2016). "The Chinese Music Industries: Top Down in the Bottom-up Age". In P. Wikström & R.t DeFillippi (eds), *Business Innovation and Disruption in the Music Industry*, 133–50. Cheltenham: Edward Elgar.

Moskowitz, D. & S. Hershberger (2012). *Modeling Intraindividual Variability with Repeated Measures Data: Methods and Applications*. New York: Psychology Press.

Mulligan, M. & K. Jopling 2019. "Independent Artists: The Age of Empowerment". MIDiA Research/Amuse. https://www.midiaresearch.com/blog/independent-artists-the-age-of-empowerment.

Murphy, S. & M. Hume (2022). "Market Readiness for the Digital Music Industries: A Case Study of Independent Artists". In G. Morrow, D. Nordgård & P. Tschmuck (eds), *Rethinking the Music Business*, 215–37. Cham, CH: Springer.

Musgrave, G. (2023a). "Music and Wellbeing vs. Musicians' Wellbeing: Examining the Paradox of Music-Making Positively Impacting Wellbeing, but Musicians Suffering from Poor Mental Health". *Cultural Trends* 32(3): 280–95. https://doi.org/10.1080/09548963.2022.2058354.

Musgrave, G. (2023b). "Musicians, Their Relationships, and Their Wellbeing: Creative Labour, Relational Work". *Poetics* 96 (Feb): 101762. https://doi.org/10.1016/j.poetic.2023.101762.

Music Business Worldwide (2022). "Spotify Just Dropped a Stat That Changes Everything about How You Should Judge the Streaming Economy". Music Business Worldwide blog. https://www.musicbusinessworldwide.com/podcast/spotify-just-dropped-stat-changes-everything-about-how-we-should-judge-the-streaming-economy/.

MusicAlly (2019). "Fresh Start: Rightsholders Want to Nurture the next Generation of Inventive Music/Tech Startups – So How Well Are They Doing?" https://musically.com/wp-content/uploads/2019/08/Report-424-169704300.pdf.

Musicians' Union (2020). "Lobbying Update: SEISS and Furlough Extensions Confirmed". Musicians' Union blog, 28 April. https://musiciansunion.org.uk/news/lobbying-update-seiss-and-furlough-extensions-confirmed.

Musmann, H. (2006). "Genesis of the MP3 Audio Coding Standard". *IEEE Transactions on Consumer Electronics* 52(3): 1043–9. https://doi.org/10.1109/TCE.2006.1706505.

Naveed, K., C. Watanabe & P. Neittaanmäki (2017). "Co-Evolution between Streaming and Live Music Leads a Way to the Sustainable Growth of Music Industry – Lessons from the US Experiences". *Technology in Society* 50 (Aug): 1–19. https://doi.org/10.1016/j.techsoc.2017.03.005.

Negus, K. (2019). "From Creator to Data: The Post-Record Music Industry and the Digital Conglomerates". *Media, Culture & Society* 41(3): 367–84. https://doi.org/10.1177/0163443718799395.

Nickell, C. (2020). "Promises and Pitfalls: The Two-Faced Nature of Streaming and Social Media Platforms for Beirut-Based Independent Musicians". *Popular Communication* 18(1): 48–64. https://doi.org/10.1080/15405702.2019.1637523.

Nieborg, D. & T. Poell (2018). "The Platformization of Cultural Production: Theorizing the Contingent Cultural Commodity". *New Media & Society* 20(11): 4275–92. https://doi.org/10.1177/1461444818769694.

Nieborg, D., T. Poell & J. Van Dijck (2022). "Platforms and Platformization". In T. Flew, J. Holt & J. Thomas (eds), *The SAGE Handbook of the Digital Media Economy*, 29–49. London: Sage.

Nielsen, R. & S. Ganter (2022). *The Power of Platforms: Shaping Media and Society*. New York: Oxford University Press.

Nørholm Lundin, A. (2023). "'Where Is Your Fixed Point?' Dealing with Ambiguous Freelance Musician Careers". *Cultural Trends* 32(3): 231–46. https://doi.org/10.1080/09548963.2022.2075715.

O'Dair, M. & R. Owen (2019). "Financing New Creative Enterprise through Blockchain Technology: Opportunities and Policy Implications". *Strategic Change* 28(1): 9–17. https://doi.org/10.1002/jsc.2242.

O'Dair, M. *et al.* (2016). "Music On The Blockchain". Blockchain For Creative Industries Research Cluster, Middlesex University. http://austiny.snu.ac.kr/down/block/Music-On-The-Blockchain.pdf.

O'Dwyer, R. (2023). *Tokens: The Future of Money in the Age of the Platform*. London: Verso.

Ozimek, A. (2021). "Skills Shortages, Gaps and Training Needs in the Screen Industries in Yorkshire and the Humber: Scoping Report". https://screen-network.org.uk/wp-content/uploads/2021/03/Skills-shortages-gaps-and-training-needs-in-the-screen-industries-in-YH-report-January-2021.pdf.

Pagano, U. (2014). "The Crisis of Intellectual Monopoly Capitalism". *Cambridge Journal of Economics* 38(6): 1409–29. https://doi.org/10.1093/cje/beu025.

Page, W. (2020). "Streaming Is Stalling: Can Music Keep up in the Attention Economy?" Billboard. https://www.billboard.com/articles/business/9500546/streaming-music-growth-stalled-factors-attention-economy/.

Page, W. (2024). "Music smashes box office records: global value of music copyright soars to $45.5 billion, now worth more than cinema". *Pivotal Economics*, 25 November. https://pivotaleconomics.com/undercurrents/music-copyright-2023.

Paine, A. (2017). "Kobalt Capital Acquires Songs Music Publishing Catalogue". Music Week blog, 8 December. https://www.musicweek.com/publishing/read/kobalt-capital-acquires-songs-music-publishing-catalogue/070786.

Parales, J. (2002). "David Bowie, 21st-Century Entrepreneur". *New York Times*, 9 June. https://www.nytimes.com/2002/06/09/arts/david-bowie-21st-century-entrepreneur.html.

Parker, G., M. Van Alstyne & S. Choudary (2016). *Platform Revolution: How Networked Markets Are Transforming the Economy and How to Make Them Work for You*. New York: Norton.

Paterno, T. & L. Deneen (2024). "AI Threats Emerge In Music Publishers' Battle With Big Tech (Guest Column)". *The Hollywood Reporter*, 5 January. https://www.hollywood

reporter.com/business/business-news/ai-threats-music-publishers-big-tech-12357 67692/.

Patrickson, B. (2021). "What Do Blockchain Technologies Imply for Digital Creative Industries?" *Creativity and Innovation Management* 30(3): 585–95. https://doi.org/10.1111/caim.12456.

Peitz, M. & P. Waelbrock (2006). "Digital Music". In G. Illing & M. Peitz (eds), *Industrial Organization and the Digital Economy*. Cambridge, MA: MIT Press.

Peoples, G. (2023). "South Korea's Beyond Music Raises Another $170 Million for Catalog Acquisitions". Billboard, 6 May. https://www.billboard.com/pro/south-korean-investment-firm-beyond-music-raises-170m-buy-catalogs/.

Peters, J. (2023). "Downtown Music Publishing and Songtrust". *Entrepreneurship Education and Pedagogy* 6(1): 148–60. https://doi.org/10.1177/25151274211040418.

Poell, T. (2020). "Three Challenges for Media Studies in the Age of Platforms". *Television & New Media* 21(6): 650–57. https://doi.org/10.1177/1527476420918833.

Poell, T., D. Nieborg & J. Van Dijck (2019). "Platformisation". *Internet Policy Review* 8(4). https://doi.org/10.14763/2019.4.1425.

Polak, N. & J. Schaap (2024). "Write, Record, Optimize? How Musicians Reflect on Music Optimization Strategies in the Creative Production Process". *New Media & Society* (Apr): 14614448241243095. https://doi.org/10.1177/14614448241243095.

Potts, J. & E. Rennie (2019). "Web3 and the Creative Industries: How Blockchains Are Reshaping Business Models". In S. Cunningham & T. Flew (eds), *A Research Agenda for Creative Industries*, 93–111. Cheltenham: Edward Elgar.

Power, D. & D. Hallencreutz (2002). "Profiting from Creativity? The Music Industry in Stockholm, Sweden and Kingston, Jamaica". *Environment and Planning A: Economy and Space* 34(10): 1833–54. https://doi.org/10.1068/a3529.

Prey, R. (2018). "Nothing Personal: Algorithmic Individuation on Music Streaming Platforms". *Media, Culture & Society* 40(7): 1086–100. https://doi.org/10.1177/0163443717745147.

PRS for Music (2019). "UK Songwriters and Composers Generate a Record £746 m in Music Royalties". https://www.prsformusic.com/press/2019/uk-songwriters-generate-record–746m-music-royalties.

Pussinen, P., A. Wallin & J. Hemilä (2023). "The Hope of Exponential Growth – Systems Mapping Perspective on Birth of Platform Business". *Digital Business* 3(2): 100060. https://doi.org/10.1016/j.digbus.2023.100060.

Qu, S., D. Hesmondhalgh & J. Xiao (2023). "Music Streaming Platforms and Self-Releasing Musicians: The Case of China". *Information, Communication & Society* 26(4): 699–715. https://doi.org/10.1080/1369118X.2021.1971280.

Ramiro, A. & R. de Queiroz (2022). "Cypherpunk". *Internet Policy Review* 11(2): no pagination.

Rauchberg, J. (2022). "A Different Girl, but She's Nothing New: Olivia Rodrigo and Posting Imitation Pop on TikTok". *Feminist Media Studies* 22(5): 1290–94. https://doi.org/10.1080/14680777.2022.2093251.

Rendell, J. (2021). "Staying in, Rocking out: Online Live Music Portal Shows during the Coronavirus Pandemic". *Convergence: The International Journal of Research into New Media Technologies* 27(4): 1092–111. https://doi.org/10.1177/1354856520976451.

Rheingold, H. (2002). *Smart Mobs: The Next Social Revolution.* New York: Basic Books.

RIAA (2017). "Five Stubborn Truths About YouTube and The Value Gap". *Medium*, 18 August. https://riaa.medium.com/five-stubborn-truths-about-youtube-and-value-gap-4faff133271f.

Rigi, J. & R. Prey (2015). "Value, Rent, and the Political Economy of Social Media". *The Information Society* 31(5): 392–406. https://doi.org/10.1080/01972243.2015.1069769.

Riom, L. (2023). "(Un)Playing Music at Sofar Sounds: Some Elements of an Ethno(Methodo)Musicology of Live Performances". *Ethnomusicology Review* 24. https://ethnomusicologyreview.ucla.edu/journal/volume/24/piece/1098.

Rogers, R. (2018). "Otherwise Engaged: Social Media from Vanity Metrics to Critical Analytics". *International Journal of Communication* 12: 450–72.

Rosen, S. (1981). "The Economics of Superstars". *American Economic Review* 71: 845–58.

Sandvoss, C. (2005). *Fans: The Mirror of Consumption.* Cambridge: Polity.

Sargent, C. (2009). "Local Musicians Building Global Audiences: Social Capital and the Distribution of User-Created Content On- and Off-Line". *Information, Communication & Society* 12(4): 469–87. https://doi.org/10.1080/13691180902857660.

Savage, M. (2021). "Elvis Costello Defends Olivia Rodrigo over Brutal Plagiarism Claim". BBC News, 29 June. https://www.bbc.co.uk/news/entertainment-arts-57650176.

Sayer, A. (2007). "Moral Economy as Critique". *New Political Economy* 12(2): 261–70. https://doi.org/10.1080/13563460701303008.

Scharf, N. (2022). "The Evolution and Consequences of Digital Rights Management in Relation to Online Music Streaming". *Legal Studies* 42(1): 61–80. https://doi.org/10.1017/lst.2021.26.

Schechter, A. (2017). "Google Is as Close to a Natural Monopoly as the Bell System Was in 1956". ProMarket blog, 9 May. https://promarket.org/ 2017/05/09/google-close-natural-monopolybell-system-1956/.

Schneider, N. (2022). "Foreword: Practice Upwards". In R. Catlow & P. Rafferty (eds), *Radical Friends: Decentralised Autonomous Organisations & the Arts*, 20–23. Torgue Editions.

Scolere, L., U. Pruchniewska & B. Duffy (2018). "Constructing the Platform-Specific Self-Brand: The Labor of Social Media Promotion". *Social Media + Society* 4 (3): 2056305118784768. https://doi.org/10.1177/2056305118784768.

Scott, M. (2012). "Cultural Entrepreneurs, Cultural Entrepreneurship: Music Producers Mobilising and Converting Bourdieu's Alternative Capitals". *Poetics* 40(3): 237–55. https://doi.org/10.1016/j.poetic.2012.03.002.

Seabrook, J. (2024). "Inside the Music Industry's High-Stakes A.I. Experiments". *The New Yorker*, 29 January. https://www.newyorker.com/magazine/2024/02/05/inside-the-music-industrys-high-stakes-ai-experiments.

Semenzin, S. (2023). "'Blockchain for Good': Exploring the Notion of Social Good inside the Blockchain Scene". *Big Data & Society* 10(2): 20539517231205479. https://doi.org/10.1177/20539517231205479.

Shapiro, C. & H. Varian (1999). *Information Rules: A Strategic Guide to the Network Economy.* Boston, MA: Harvard Business School Press.

Siles, I. *et al.* (2022). "Playing Spotify's Game: Artists' Approaches to Playlisting in Latin America". *Journal of Cultural Economy* 15(5): 551–67. https://doi.org/10.1080/17530350.2022.2058061.

Simon, J. (2019). "New Players in the Music Industry: Lifeboats or Killer Whales? The Role of Streaming Platforms". *Digital Policy, Regulation and Governance* 21(6): 525–49. https://doi.org/10.1108/DPRG-06-2019-0041.

Singh, S. (2024) "The Pretenders' Chrissie Hynde doesn't want to see the same fans in the front row at multiple shows: 'Give local fans a chance'". *NME*, 18 October. https://www.nme.com/news/music/he-pretenders-chrissie-hynde-doesnt-want-to-see-the-same-fans-in-the-front-row-at-multiple-shows-give-local-fans-a-chance-3803931.

Sisario, B. (2024a). "Music Catalog Giant Hipgnosis Agrees to $1.4 Billion Sale to Concord". *New York Times*, 18 April. https://www.nytimes.com/2024/04/18/arts/music/hipgnosis-songs-fund-sell-concord.html.

Sisario, B. (2024b). "Music Catalog Giant Hipgnosis Is Sold, and Merck Mercuriadis Exits". *New York Times*, 9 June. https://www.nytimes.com/2024/07/09/arts/music/hipgnosis-sold-blackstone-merck-mercuriadis.html?searchResultPosition=3.

Sjöblom, M. *et al.* (2019). "The Ingredients of Twitch Streaming: Affordances of Game Streams". *Computers in Human Behavior* 92: 20–28. https://doi.org/10.1016/j.chb.2018.10.012.

Smith, D. (2024a). "European Parliament Passes Landmark AI Act – IFPI and Others Shift the Focus to 'Meaningful and Effective' Enforcement". *Digital Music News*, 13 March. https://www.digitalmusicnews.com/2024/03/13/ai-act-music-industry-response/.

Smith, D. (2024b). "Kobalt 'Funding Capacity' Tops $1 Billion Following Royalties-Backed Securitization 'Execution' and Refinancing". *Digital Music News*, 19 March. https://www.digitalmusicnews.com/2024/03/19/kobalt-funding-march-2024/.

Srnicek, N. (2016). *Platform Capitalism*. Cambridge: Polity.

Stahl, M. (2013). *Unfree Masters: Recording Artists and the Politics of Work*. Durham, NC: Duke University Press.

Stahl, M. & L. Meier (2012). "The Firm Foundation of Organizational Flexibility: The 360 Contract in the Digitalizing Music Industry". *Canadian Journal of Communication* 37(3): 441–58. https://doi.org/10.22230/cjc.2012v37n3a2544.

Stark, L. & K. Crawford (2019). "The Work of Art in the Age of Artificial Intelligence: What Artists Can Teach Us About the Ethics of Data Practice". *Surveillance and Society* 17(3/4): 442–55. https://doi.org/10.24908/ss.v17i3/4.10821.

Stassen, M. (2023). "There Are Now 120,000 New Tracks Hitting Music Streaming Services Each Day". Music Business Worldwide, 25 May. https://www.musicbusinessworldwide.com/there-are-now-120000-new-tracks-hitting-music-streaming-services-each-day/.

Stockholm Business Region (2016). "Stockholm – the Powerhouse of Sound: The Birthplace of MusicTech Innovation". Stockholm Business Region.

Strachan, R. (2007). "Micro-Independent Record Labels in the UK: Discourse, DIY Cultural Production and the Music Industry". *European Journal of Cultural Studies* 10(2): 245–65. https://doi.org/10.1177/1367549407075916.

Strauss, N. (1995). "Pennies That Add up to $16.98: Why CDs Cost so Much". *New York Times*, 5 June. https://www.nytimes.com/1995/07/05/arts/pennies-that-add-up-to-16.98-why-cd-s-cost-so-much.

Sturm, B. *et al.* (2019). "Artificial Intelligence and Music: Open Questions of Copyright Law and Engineering Praxis". *Arts* 8(3): 115. https://doi.org/10.3390/arts8030115.

Sun, H. (2019). "Paradox of Celestial Jukebox: Resurgence of Market Control". *Creative Industries Journal* 12(1): 105–24. https://doi.org/10.1080/17510694.2018.1554944.

Sundararajan, A. (2016). *The Sharing Economy: The End of Employment and the Rise of Crowd-Based Capitalism*. Cambridge, MA: MIT Press.

Tang, D. & R. Lyons (2016). "An Ecosystem Lens: Putting China's Digital Music Industry into Focus". *Global Media and China* 1(4): 350–71. https://doi.org/10.1177/2059436416685101.

Taplin, J. (2012). "The Band's Ex-Tour Manager Blasts Reddit Founder Alexi Ohanian, Kim Dotcom, The Kickstarter 'Begging Bowl'". Fast Company, 23 April. www.fastcompany.com/1834866/bands-ex-tour-manager-blasts-reddit-founder-alexis-ohanian-kim-dotcom-kickstarter-begging-bo.

Taplin, J. (2017). *Move Fast and Break Things: How Facebook, Google, and Amazon Cornered Culture and Undermined Democracy*. New York: Little, Brown.

Taylor, T. (2018). *Watch Me Play: Twitch and the Rise of Game Live Streaming*. Princeton, NJ: Princeton University Press.

Teipen, C. (2008). "Work and Employment in Creative Industries: The Video Games Industry in Germany, Sweden and Poland". *Economic and Industrial Democracy* 29(3): 309–35. https://doi.org/10.1177/0143831X08092459.

Tencer, D. (2025). "10,000 AI tracks uploaded daily to Deezer, platform reveals, as it files two patent for AI detection tool". Music Business Worldwide, 24 January. https://www.musicbusinessworldwide.com/10000-ai-tracks-are-uploaded-daily-to-deezer-platform-reveals-as-it-files-two-patents-for-new-ai-detection-tool/.

Tessler, H. & M. Flynn (2016). "From DIY to D2F: Contextualizing Entrepreneurship for the Artist/Musician". In A. Dumbreck & G. McPherson (eds), *Music Entrepreneurship*, 47–74. London: Bloomsbury.

Théberge, P. (2006). "Everyday Fandom: Fan Clubs, Blogging, and the Quotidian Rhythms of the Internet". *Canadian Journal of Communication* 30(4): 485–502. https://doi.org/10.22230/cjc.2005v30n4a1673.

Thomas, D. (2024). "Hipgnosis Cuts Value of Music Portfolio by over a Quarter". *Financial Times*, 4 March. https://www.ft.com/content/030cf28e-3ba9-4ffb-b3f1-70bfce9176cd.

Thomes, T. (2013). "An economic analysis of online streaming music services". *Information Economics and Policy* 25(2): 81–91. https://doi.org/10.1016/j.infoecopol.2013.04.001.

Threadgold, S. (2018). "Creativity, Precarity and Illusio: DIY Cultures and 'Choosing Poverty'". *Cultural Sociology* 12(2): 156–73. https://doi.org/10.1177/1749975517722475.

Tooze, A. (2021). *Shutdown: How Covid Shook the World's Economy*. London: Allen Lane.

Towse, R. (2011). *A Textbook of Cultural Economics*. Cambridge: Cambridge University Press.

Towse, R. (2020). "Dealing with Digital: The Economic Organisation of Streamed Music". *Media, Culture & Society* 42(7/8): 1461–78. https://doi.org/10.1177/01634437209 19376.

Truby, J. (2020). "Fintech and the City: Sandbox 2.0 Policy and Regulatory Reform Proposals". *International Review of Law, Computers & Technology* 34(3): 277–309. https://doi.org/10.1080/13600869.2018.1546542.

Tschmuck, P. (2017). *The Economics of Music*. Newcastle upon Tyne: Agenda Publishing.

Turchet, L. (2023). "Musical Metaverse: Vision, Opportunities, and Challenges". *Personal and Ubiquitous Computing* 27(5): 1811–27. https://doi.org/10.1007/s00779-023-01708-1.

Umney, C. & L. Kretsos (2015). "'That's the Experience': Passion, Work Precarity, and Life Transitions Among London Jazz Musicians". *Work and Occupations* 42(3): 313–34. https://doi.org/10.1177/0730888415573634.

Vandenberg, F. (2022). "Put Your 'Hand Emotes in the Air': Twitch Concerts as Unsuccessful Large-Scale Interaction Rituals". *Symbolic Interaction* 45(3): 425–48. https://doi.org/10.1002/symb.605.

Vandenberg, F., M. Berghman & J. Schaap (2021). "The 'Lonely Raver': Music Livestreams during COVID-19 as a Hotline to Collective Consciousness?" *European Societies* 23 (sup1): S141–52. https://doi.org/10.1080/14616696.2020.1818271.

Verboord, M. & S. Van Noord (2016). "The Online Place of Popular Music: Exploring the Impact of Geography and Social Media on Pop Artists' Mainstream Media Attention". *Popular Communication* 14(2): 59–72. https://doi.org/10.1080/15405702.2015.1019073.

Vonderau, P. (2019). "The Spotify Effect: Digital Distribution and Financial Growth". *Television & New Media* 20(1): 3–19. https://doi.org/10.1177/1527476417741200.

Voshmgir, S. (2020). *Token Economy: How the Web3 Reinvents the Internet*. Second edition. Token Kitchen.

Wallis, R. (2006). "The Changing Structure of the Music Industry". In S. Brown & U. Volgsten (eds), *Music and Manipulation: On the Social Uses and Social Control of Music*, 287–311. Oxford: Berghann.

Walzer, D. (2017). "Independent Music Production: How Individuality, Technology and Creative Entrepreneurship Influence Contemporary Music Industry Practices". *Creative Industries Journal* 10(1): 21–39. https://doi.org/10.1080/17510694.2016.1247626.

Watson, A. (2008). "Global Music City: Knowledge and Geographical Proximity in London's Recorded Music Industry". *Area* 40(1): 12–23. https://doi.org/10.1111/j.1475-4762.2008.00793.x.

Watson, A. (2014). *Cultural Production In and Beyond the Recording Studio*. Abingdon: Routledge.

Watson, A. (2016). "Digital Disruption and Recording Studio Diversification: Changing Business Models for the Digital Age". In P. Wikström & R. DeFillippi (eds), *Business Innovation and Disruption in the Music Industry*. Cheltenham: Edward Elgar.

Watson, A. & J. Beaverstock (2016). "Transnational Freelancing: Ephemeral Creative Projects and Mobility in the Music Recording Industry". *Environment and Planning A: Economy and Space* 48(7): 1428–46. https://doi.org/10.1177/0308518X16641412.

Weber, S. (2004). *The Success of Open Source*. Cambridge, MA: Harvard University Press.

White, A. (2023). "The DCMS Committee's Inquiry on the Economics of Music Streaming and Its Implications for Artists". *Cultural Trends* 32(3): 325–39. https://doi.org/10.1080/09548963.2022.2156267.

Wikström, P. (2009). "The Adaptive Behavior of Music Firms: A Music Industry Feedback Model". *Journal of Media Business Studies* 6(2): 67–96. https://doi.org/10.1080/16522354.2009.11073485.

Wikström, P. (2020). *The Music Industry: Music in the Cloud*. Third edition. Cambridge: Polity.

Williamson, J. & M. Cloonan (2007). "Rethinking the Music Industry". *Popular Music* 26(2): 305–22. https://doi.org/10.1017/S0261143007001262.

Witt, S. (2015). *How Music Got Free: What Happens When an Entire Generation Commits the Same Crime?* London: Bodley Head.

Wójcik, D. (2021). "Financial Geography II: The Impacts of FinTech – Financial Sector and Centres, Regulation and Stability, Inclusion and Governance". *Progress in Human Geography* 45(4): 878–89. https://doi.org/10.1177/0309132520959825.

Woodcock, J. & M. Johnson (2019). "The Affective Labor and Performance of Live Streaming on Twitch.Tv". *Television & New Media* 20(8): 813–23. https://doi.org/10.1177/1527476419851077.

Wooldridge, M. (2021). *The Road to Conscious Machines: The Story of AI*. London: Pelican.

Wu, T. (2016). *The Attention Merchants: The Epic Scramble to Get inside Our Heads*. New York: Knopf.

Zhang, M. & Z. Xiao (2023). "Platform-Mediated Live Musical Performance in China: New Social Practices and Urban Cultural Spaces". *Geoforum* 140: 103723. https://doi.org/10.1016/j.geoforum.2023.103723.

Zhang, Q. & K. Negus (2020). "East Asian Pop Music Idol Production and the Emergence of Data Fandom in China". *International Journal of Cultural Studies* 23(4): 493–511. https://doi.org/10.1177/1367877920904064.

Zhang, Q. & K. Negus (2021). "Stages, Platforms, Streams: The Economies and Industries of Live Music after Digitalization". *Popular Music and Society* 44(5): 539–57. https://doi.org/10.1080/03007766.2021.1921909.

Zhang, Q. & K. Negus (2024). "From Cultural Intermediaries to Platform Adaptors: The Transformation of Music Planning and Artist Acquisition in the Chinese Music Industry". *New Media & Society*. https://doi.org/10.1177/14614448241232086.

INDEX